Verses marked KJS are taken from the King James Version of the Bible.

Scripture quotations identified as ASV are from the *American Standard Version New Testament,* © Thomas Nelson & Sons, 1901, 1929.

Scripture quotations identified as YLT are from *Young's Literal Translation Of The Holy Bible* (Robert Young). Grand Rapids: Baker Book House, 1976.

Scripture quotations identified as DBY are from *The Holy Scriptures, A New Translation from The Original Languages* (J. N. Darby). Lancing, Sussex: Kingston Bible Trust, 1980.

...utes of God
...ight ©2003 Ron Ricley
...ts reserved

...Design by Alpha Advertising
...design by Pine Hill Graphics

...by ACW Press
...th Ave., #502
...Arizona 85013
...ress.com
...expressed or implied in this work do not necessarily reflect those of ACW Press.
...esign, content, and editorial accuracy of this work is the responsibility of the

...ongress Cataloging-in-Publication Data
...Quality Books, Inc.)

...l.
...tes of God / by Ronald Ricley. -- 1st ed.

...liographical references.
...25-96-8

...cal teaching.   I. Title.

231
QBI33-774

...d. No part of this book may be reproduced, stored in a retrieval system,
...ny form or by any means—electronic, mechanical, photocopying,
...wise–without prior permission in writing from the copyright holder
...by USA copyright law.

...d States of America.

RONALD RICL

The Absolu
of God

Principles for Building a Solid
in our Christian Lif

**Absol
Copyr
All rig

Cover I
Interior

Packaged
5501 N.
Phoenix,
www.acw
The views
Ultimate d
author(s).

Library of C
(Provided by

Ricley, Ronal
The absolu
p. cm.
Includes bib
ISBN 1-892

1. God--Bibli

BS544.R53 2002

**All rights reserve
or transmitted in
recording, or othe
except as provided

Printed in the Unit

Contents

Introduction

It would be a miracle if a single book could confront the present confusion in Christendom and make a difference. Nevertheless, God is a God of miracles! This book is about the Word of God and its building blocks of truth that have been forgotten or misplaced. The writer of Hebrews calls them "the first principles of the oracles of God" (Heb. 5:12).

Our everyday lives find structure in the thousands of things we accept as truths, from the numbers we use to the names of colors and textures. Christ introduced His disciples to absolute truths as He added spiritual understanding to the things that He wanted them to know. There are absolutes in the Bible, and they are constants in the spiritual realm, as "2+2" is a constant in the physical realm. The problem we have with understanding spiritual things is excluding God from the equation. Only God can establish meanings for the things He says. Without the voice of His authority, values can be changed arbitrarily. Because the natural man knows nothing about spiritual things, any man can proclaim himself an expert.

The Bible is the Word of God and, therefore, the foundation of the Church. Because we fail to acknowledge the Spirit of God as the *only* authority able to interpret the Word, the absolutes get lost and truth becomes conjecture. With an eroded foundation, the Church is now in a place where any idea is as valid as the next. Relativity has infiltrated the Body of Christ.

The Bible is a compilation of holy, inspired writings. As such, it constitutes the revelation of the divine personality of the One and only Creator, God. The Bible is written to the Church, not to the world, because the same heavenly inspiration is required to read it as was to write it, (and the world had no access to divine inspiration outside of God). God gave the Bible to the Church because it is there the great truths of Scripture are to be lived and declared to the uninformed and lost.

My prayer is that this book be received as a gift from God to His children. The very premise of this work is too large a task for any man to undertake.

The Bible stands over and above any other book, because it is not just *a* book, it is *the* Book! It is an eternal declaration of light. By that light, we can see a God who is Spirit. The Word is the only place in the expanse of the universe where a man can stand and see God.

God's desire is that the words He spoke become alive in His people so that He is seen in His Church. God wants to be visible, not only to His Church but also to the whole world. He wants to see truth believed in and lived out in front of the entire world.

The Bible is not like the writings of mere mortals—intellectual critique of it has no value. It is the voice of God, age after age, crying, "Adam, where are you?" After the lost are found, it is the fellowship of the Spirit, long talks with the Father as we walk the road home. From its pages, we hear the voice of God for the first time and encounter the precious fragrance of His love. He touches us through its message. Because of its promises, we reach up and cling to an amnesty so vast and free that our earthbound minds cannot take in the depth and breadth of His mercy and grace. He births us anew of His Spirit, knowing that we need His indwelling in order to understand what we see and hear and feel when we encounter His presence in the message that He sent—the precious revelation of God.

Ron Ricley
Lecompton, Kansas

What Are Absolutes?

The twenty-first century Church of Jesus Christ is divided by opinions and adrift upon a sea of doctrines. Anyone who claims to be an expert or a critic can hold court and sway opinions. Believers have grouped themselves together in clusters of opinion, distrusting anyone who does not see things their way. No one seems to know how to resolve the confusion.

Meanwhile, the world looks on in dismay, waiting for answers that the Church does not provide. Religious fervor is not the same thing as Christianity, and substitutes for true faith will never do. As truth gets lost amidst the clamoring voices of conflicting views, little else that is spoken to the world matters. The Church is trying to lift up Christ so that men are drawn to Him, but in all the confusion, Jesus is being misrepresented. It is time for a reformation.

Jesus said that the world would know His disciples by the love they have one for another. Instead of displaying love, we Christians have been busy congratulating ourselves for just sitting together in the same room without throwing punches! Have we forgotten Jesus' high priestly prayer in John 17, asking that we become *one* as He and the Father are one? God says that two cannot walk together except they agree (Amos 3:3). God is talking to the Church right now through what Paul wrote in 1 Corinthians 1:10:

> *Now I beseech you, brethren, by the name of our Lord Jesus Christ,*
> *that ye all speak the same thing, and that there be no divisions among*
> *you; but that ye be perfectly joined together in the same mind and in*
> *the same judgment.* 1 Corinthians 1:10 (KJS)

This Scripture demands an answer from today's Church. Discussing religion, especially with a vision for reformation, has always been a dangerous thing to do. Believers tend to be very protective of the doctrines they hold dear, and critics who are simply being critical abound. However, true love for the true Church of Jesus Christ does not demand silence. Quite the opposite, love demands judgment so that the Church can once again be pure. Truth is light and light dispels darkness. It is necessary to expose the problems so that we can seek God's answers. Denying that problems exist is no solution.

First, a Look at Some of the Problems

The Church has committed two evils: she has forsaken the fountain of living waters and has hewn out broken cisterns that can hold no water (Jer. 2:13). **The fountain of living waters is the spontaneous flow of the presence of God. Jesus is the Fountain of living waters!** Today, the cloud of God's presence is not even expected, and the spontaneity that allows Him to work has been cut off. We forsake the Fountain to our own demise. It is only when God's will is sought and followed in our lives and in the assembly of the saints that the enemy's lies are effectively confronted and strongholds in our hearts torn down. God's specific word for any given occasion is what the Church should be seeking, for it contains a life-giving flow that man cannot duplicate.

Think of any gathering of God's saints as a grand banquet. From a heart that has all wisdom and understanding, our loving Father desires to feed us exactly what we need at the time. He wants to nurture us and protect us, to admonish us and mold us. The minister's job is to simply be a vessel God can move through in order to lead His people on.

Ministers learn to make good sermons in Bible school. Sprinkled with Scriptures, such sermons sound like heaven's own message. However, more often than not they are only broken cisterns. Such sermons may be full of enticing words of men's wisdom, but they lack divine power (1 Cor. 2:4). Sadly, worldly wisdom is often passed off as God's message to the Church. Old sermons are reheated and writers are hired to replace the anointing oil of God with quips and quotes and jokes. Sunday after Sunday, God's power is nowhere in sight. We need to let the Holy Spirit do His job!

The Holy Spirit is the "Teacher sent from God." Jesus said that the Holy Spirit would guide us into all truth (John 16:13). The Holy Spirit is also called the Spirit of Truth. Again, in John10 Jesus said, "My sheep hear my voice, and the voice of a stranger they will not follow." By the Spirit's anointing, the Word of God becomes more than words. It becomes the voice of God.

The human intellect has replaced the Holy Ghost as teacher with disastrous results. In the absence of divine guidance, the Bible's spiritual precepts lose their simplicity. Religious knowledge becomes tangled webs spun by mental gymnastics. These webs become so twisted and intimidating that they may go unchallenged for centuries. This does not happen when the Holy Ghost is the one doing the teaching. Religious knowledge is not the same as revelation knowledge.

Not content to usurp the office of the Holy Ghost, man has also made himself the head of the Church. Man took over the daily operations of the Church, but it was a hostile takeover. Without reference to God's will, men have decided the course for the Church and policy meetings have become political power forums. Men have increased the speed of travel but they are going away from God.

Under man's leadership, the world has seen many churches built. Unprecedented numbers attend Bible schools around the world. For every Bible school there is another school of thought. Man can certainly build but he cannot unify. We have fooled ourselves into believing that red-hot programs and exciting headliners can change lives. They cannot. The Church has lost her expectation of the miraculous. Week after week of "self-help" theology can never replace prayer that seeks God's intervention. The Church must return to the Fountain of living waters.

The transition from theocracy to democracy has changed the attitude of the Bride and put the vote where submission should have been. Man's arrogance stands in defiance of the established order of God and the woman (the church congregation) can hire or fire the man whom God sends to minister. The Church is not supposed to operate that way.

The only Head ordained to lead the Church is Jesus Christ. His banner over her is love. He spoke His word *about* her as much as *to* her because His word has creative power. The Church is not about running a business or building awe-inspiring cathedrals, it is about light coming out of darkness and order out of chaos. The gospel of Jesus was not sent to influence man, it was sent to impregnate the soul. The Church is not an organization it is an organism. God is not after a worldwide corporation He wants a Bride.

Self-righteousness is pandemic in the Church, and that is not what Jesus is after. The Bible promises a victorious Church without spot or wrinkle, a Church the gates of Hell will not prevail against. God is now awakening that Church. Under the rightful leadership of Jesus, she will triumph over every obstacle. The victorious Church walks in absolute truth because Jesus is absolute truth.

Another problem is that the Church has forsaken the absolutes of truth. Truth anchored the Church of Acts. She had knowledge from on high and walked in the Spirit of revelation.

The atoms of knowledge are the fundamental building blocks that must be absolutes. Where there are absolutes a foundation is formed that clears the way for deeper understanding (i.e., 2+2=4). Absolutes demand consistency and produce predictable results. Dividing 7,256 into 9,385,145 produces only one true answer. The beauty of constants is that anyone in the world can solve that problem the same way.

God gave the Church absolutes, truths that are like atoms of knowledge. In the early Church, the written Word of God revealed by the Spirit of God produced such a firm foundation that Jesus said, "On this rock (revelation from God) I will build my Church, and the gates of Hell cannot prevail against it" (Matthew 16:18). The Church must remember that she has an adversary who is the father of lies. One lie leads to another, and Satan knows that lies set the Church adrift. Without an anchor of truth, any wind of doctrine will blow her (Ephesians 4:14).

The word "absolute" is defined as the following: 1. being entirely without flaw and meeting supreme standards of excellence; 2. pure; 3. free from restrictions; 4. definite. It also means existing in or based on fact. Synonyms of "absolute" are factual, genuine, and perfect.

God is an absolute. He is pure, He is perfect, He is entirely without flaw, and He exceeds beyond comparison any standard of excellence. His existence is based on fact. He is free from restrictions, but He cannot lie. Not only is He a God of truth, He is Truth! He is a God of His word and He is the Word of God.

It is perfectly natural to trust in things that do not change. God does not change. Confidence in God, the unchanging absolute, inspires rest as nothing else does. The psalmist David described resting in God when he said, "Thou preparest a table before me in the presence of mine enemies: thou anointest my head with oil; my cup runneth over" (Psalms 23:5). It would be impossible to sit down and eat in front of our enemies unless we knew they were held at bay by a very powerful force.

Jesus said, "Come unto me, all ye that labor and are heavy laden, and I will give you rest. Take my yoke upon you, and learn of me; for I am meek and lowly in heart: and ye shall find rest unto your souls. For my yoke is easy, and my burden is light" (Matthew 11:28-30). Trusting that He can conform us to His unchanging image gives us rest.

God has declared that He will have a Church that is an absolute. The Church is the glory of God's creation. Through His plan of salvation, man can return to the original pattern that God used when He made Adam in the Garden of Eden.

The Lord has led me to address seven absolutes that the Church has ignored, thereby leaving the truth she was to guard unprotected. These absolutes are the necessary building blocks of knowledge. Right now, the Church is in confusion because she has rejected God's knowledge and embraced man's knowledge. The difference between the two is vast. The Church is filled with man's knowledge today, and the absolutes of God confront accepted human wisdom.

> *My people are destroyed for lack of knowledge: because thou hast rejected knowledge, I will also reject thee, that thou shalt be no priest to me: seeing thou hast forgotten the law of thy God, I will also forget thy children.* Hosea 4:6 (KJS)

Below are a few of the absolutes of the Word of God. They will confront lies and illuminate the way for us to go.

1. **God's will for man is that he be perfect in Christ Jesus.** *God created Adam as a perfect man. Until he became the judge of what was good and what was evil, Adam walked with God as a perfect son. Jesus succeeded in walking perfectly in the flesh to show God's ability to do such a miraculous thing in man.*
2. **The knowledge of good and evil does not produce godly believers or healthy Christians.** *Adam could not eat of both the tree of life and the tree of the knowledge of good and evil.*
3. **The natural man does not receive the things of God.** *Jesus told Nicodemus that unless you are born again of the Spirit you cannot see the Kingdom of God.*

4. **Every believer must know the voice of Jesus.** *Jesus said that His sheep will know His voice, and the voice of a stranger they will not follow.*

5. **The Holy Ghost is the teacher sent from God to indwell every believer.** *Jesus calls the Holy Ghost the Spirit of Truth. Sent to indwell us, only He can teach every Christian the truths of the Word of God.*

6. **Once we repent of our sins, we become His workmanship, created in Christ Jesus.** *Trusting that Jesus is truly working in us and for us every day, and that we are not our own workmanship, restores our peace with God and returns joy. Our faith grows, and faith can move things out of our lives that nothing else can.*

7. **The Bible was written both historically and spiritually.** *The spiritual aspect of the Bible was sealed. The Bible contains truths that we cannot understand unless a revelation of God opens them up. Peter knew that Jesus was the Christ and the Son of God by divine revelation. God must open the Bible to us in the same way.*

These absolutes are some of the atoms of knowledge that anchor the Church. Discussing them will doubtless produce an array of responses in Christians. Instead of receiving these truths by Holy Spirit revelation, the natural man regards them as merely religious jargon open to debate. The Church is in desperate need of a sure foundation. A willingness to know the will of God and seek it in our lives will cause these building blocks of truth to form that foundation.

Summary

We live in a world that is very hostile to the idea of absolutes. More than she knows, the Church has allowed the world's mindset to deeply infiltrate and corrupt the foundation God gave her to live by in His Word. God commands, "Come out from among them and be ye separate" (2 Cor. 6:17). We must ask God to reveal the worldliness in the Church and in our hearts if we are to receive the truth and return to the fundamental concepts necessary to live a normal Christian life. What most Christian's today view as a "normal" walk of faith is far removed from what God defines as normal for His sons and daughters. If we can only forsake our wrong ideas and lifestyles and open our ears and eyes to embrace what the Spirit says to the Church, we can give God the liberty He desires to present a spotless Bride to His Son. He is waiting on us to believe His promises.

Not only is He waiting, all of creation groans for the manifestation of the sons of God (Romans 8:19-22)!

Study Questions

1. *Why is it so bad that the Church has forsaken the fountain of living waters and hewn out broken cisterns that can hold no water?*
2. *What is the purpose of the Holy Spirit and why do we need Him so much in our churches?*
3. *Why is man's leadership so destructive to the Church?*
4. *What should man's leadership be replaced with—and how do we do that?*
5. *Define the true Church of Christ.*
6. *Why is truth so important to the Church?*
7. *What is an absolute?*
8. *What will bring the Church back to a firm foundation?*

ONE

God's Will for Man Is That He Be Perfect in Christ Jesus

The Sermon on the Mount is the great manifesto of the King of kings. In it, we find the commandment, "Be ye therefore perfect, even as your Father in heaven is perfect" (Matthew 5:48). Man recoils from such a statement in doubt. It is too wide and high and vast to figure out. The "giants" of our hearts drive us back from God's promise of victory because we see ourselves as the warriors and know we would lose the fight. The carnal man will always respond this way to the concept of perfection because the natural man is unable to grasp it as God's promise of victory. From Genesis to Revelation, God shows us that the flesh is faithless. God tells us that the carnal mind is not subject to the laws of God, neither indeed can it be, so then they that are in the flesh cannot please God (Romans 8:8).

God issued this command to be perfect within the perfect context! Jesus began His sermon with a promise of divine intervention, not divine expectations. The word "perfect" demands attention, yet it is situated within a context that first comforts us by speaking a proclamation of amnesty, thus setting this jewel in gold, not clay. The first words of the sermon set the tone for the subsequent demands: "Blessed [are] the poor in spirit: for theirs is the kingdom of heaven" (Matt. 5:3).

The perfect man can only come from the perfect grace. The promise is from heaven; it comes from the mouth of the perfect Son, whose perfect sacrifice procured the perfect seed to impregnate the soul of man at the perfect moment. The promise is about harvesting the results of the perfect salvation, so that the Kingdom of the perfect King will be inhabited by a people whose perfect praise will come from understanding that the perfect work was not their doing. They will be grateful for salvation, grateful that the new man grew to maturity, and grateful for the loving grace that finished the work. It is not a work accomplished by physical means, but a creative work accomplished by the voice of God.

Perfection is no one's business but God's business. Perfection is possible, even though the carnal mind disagrees. Perfection is not about the elevation of the flesh for the glory of men. It is about Christ in us, the hope of glory (Col. 1:27)!

In the first words of His sermon, Jesus revealed the blessedness of the grieving, repentant heart. Anyone who knows that he is in debt to God because of inability to keep God's commands is astounded to hear such words. Feeling the weight of failure, we embrace these words of hope as a beacon in the night. After Jesus arrived, the long night of failure was over! Jesus as Victor did not come by earthly powers, but by His Word. Jesus did not merely talk about salvation from sin He was (and is) Salvation from sin.

Only the Savior can give such amnesty, and only the Savior can give such commands. The order to be perfect staggers every mind into awe. This demand is different from the law, and its fulfillment is more than improbable, it is impossible for man! Enter the King, high and lifted up with His train filling the temple—with God as the Workman, all things are possible. The Kingdom truly is His glory!

Some believe that the word translated as "perfect" in the King James Bible means "mature." In order to gain a better understanding of the word, we shall look at an objective translation of the Greek.

Thayers #5046 teleios (tel'-i-os) from 5056; TDNT - 8:67,1161; adj AV - perfect 17, man 1, of full age 1; 19

1) brought to its end, finished; 2) wanting nothing necessary to completeness; 3) perfect; 4) that which is perfect; 4a) consummate human integrity and virtue; 4b) of men; 4b1) full grown, adult, of full age, mature

The Greek word *teleios* is from the root word *telos* (to set out for a definite point or goal). It was translated thirty-five times in the New Testament as "end."

1) end; 1a) termination, the limit at which something ceases to be. (always at the end of some act or state, but not a period of time); 1c) that by which a thing is finished; 1d) the end to which all things relate, the aim, purpose.

For the sake of those claiming right-of-translation, let's insert the word "mature" into a couple of scriptural contexts to see whether or not it negates the concept of a Church without spot or wrinkle.

Be ye therefore perfect, even as your Father which is in heaven is <u>perfect</u>. *Matthew 5:48 (KJS)*

or

Be ye therefore "<u>mature</u>," even as your Father which is in heaven is "<u>mature</u>."

Again, using this word *teleios*, let's look at another place in the New Testament where it is used:

1 I beseech you therefore, brethren, by the mercies of God, that ye present your bodies a living sacrifice, holy, acceptable unto God, [which is] your reasonable service. 2 And be not conformed to this world: but be ye transformed by the renewing of your mind, that ye may prove what [is] that good, and acceptable, and <u>perfect</u> will of God. 3 For I say, through the grace given unto me, to every man that is among you, not to think [of himself] more highly than he ought to think; but to think soberly, according as God hath dealt to every man the measure of faith. Romans 12:1-3 (KJS)

or

...that ye may prove what is that good, and acceptable, and "<u>mature</u>" will of God.

17

Man's understanding of "mature" cannot fit into either of these Scriptures without doing damage to God as Supreme. Nothing less than perfection will fulfill the will of God. What, then, is the fulfillment of the will of God? What is the end of what God wants? In Genesis, we read that God created Adam as a perfect man. No one believes that he was sinning in the garden before Eve was tempted to eat of the forbidden fruit. God created man as He wanted man to be. Satan, in his jealousy, sought to destroy the beauty of God's creative masterpiece.

In Hebrews 7:19, God said, "For the law made nothing perfect, but the bringing in of a better hope did, by the which we draw nigh unto God." This "better hope" is Jesus! The sinless life that He lived is now imparted to us if we invite Him into our hearts. A believer must be born again, and the new man is a new creation in Christ (2 Cor. 5:17). When the new man, who begins as a baby, grows to maturity, it affects the believer in a victorious way. The old argument says that God did not mean "sinless" when he said, "Be ye therefore perfect." In 1 John 3:9, the Spirit of Truth says, "Whosoever is born of God doth not commit sin; for his seed remaineth in him: and he cannot sin, because he is born of God."

When the new man, who cannot sin, matures, will we be mature or sinless? We will be both! The new creation that lives in a believer after his conversion is perfect from birth. However, this spirit man is not in control of the old nature instantly. As he grows, he gradually takes over (remember, the new man is Christ in you; it is Him, not you, doing the work). Understanding these things keeps us from feeling condemnation for not doing better (condemnation originates with self-righteousness). Just as a mother should not compare the abilities of her older, stronger children to her smaller ones lest she discourage them, the ministers of God should know that age certainly makes a difference.

Even though God does the work, young believers are often anxious to grow and change. Feeling like they have failed to measure up to a certain standard of behavior defeats their faith. Satan, as the adversary of the soul, knows that it is easy to accuse a baby Christian of being small. He is small! He should be small until time passes and he grows. If God's ministers will feed babies the Word of God (which is spiritual food), those babies will grow. This is what Jesus commanded Peter to do. The Lord found that Peter had returned to fishing after the crucifixion and resurrection. Jesus called him back by saying, "Feed my sheep" (John 21:17).

What encouragement to know that as the new man grows up the old man loses his place of control. As a baby, the new man has no knowledge of the power he possesses. A newborn may grow up to be an Olympic champion, but as a baby, he is weak; he must gain strength over time. The same is true of spiritual babies. The apostle Paul talked about this in his great passage on love, 1 Corinthians 13. Loving as God does, after all, is a sign of maturity in a believer. Paul's own life is a good example.

> *8 Charity never faileth: but whether [there be] prophecies, they shall fail; whether [there be] tongues, they shall cease; whether [there be] knowledge, it shall vanish away. 9 For we know in part, and we prophesy in part. 10 But when that which is perfect is come, then that which is in part shall be done away. 11 When I was a child, I spake as a child, I understood as a child, I thought as a child: but when I became a man, I put away childish things. 12 For now we see through a glass, darkly; but then face to face: now I know in part; but then shall I know even as also I am known. 13 And now abideth faith, hope, charity, these three; but the greatest of these [is] charity.* 1 Corinthians 13:8-13 (KJS)

Love never fails! This is what God's heart is all about—never failing love. God, who knows man better than man knows himself, loves him unconditionally and unfailingly. When the Church can forgive as Jesus instructed Peter to forgive—"seventy times seven" instances in a single day—the Church will be mature.

Paul's words are a good reminder. "We know in part (often, our condemnation of others occurs because we know only part of what God knows). We prophesy in part (again, we are reminded that even the gifts of the Spirit are limited by flesh and the carnal mind). But, when that which is *perfect* is come, that which is in part shall be done away with." The Church should not deny God's promise of perfection. Instead, she should rejoice. The new man, who cannot sin, is ground zero for the Church that is to "overcome the world."

Paul said, "When I was a child, I spake as a child, I understood as a child, but when I became a man, I put away childish things." It is time for the Church of Jesus Christ to become a man, to put away childish things. If we define perfection as merely becoming a mature man, the word has little effect on the unbelieving, carnal-minded leadership of the "self-help" church of the natural man. Defining the word correctly most certainly does have an effect.

The new man cannot sin! What does that mean? It does not mean the old man after conversion and forty-odd years of "doing better," it means the new man. There is a body celestial and there is a body terrestrial. Feed whichever one you will and it will become the stronger one. Deny whichever one you will and it will become the weaker one.

> 40[There are] also celestial bodies, and bodies terrestrial: but the glory of the celestial [is] one, and the [glory] of the terrestrial [is] another. 41 [There is] one glory of the sun, and another glory of the moon, and another glory of the stars: for [one] star differeth from [another] star in glory. 42 So also [is] the resurrection of the dead. It is sown in corruption; it is raised in incorruption: 43 It is sown in dishonour; it is raised in glory: it is sown in weakness; it is raised in power: 44 It is sown a natural body; it is raised a spiritual body. There is a natural body, and there is a spiritual body. 45 And so it is written, The first man Adam was made a living soul; the last Adam [was made] a quickening spirit. 46 Howbeit that [was] not first which is spiritual, but that which is natural; and afterward that which is spiritual. 1 Corinthians 15:40-46 (KJS)

The new man is the body celestial. He is the perfect image of the Son of God, begotten of Him. In verse 45, Paul said that Jesus is the last Adam, a quickening spirit. Why does Paul say that He is the last Adam? The two Adams stand for humanity. All of their attributes are endowed to us. The first Adam passed to all the plague of failing to obey; the Last Adam passed to all the power to obey. Even more importantly, Jesus is a quickening Spirit. This Last Adam comes to us as a quickening spirit, to indwell and quicken the believer. The power is in the quickening.

The body celestial does not come first. This is Paul's explanation for why the body terrestrial is obviously in control, even after our rebirth. The natural man is first in control and he must be displaced. The spirit man must grow, and growth demands a process that requires time. Still, God has given us the promise of victory over the terrestrial.

John wrote, "To as many as received him to them gave he power to become the sons of God" (John 1:12). When the children of God are mature, the Spirit of God will be able to lead them. They will become the *sons* of God! Jesus is the first born of many brethren (Rom. 8:29). The whole world is waiting on the manifestation of the sons of God.

> *18 For I reckon that the sufferings of this present time [are] not worthy [to be compared] with the glory which shall be revealed in us. 19 For the earnest expectation of the creature waiteth for the manifestation of the sons of God. 20 For the creature was made subject to vanity, not willingly, but by reason of him who hath subjected [the same] in hope, 21 Because the creature itself also shall be delivered from the bondage of corruption into the glorious liberty of the children of God.* Romans 8:18 (KJS)

The new man , led by the Spirit of God, and the old man, delivered from the bondage of corruption, shall come into the glorious liberty of the children of God. This is the definition of the perfect man!

We see, then, two bodies. One is earthly, the other heavenly. Man cannot and does not make either body all that it is or all that it will be. Jesus said that a man could not add one cubit to his stature by taking thought (Matt. 6:27, Luke 12:25). How much less, then, can man make himself into that which glorifies God?

A tiny seed contains all the power of its nature. Whether it is an oak seed or a wheat seed, it is full of the growth potential that its nature contains. The same holds true for man; the natural man and the spirit man both begin as seeds of potential. Man, over time, has come to believe that he is in control of the process, but he is not. Paul prayed that he might know Christ in the power of the resurrection (in incorruption), being made conformable to His death. Do we forget when we read this that Paul also talked about being dead with Christ and buried with Him in baptism? He was dead with Christ, dead to sin, and dead to self!

Because of this glorious truth, a person born anew of the Spirit could enter into eternity the next minute and be saved for all eternity. This maturing process is not about going to heaven, it is about God's glory in His Kingdom within us on the earth. If a Christian lives for forty years or more after conversion, he should by then be a creature of faith, full of the fruit of the Spirit of God and unshakable in his knowledge of the Word. He should see Christ in His revealed glory and hear His voice clearly. This is not necessarily the idea of perfection we get from the tree of the knowledge of good and evil!

Being Blameless under the Law Is Not Perfection

Let's consider the following passage:

6 Concerning zeal, persecuting the church; touching the righteousness which is in the law, blameless. 7 But what things were gain to me, those I counted loss for Christ. 8 Yea doubtless, and I count all things [but] loss for the excellency of the knowledge of Christ Jesus my Lord: for whom I have suffered the loss of all things, and do count them [but] dung, that I may win Christ, 9 And be found in him, not having mine own righteousness, which is of the law, but that which is through the faith of Christ, the righteousness which is of God by faith: 10 That I may know him, and the power of his resurrection, and the fellowship of his sufferings, being made conformable unto his death; 11 If by any means I might attain unto the resurrection of the dead. 12 Not as though I had already attained, either were already perfect: but I follow after, if that I may apprehend that for which also I am apprehended of Christ Jesus. 13 Brethren, I count not myself to have apprehended: but [this] one thing [I do], forgetting those things which are behind, and reaching forth unto those things which are before, 14 I press toward the mark for the prize of the high calling of God in Christ Jesus. Philippians 3:6-14 (KJS)

In verse 12, Paul said, "Not as though I had already attained (the resurrection), either were already perfect." Obviously, he was not talking about the same resurrection that man talks about now. Why would he say, while he was still walking around in his body, that he had not already attained resurrection? Was he worried that those standing next to him would not notice that he was still with them? Why did he tie this resurrection to being "already perfect" if it was not possible? While saying that he had not already attained, he also said that he was pressing for the mark of the prize of the high calling of God in Christ Jesus.

Later in his life, Paul said that he had finished his course. He had run his race, fought a good fight, and kept the faith. He knew there was a crown laid up for him, meaning he had won (like an Olympic champion). The word *teleos* means "end." It means the will of God for man brought to pass in a man. To God, that is success. Jesus lived the perfect life of a Son for our example, but we can also see it in the lives of others!

What about the flesh, what is to be done to it? The Bible says that the flesh died at Calvary with Jesus. We must accept this promise by faith because we do not see it with our carnal eyes. It is as tangible as Sarah's baby, but is also as unseen as Isaac was until his appointed time.

14 But God forbid that I should glory, save in the cross of our Lord Jesus Christ, by whom the world is crucified unto me, and I unto the world. 15 For in Christ Jesus neither circumcision availeth any thing, nor uncircumcision, but a new creature. Galatians 6:14-15 (KJS)

Like Paul, we are crucified to the world and the world is crucified to us. In Christ Jesus, neither circumcision (keeping ordinances) avails anything, nor uncircumcision (not keeping ordinances), but a new creature!

In Colossians, Paul boldly declared the flesh finished and buried with Christ.

21 And you, that were sometime alienated and enemies in [your] mind by wicked works, yet now hath he reconciled 22 In the body of his flesh through death, to present you holy and unblameable and unreproveable in his sight: 23 If ye continue in the faith grounded and settled, and [be] not moved away from the hope of the gospel, which ye have heard, [and] which was preached to every creature which is under heaven; whereof I Paul am made a minister. Colossians 1:21-23 (KJS)

If, as some say, a Christian cannot attain sinless perfection, he might settle for what verse 22 says Christ does for us! We are reconciled in His body of flesh through His death so that He might present us holy, unreproveable, and unblameable in His sight. In the Greek, it says "without blemish" and unreproveable. We must have the Spirit of wisdom and revelation so that we can receive the things that the Spirit teaches. We are reconciled in the body of His flesh! We are reconciled through His death so that we can be presented "holy, unblameable, and unreproveable in His sight: *if* ye continue in the faith grounded and settled, not moved away from the hope of the gospel."

The Church is to be filled with believers who are holy, unblameable, and unreproveable in whose sight? In God's sight! Would it matter what others said about you if you knew that you were holy, without blame,

23

and not needing reproof in God's sight? No! Bear in mind, this is the same God who knows what a man thinks and does when no one else is around!

How does man become such a pure being? What do the Scriptures say? Notice, God starts with the mind, the place where wicked things can go unseen by others for a long time. God saw that wickedness from the beginning and set in motion His salvation plan, reconciling us "*in*" the body of "*His flesh*" through death, to present us holy. Remember, He is telling us that this is already done. There is a clause to this bold statement if we continue reading. Paul said: "*if*" you continue in the faith, grounded and settled, and not moved away from that hope of the gospel which you have heard. Hold on as Abraham held to his promise. Take the truth and hold on to it. That's all? It sounds too simple, but the Gospel *is* simple. If the Bible says that believers are holy because of Christ's actions and not the believer's actions, without blemish and unreproveable, it sounds again as though God's idea of the Church perfected means *without sin*.

Sin Shall Not Have Dominion over You!

> *11 Likewise reckon ye also yourselves to be dead indeed unto sin, but alive unto God through Jesus Christ our Lord. 12 Let not sin therefore reign in your mortal body, that ye should obey it in the lusts thereof. 13 Neither yield ye your members [as] instruments of unrighteousness unto sin: but yield yourselves unto God, as those that are alive from the dead, and your members [as] instruments of righteousness unto God. 14 For sin shall not have dominion over you: for ye are not under the law, but under grace. 15 What then? shall we sin, because we are not under the law, but under grace? God forbid. 16 Know ye not, that to whom ye yield yourselves servants to obey, his servants ye are to whom ye obey; whether of sin unto death, or of obedience unto righteousness? 17 But God be thanked, that ye were the servants of sin, but ye have obeyed from the heart that form of doctrine which was delivered you. 18 Being then made free from sin, ye became the servants of righteousness.* Romans 6:11-18 (KJS)

Is the Church of Jesus Christ free from sin? The Bible says yes! Sin does not have dominion over us. We can yield ourselves to righteousness.

Make no mistake, we are talking here about sin not having dominion over our mortal, not our immortal, bodies.

Jesus instructed us to pray for this very thing. He told His disciples to pray, "Thy kingdom come (the Kingdom of God comes not with observation, for the Kingdom of God is within you), Thy will be done in earth as it is in heaven." Can God's will be done on earth as it is in heaven? Men have tried to live perfect lives and failed; they shall continue to fail. However, God answers prayer.

If we pray for the blind to see, do we expect to bring it to pass ourselves? No. We pray because God can do what no other power can do. When we pray for something, we must leave it in God's hands. Only faith can do that. Faith sees God's promises in the Bible about His will being done in us and believes what cannot be seen temporally.

Remember, Jesus commands us to be perfect. God showed Paul that only He has the ability to perfect man. He proclaimed it as a finished work. The writer of Hebrews lamented that the law made nothing perfect. If perfect meant only mature or complete, that Scripture would be false and the law would be our savior. Only Jesus fulfilled the law! Paul said that he was blameless concerning the law— not perfect, but *blameless* under the law. The Levites waited until they were thirty years old to begin ministering, a picture of maturity under the law.

> For the law made nothing perfect, but the bringing in of a better hope
> [did]; by the which we draw nigh unto God. Hebrews 7:19 (KJS)

The law made nothing perfect, but the bringing in of a better hope did! The new hope did make something perfect! It is by that better hope that we draw nigh unto God. If we draw near to Him, He will draw near to us (James 4:8).

Man constantly looks for a formula he can apply to the perfecting of the Church, but he cannot find one. God gives us no formulas because He intends to start and finish the work in Christ Jesus alone. The Bible tells us that Jesus is the Author and Finisher of our faith. He is the Alpha and the Omega (Greek for beginning and end). He is the Workman and we are His workmanship.

If believers are still under the dominion of sin, then James told us a strange thing in chapter 1 of his epistle.

> *Pure religion and undefiled before God and the Father is this, To visit the fatherless and widows in their affliction, [and] to keep himself unspotted from the world.* James 1:27 (KJS)

Pure and undefiled religion is what? It is to visit the fatherless and widows in their affliction and to keep ourselves unspotted from the world. John started his first epistle with the same thought.

> *1 My little children, these things write I unto you, that ye sin not. And if any man sin, we have an advocate with the Father, Jesus Christ the righteous: 2 And he is the propitiation for our sins: and not for ours only, but also for [the sins of] the whole world.* 1 John 2:1-2 (KJS)

Notice, John wrote these things so that we "sin not." Saying "*if*" and not "*when*" we sin is a clear implication that sin is not expected to be part of a Christian's life. John ministered according to the concept that the Church would not sin. If a believer does sin, he has an advocate with the Father, Jesus Christ the righteous. God is not finished with a believer the day he repents, and Jesus is his High Priest and Advocate. It is important to differentiate between the old man and the new man. One sins and one does not. God said the old man died at Calvary with Jesus and the new man is spiritual.

> *8 If we say that we have no sin, we deceive ourselves, and the truth is not in us. 9 If we confess our sins, he is faithful and just to forgive us [our] sins, and to cleanse us from all unrighteousness. 10 If we say that we have not sinned, we make him a liar, and his word is not in us.* 1 John 1:8-10 (KJS)

Verse 8 is the battle cry of everyone who still believes that sin has dominion over believers. We must understand that John was talking about the flesh man. **He that is born of God does not commit sin!** It is precious to know that God is not finished with us the moment we are born again. We are not strong enough in faith at that point to appropriate all that God gives us. Think of the children of Israel who entered the promised land. They did not conquer all of the land in the first battle. However, God gave them the entire land and that is a matter of truth.

If we confess our sins, we are told that He will be faithful and just to forgive our sins and cleanse us of all unrighteousness. Who cleanses us? Do we promise not to sin again? We certainly hate the sin, but the Bible teaches that *He* cleanses us from all unrighteousness. Again, He does the work if only we will believe. Cleansing *all unrighteousness* is a tall order. Can you receive the promise that He will do that work in you?

The Fivefold Ministry and the Perfected Church

10 He that descended is the same also that ascended up far above all heavens, that he might fill all things.) 11 And he gave some, apostles; and some, prophets; and some, evangelists; and some, pastors and teachers; 12 For the perfecting of the saints, for the work of the ministry, for the edifying of the body of Christ: 13 Till we all come in the unity of the faith, and of the knowledge of the Son of God, unto a perfect man, unto the measure of the stature of the fulness of Christ: 14 That we [henceforth] be no more children, tossed to and fro, and carried about with every wind of doctrine, by the sleight of men, [and] cunning craftiness, whereby they lie in wait to deceive.
Ephesians 4:10-14 (KJS)

God gives the ministries of God to the Church for one purpose: the perfecting of the saints. The word translated "saints" means holy ones. God ordains ministers; their work is the perfecting of the holy ones. These ministers are given for the work of the ministry, and they are to edify the Body of Christ. We know that the Church is the Body of Christ, and the body of Christ was sinless while on the earth.

To edify means to build up. The leaders of the Church are to build up the Body of Christ. Will that Body, called by such a pure name, be full of sin and wickedness? The Bible says that it will not. As we read on, we see in clear detail the plan of God for His people, the Church. God's ministries will work "till we all come into the **unity of the faith,** and the **knowledge of the Son** of God, unto a **perfect man**."

Here, we glimpse two miracles. They are made possible by knowing who Jesus is and what He did, and still does, for us. The first miracle is unity (and what a blessing that would be for the Church, when a house

27

or kingdom divided will not stand). The second miracle is a perfect man. The power contained in verse 13 is the finished product that unity and perfect knowledge introduce, a perfect man. The Church is to be a perfect man, not perfect men. This is about the Body coming to life, and the Body *is* Christ!

To stop all arguments, God tells us what He expects His Word to accomplish—"the full stature of the man Christ Jesus." Does this stop all arguments? It should, but not all men who teach the Church are born of the Spirit, and not all men have ears to hear what the Spirit says to the Church.

Jesus said, "To him that overcometh will I grant to sit with Me in My throne even as I overcame and am set down with My Father in His throne" (Rev. 3:21) …Overcome what? He also said, "To him that overcometh will I make a pillar in the temple of My God" (Rev. 3:12) …and the list goes on. What action on the part of a believer overcomes the world? Believing does. Unbelief is what we shall overcome.

> *4 For whatsoever is born of God overcometh the world: and this is the victory that overcometh the world, [even] our faith. 5 Who is he that overcometh the world, but he that believeth that Jesus is the Son of God?* 1 John 5:4-5 (KJS)

See how positively these promises are proclaimed? **"For whatsoever is born of God overcomes the world: and this is the victory that overcomes the world, even our faith."** The Bible tells us what "the world" means:

> *15 Love not the world, neither the things [that are] in the world. If any man love the world, the love of the Father is not in him. 16 For all that [is] in the world, the lust of the flesh, and the lust of the eyes, and the pride of life, is not of the Father, but is of the world. 17 And the world passeth away, and the lust thereof: but he that doeth the will of God abideth for ever.* 1 John 2:15-17 (KJS)

Our faith in Jesus and in His work within us overcomes all that the world is. We cannot overcome by works, but by a new birth. The Bible says whatsoever is born of God overcomes, not whatsoever keeps every ordinance.

True or False: As Long as We Are in the Flesh We Will Sin...

The answer to every doubt about perfection is this: God can do it. As long as Christians have misconceptions about sin and how to deal with it, the word "perfection" will fall into the cavern of false understanding. If we feed the wrong information into an equation, we will get wrong information out.

> 1 [There is] therefore now no condemnation to them which are in Christ Jesus, who walk not after the flesh, but after the Spirit. 2 For the law of the Spirit of life in Christ Jesus hath made me free from the law of sin and death. 3 For what the law could not do, in that it was weak through the flesh, God sending his own Son in the likeness of sinful flesh, and for sin, condemned sin in the flesh: 4 That the righteousness of the law might be fulfilled in us, who walk not after the flesh, but after the Spirit. 5 For they that are after the flesh do mind the things of the flesh; but they that are after the Spirit the things of the Spirit. 6 For to be carnally minded [is] death; but to be spiritually minded [is] life and peace. 7 Because the carnal mind [is] enmity against God: for it is not subject to the law of God, neither indeed can be. 8 So then they that are in the flesh cannot please God. 9 But ye are not in the flesh, but in the Spirit, if so be that the Spirit of God dwell in you. Now if any man have not the Spirit of Christ, he is none of his. Romans 8:1-9 (KJS)

This passage answers the argument that as long as a man is in the flesh he will sin. Romans 8:8 says, "So then they that are in the flesh cannot please God." The Bible scholars who believe that they are their own potters have this verse memorized. If man is the potter, he must stop at that verse. However, if God is the potter, we may move on to the next verse. Does it say that you are not in the flesh because you have kept every commandment, observed every ordinance, no matter how trivial, fasted twice a week, and were circumcised on the eighth day? No, it says that you are not in the flesh if so be that the Spirit of God dwells in you. It says just that, nothing more. No matter how excited the flesh gets about its accomplishments in religious things, only the indwelling Spirit pleases God. Christ in us is the only thing that makes a difference.

We should not misconstrue sinless perfection to mean equality to God. Rather, it is His creative masterpiece. Man was not created by God to be the slave of sin, he was created to reign with God. God's glory is not made bright by darkness ruling over His children.

Ministers who seek validation from their peers and fear reproach will choose the path of least resistance. They will not suffer the reproach of Christ because they will not esteem it greater riches than the treasures of Egypt (Heb. 11:26).

When Paul said that he would only preach Jesus Christ and Him crucified, he meant it. He did not preach doctrines of works for righteousness and made no claim to heaven by any other victory than Christ's. The Church that the gates of Hell cannot prevail against stands on the name of Jesus, and that name only.

Summary

Of the commands of Jesus, Andrew Murray said, "They are the command of love, which is ever only a promise in a different shape." Let us know that the great command of the Sermon on the Mount is the promise of Christ to His Bride! Through God's plan of salvation, we can return to the original pattern God used when He created man: Adam was a son of God, Jesus is the Son of God, and we, as believers, have been adopted as Sons of God, crying, "Abba, Father!" We are fellow heirs with Christ (Romans 8:15-17)! The new man within a regenerated Christian is no less a perfect Son than Jesus is. Jesus said that we would do greater things on the earth than He did because He is now glorified and is come in a many-membered Body. Jesus succeeded in walking perfectly in the flesh to demonstrate God's ability to do such a miraculous thing in man. In the flesh, Jesus walked perfectly in a single body. How much greater that He can walk perfectly on the earth in His Body, the Church! The work of the Church is to believe in sinless perfection and thereby yield to righteousness.

Study Questions

9. *What is God's promise of victory?*
10. *What is Christ's command about perfection in the sermon on the Mount*
11. *Did Jesus expect His followers to keep that command by their own power of commitment? If not why did he speak it?*
12. *Explain why "mature" and "perfect" which are translations of the same Greek word require context to define different concepts.*
13. *What does it mean to be born again?*

14. *Explain the difference between the old man and the new man.*
15. *What can't the new man do according to God's word?*
16. *What provision has God made to help us grow stronger spiritually? How is that growth accomplished?*
17. *What is the difference between the first Adam and the last Adam?*
18. *What is the difference between being "blameless" and being "perfect"?*
19. *How are we reconciled to God?*
20. *What if we do sin after we become Christians?*
21. *What is the purpose of the fivefold ministry?*
22. *What are the two miracles born of God's fivefold ministry?*
23. *How do we overcome the world?*
24. *Is it true that a Christian will sin as long as he is living on the earth? Is a Christian in the flesh just because he is alive?*

TWO

The Knowledge of Good and Evil Does Not Produce Healthy Christians or Godly Believers

In the opening chapters of the Bible, God explains the terrible calamity that befell His son Adam and the way He intervened to save him. Those early chapters foretold the rise of religions. Once Adam accepted the premise contained in Satan's challenge (the premise that knowledge of good and evil was the missing ingredient for becoming like God), religions were the certain outcome. Because of man's fears, religion's claims over him continue to multiply, fostered by the need to please gods of uncertain desires. *God created Adam in His own image because He wanted a son like Himself.* Satan wanted Adam to trade his father-son, faith-based, intimate relationship with God for one based instead on the value that Adam's actions could create—this is the basis of religion.

There were two trees noted in the Garden of Eden. One was the tree of life. The other, which Adam and Eve were forbidden to eat from, was the tree of the knowledge of good and evil. In the biblical account, Satan the liar used God's own words to lend credibility to his own twisted version of reality. He called God the liar, and insisted that Eve could become like God if she only acquired the knowledge of good and evil. Satan suggested that disobeying God was the key to becoming more like God! We need to remember that nothing could be further from the truth. This was and is a lie.

Adam and Eve left the security of a relationship that asked for obedience in only one thing and made themselves the judges in a system that relies solely upon the finite human brain. There was no constitution or legal system of any kind in place, and they had no prior judicial experience to draw from. In short, when Adam and Eve ate of the tree of the knowledge of good and evil, they introduced random criteria as a foundation and judgment by conjecture as a structure, and they made the human intellect supreme judge in eternal matters.

The scope of judgment required to divide all of creation and all actions into two categories—good and evil—is grand by any standard. The Christian Church can no longer ignore the impact that this forbidden fruit still exerts against faith in God's plan of salvation by grace.

The highest authority in any civilization is a supreme court. Laws must form the basis of any society, and laws that are put in place must stem from a framework of righteousness and justice. Standards must exist that assure continuity, uniformity, and consistency. The only being capable of setting up such a system is God. He had not done so in the Garden of Eden.

There is always a measure of truth within a lying statement because Satan knows that partial truth throws off any skeptic, creating a sense of credibility. He did exactly that when he tempted Eve:

> *1 Now the serpent was more subtle than any beast of the field which Jehovah God had made. And he said unto the woman, Yea, hath God said, Ye shall not eat of any tree of the garden? 2 And the woman said unto the serpent, Of the fruit of the trees of the garden we may eat: 3 but of the fruit of the tree which is in the midst of the garden, God hath said, Ye shall not eat of it, neither shall ye touch it, lest ye die. 4 And the serpent said unto the woman, Ye shall not surely die: 5 for God doth know that in the day ye eat thereof, then your eyes shall be opened, and ye shall be as God, knowing good and evil. 6 And when the woman saw that the tree was good for food, and that it was a*

delight to the eyes, and that the tree was to be desired to make one wise, she took of the fruit thereof, and did eat; and she gave also unto her husband with her, and he did eat. Genesis 3:1-6 (ASV)

Satan knew that the knowledge of good and evil belonged only to God—this much was true. Such knowledge, without the mind of God, was only an invitation to invention. Man rose to the occasion and was immediately ensnared in Satan's vicious trap.

Through the ages, man has made fun of the apple (which has become symbolic of the fruit of the knowledge of good and evil) as though God did not want Adam to be intelligent. The truth is that God knew the deep and lasting consequences of eating that fruit, not in Adam's stomach but in his mind. This tree did not contain the fruit of intelligence, but of judgment. Because it provided knowledge about what is good and what is evil but did not provide guidelines, it was a dangerous power to consume. It was like taking the keys to start a racecar that has no steering wheel.

Adam and Eve were not created with the understanding necessary to establish criteria to judge by. Only an adversary would want them to possess such a power with no perimeters. Once Adam possessed the knowledge of good and evil, he became the sole judge of what was good and what was evil. Today, we can see what a disaster this has become.

When man is the judge of what is good or evil, his concept of it depends upon his own limited sphere of experience and what he learns from his environment. When a society is subjected to constantly declining morality, things that were once offensive eventually become acceptable. A conditioning to violence leaves even young people void of feeling and, even worse, without a conscience. Relativity regarding right and wrong, which shifts with the accepted norms of a society, leads that society down a road ending with extermination camps and abortion clinics.

Satan knows all of this. He knew that Adam wanted to please God, his Father, and that Adam was willing to make himself pleasing to God by any means he believed were right. Through the ages, men have sacrificed their children to please gods of their own making. They have sacrificed their wives, mutilated their own bodies, and even taken their own lives, all to please an image made with hands. Once a man believes something is right to do, he does it regardless of the cost.

35

The same goes for evil. When men are taught that something is evil, they will henceforth look upon that thing as evil. At one time, many believed that translating the Bible into the common languages was evil. Men who believed otherwise lost their lives. Satan does not want men to read the Bible because it leads to Satan's ultimate demise.

When Adam and Eve ate of the forbidden tree, they introduced random criteria to the world. Without absolutes, randomness is the only point from which we can judge. That day in the garden, human reasoning began to provide the guidelines for judgment. Adam, seeing that he and Eve were naked, made his first assessment as to what he thought was evil. Instantly, he began to fear his Father.

Satan accomplished exactly what he wanted. Man, judging himself as evil, lost his faith in God's love for him. After his mind was impregnated with that deadly fruit, just seeing his own naked body made him fear that he could no longer walk in God's love. From thenceforth, his mind demanded that he do something religious to please God. What is the truth in all of this? Adam *was* pleasing to the Father, unconditionally loved and cherished as the master work of the Potter. God knew what His expectations for Adam were, for He created him in His own image. Adam was naked and had nothing to hide before he disobeyed. Knowing good and evil was never the key to becoming like God.

In a church service, a friend once told of her sorrow upon buying her son a gift and then overhearing him tell others that he had paid for it himself. The joy of giving is in the joy of receiving. The knowledge of good and evil causes us to insist upon earning, by arbitrary standards, anything that comes from God.

The Two Trees

The fruit of the righteous [is] a tree of life; and he that winneth souls [is] wise. Proverbs 11:30 (KJS)

It is the spirit that quickeneth; the flesh profiteth nothing: the words that I speak unto you, [they] are spirit, and [they] are life. John 6:63 (KJS)

The two trees mentioned in Genesis symbolize the two conflicting ways by which the Church tries to live, but cannot—the tree of life and the tree of the knowledge of good and evil. She must hold to one and forget the other. Just like Adam, she cannot eat of both. The tree of life represents the way of faith in the Word of God. The tree of the knowledge of good and evil represents the way of works not based upon the will of God. The Church of the twenty-first century continues to build itself upon the knowledge of good and evil.

Christian ministers and laypeople alike ask the question: "If we do not know good and evil how can we obey God?" Man's problem is not that he knows good and evil, his problem is that he does not know God. If our knowledge of good and evil was based upon God's will, and "good" was only what He said was good, things would be different. Only God has the ability to define for us what He deems good and what He deems evil.

Adam did not hide himself because he had disobeyed God and eaten from the tree; he hid himself because he was naked. That never mattered to God, who walked with him in the cool of the evening every day. Where did that judgment come from? If it did not come from God, it must have come from Adam's mind. What was God's solution to this disaster? He killed a living sacrifice so that it could die in Adam's place. God's mercy rejoiced against God's judgment (James 2:13).

The tree of life did not accuse. The tree of life was free for the eating, available without cost. The only stipulation was that Adam could not eat of both and live. He had to make a choice: go God's way and accept God's best or go his own way and do his best.

We got a glimpse of what lay in store for mankind in Cain's life. Knowing that God accepted only a living sacrifice, Cain instead brought God his best. It was not a living sacrifice, but what Cain deemed best. God did not accept it.

How many churchgoing believers today are working according to the same illusion as Cain? They believe that if they give God their best He will be pleased. Cain was angered by the rejection of his sacrifice. He became angry enough to kill his brother, who had brought a living sacrifice and pleased God.

Paul received a revelation of God's salvation plan and he was amazed. It is not of works, lest any man should boast! We are saved by grace, through faith, and that not of ourselves. If any man had whereof to boast, Paul said that he did. Instead, he found out that righteousness is faith's prize; *"in"* Christ Jesus, he attained the righteousness of God by faith alone.

4 Though I might also have confidence in the flesh. If any other man thinketh that he hath whereof he might trust in the flesh, I more: 5 Circumcised the eighth day, of the stock of Israel, [of] the tribe of Benjamin, an Hebrew of the Hebrews; as touching the law, a Pharisee; 6 Concerning zeal, persecuting the church; touching the righteousness which is in the law, blameless. 7 But what things were gain to me, those I counted loss for Christ. 8 Yea doubtless, and I count all things [but] loss for the excellency of the knowledge of Christ Jesus my Lord: for whom I have suffered the loss of all things, and do count them [but] dung, that I may win Christ, 9 And be found in him, not having mine own righteousness, which is of the law, but that which is through the faith of Christ, the righteousness which is of God by faith: 10 That I may know him, and the power of his resurrection, and the fellowship of his sufferings, being made conformable unto his death; 11 If by any means I might attain unto the resurrection of the dead.
Philippians 3:4-11 (KJS)

Paul sought righteousness by faith; he had faith in what God did and what He will do. All of those right actions that Paul described sound like the guidelines preached from pulpits every Sunday, which believers are supposed to obey. Paul, having done those things and having been blameless under the law, saw that none of it had any merit before God. Those things that Paul once held dear became as dung to him. None of those criteria pleased God. Only faith pleases God, and Paul received that as a revelation from God.

We can see that Paul's problem did not stem from knowing good and evil, but from not knowing God. Doing what he thought was good (killing Christians) but not knowing Christ made his own righteousness of little consequence. After he met Jesus, Paul said that he not only wanted to know God, he wanted to know Him after the power of His resurrection. He wanted to know the fellowship of His sufferings and be made conformable to His death. What sublime fellowship! Only a man who truly knows God can say such things and mean them. No one can call Jesus "Lord" except by the Holy Ghost (1 Cor. 12:3).

Without the indwelling power of the Holy Ghost, there is no power in man to call Jesus "Lord." To call Him "Lord" means that the flesh and spirit are under His Lordship. The fleshly mind, with its knowledge of good and evil, cannot fully attain to that submission on its own, therefore it cannot truthfully call Jesus "Lord." In disobedience, man can call Jesus "Savior," "Counselor," or "Friend," but we see why he cannot call Him "Lord."

Justified on the Principle of Faith, Reconciled by Faith in the Blood of Christ

1 Therefore having been justified on the principle of faith, we have peace towards God through our Lord Jesus Christ; 2 by whom we have also access by faith into this favor in which we stand, and we boast in hope of the glory of God. 3 And not only [that], but we also boast in tribulations, knowing that tribulation works endurance; 4 and endurance, experience; and experience, hope; 5 and hope does not make ashamed, because the love of God is shed abroad in our hearts by [the] Holy Spirit which has been given to us: 6 for we being still without strength, in [the] due time Christ has died for [the] ungodly. 7 For scarcely for [the] just [man] will one die, for perhaps for [the] good [man] some one might also dare to die; 8 but God commends *his* love to us, in that, we being still sinners, Christ has died for us. 9 Much rather therefore, having been now justified in [the power of] his blood, we shall be saved by him from wrath. 10 For if, being enemies, we have been reconciled to God through the death of his Son, much rather, having been reconciled, we shall be saved in [the power of] his life. 11 And not only [that], but [we are] making our boast in God, through our Lord Jesus Christ, through whom now we have received the reconciliation. Romans 5:1-11 (DBY)

Notice again, all of these essential principles become real to us through faith, not actions. How are we to become more like Him if we do not practice living that which is right and shunning that which is wrong? We never will!

There are two keys to "doing right." First, we must understand that God is the Potter and we are the clay. Next, we must understand the Ten Commandments. We will address the commandments shortly, but now we shall consider the difference between the Potter and the clay. Let's look at Romans 5.

There is a process mentioned within this framework of faith, which is the secret of a believer's success. Tribulation is an important part of the equation. As God designs our walk, He proves us through times of tribulation. Tribulations lead us to endurance in our walk with God. Our Christian beliefs must hold true in times of trial.

"If I speak with the tongues of men and of angels, and have not love, it profits me nothing" (1 Cor. 13:1). We can quote the Bible all we want, but when the fire of God comes to try the Word within us, we must live it. It is then that faith, not do's and don'ts, comes under siege. Paul said that Christians must be able to endure and the Bible bears witness to that. He that continues to the end, the same shall be saved.

> *8 All these [are] the beginning of sorrows. 9 Then shall they deliver you up to be afflicted, and shall kill you: and ye shall be hated of all nations for my name's sake. 10 And then shall many be offended, and shall betray one another, and shall hate one another. 11 And many false prophets shall rise, and shall deceive many. 12 And because iniquity shall abound, the love of many shall wax cold. 13 But he that shall endure unto the end, the same shall be saved. 14 And this gospel of the kingdom shall be preached in all the world for a witness unto all nations; and then shall the end come.* Matthew 24:8-14 (KJS)

From endurance, we get experience. Our experiences in Jesus build our faith. Every believer in the Bible grew because of his or her experiences, and those experiences gave them hope. If the Church of this hour needs anything, it is hope in the reality of God's promises coming to pass. Paul said that hope does not make ashamed! **Every successful believer in the Bible succeeded because of hope in God's will coming to pass in his or her life**. Many failed miserably at times along the way, but those who held to God's forgiveness and mercy endured the tribulations and finished their lives in victory.

The Church pressures believers to project success and rejects those who fail. Ministers see no way to reconcile failures to Christ because "self-help" religion has such high expectations of the flesh. Consider what Paul said in Romans 5:10-11: "While we were enemies of God, He reconciled us to Himself through Jesus." He reconciled us while we were living in rebellion! If God loved us while we were His enemies, we must admit that His love has the power to reconcile us to Himself. We must believe it, that is our work. Certainly, expecting Him to change us is the right expectation.

Let's define reconciliation and justification according to linguistic scholarship to be certain that we are talking about the same things:

Reconciliation
BDB # 3722 kaphar (kaw-far') a primitive root; TWOT -
1023,1024,1025,1026; v AV - atonement 71, purge 7, reconciliation 4, reconcile 3, forgive 3, purge away 2, pacify 2, atonement...made 2, merciful 2, cleansed 1, disannulled 1, appease 1,
put off 1, pardon 1, pitch 1; 102
1) to cover, purge, make an atonement, make reconciliation, cover
over with pitch; 1a) (Qal) to coat or cover with pitch; 1b) (Piel);
1b1) to cover over, pacify, propitiate; 1b2) to cover over, atone for
sin, make atonement for; 1b3) to cover over, atone for sin and
persons by legal rites
1c) (Pual); 1c1) to be covered over; 1c2) to make atonement for;
1d) (Hithpael) to be covered

This word, taken from the Old Testament, means the same as atonement. Reconciliation is also the same as pitch, and we remember that
God instructed Noah to use pitch on the ark. Reconciled to God by an
act of God's atoning mercy and carried through tribulations by faith in
His incredible pronouncement—such was the life of Noah. His tribulation gave him experience, his experience gave him hope, and his hope
made him unashamed.

Justification
Thayers # 1342 (dikaios dik'-ah-yos) from 1349; TDNT -
2:182,168; adj AV - righteous 41, just 33, right 5, meet 2; 81
1) righteous, observing divine laws; 1a) in a wide sense, upright,
righteous, virtuous, keeping the commands of God; 1a1) of those
who seem to themselves to be righteous, who pride themselves to
be righteous, who pride themselves in their virtues, whether real
or imagined; 1a2) innocent, faultless, guiltless; 1a3) used of him
whose way of thinking, feeling, and acting is wholly conformed to
the will of God, and who therefore needs no rectification in the
heart or life
1a3a) only Christ truly; 1a4) approved of or acceptable of God;
1b) in a narrower sense, rendering to each his due and that in a

judicial sense, passing just judgment on others, whether expressed
in words or shown by the manner of dealing with them

Thayers # 1347 dikaiosis (dik-ah'-yo-sis) from 1344; TDNT -
2:223,168; n f AV - justification 2; 2
1) the act of God declaring men free from guilt and acceptable to
him; 2) abjuring to be righteous, justification

Faith is the substance of things hoped for and the evidence of things
not seen (Heb. 11:1). We are justified on the principle of believing that
God will do what He has promised whether we see it now or not. We
have peace with God through our Lord, Jesus Christ. By Him, we have
access through faith to the favor we stand in. Our only boast is in the
hope of the glory of God. God's glory is in His victory over the knowledge of good and evil. It is also in His atonement becoming our way to
righteousness. It is God's glory to finish His creation according to His
will and purpose for man. This is precisely what He means when He
describes Himself as the Potter.

The Ten Commandments

When Adam took upon himself the role of judge, he had no experience to guide him and no guidelines to follow. When God began the
process of reconciliation, He gave Israel the Ten Commandments in
order to provide a framework for judgment. After they were given, man
could no longer decide on his own what was "good" or "evil." God gave
him criteria to judge by and commands that were easy to follow.

To make His love and mercy stand out above the commandments,
God made a provision for the blood of animals to be a covering for sin.
"Covering" is one of the definitions for the word "reconciliation." The
Ten Commandments are important because they give man perimeters.
The Old Testament legal system formed a protective covering around
man, one he could have never created for himself. God used the law to
fashion man's hope. It was based on the blood covering and faith in
God's unmerited favor. It still is.

Instead, man placed his hope in keeping the commandments! This
is the natural result of accepting something God does but twisting it
according to the knowledge of good and evil. Consequently, man's faith

became based upon his performance. He then no longer needed unmerited favor from God.

The Ten Commandments were never obeyed according to God's intentions. God's intent was to show man that it is impossible to work our way to Him on legal terms. Man misunderstood the whole program!

Jesus understood God's will and said, "Sacrifices and offerings thou wouldest not, but a body thou hast prepared me, lo it is written in the volume of the book, I come to do thy will" (Psalm 40:6-8, Heb. 10:7). God has promised to take the Ten Commandments and write them upon the hearts of His children. Our confidence, then, is not in keeping the commandments but in the blood of Jesus. No man will go to heaven because he keeps the commands of God. He will go only if he accepts the substitutionary death of Jesus as payment for his sins. A man gets to heaven because Jesus ever lives to make intercession for him. As the perfect Workman, He makes us into what He wants us to be. We are His workmanship, created in Christ Jesus (Ephesians. 2:10).

Man as Judge and the Word of God

Even if man could keep the commandments of God by his efforts alone (which he cannot), he would still need the indwelling of the Spirit of God to lead him. The perfected Church is more than a Church without sin—the Church must be led by the Spirit of God to go where and when He would lead her. Paul talked about the law being spiritual and addressed that issue in light of his experiences in the flesh.

> *14 For we know that the law is spiritual: but I am carnal, sold under sin. 15 For that which I do I know not: for not what I would, that do I practice; but what I hate, that I do. 16 But if what I would not, that I do, I consent unto the law that it is good. 17 So now it is no more I that do it, but sin which dwelleth in me. 18 For I know that in me, that is, in my flesh, dwelleth no good thing: for to will is present with me, but to do that which is good [is] not. 19 For the good which I would I do not: but the evil which I would not, that I practice. 20 But if what I would not, that I do, it is no more I that do it, but sin which dwelleth in me. 21 I find then the law, that, to me who would do good, evil is present. 22 For I delight in the law of God after the inward man: 23*

but I see a different law in my members, warring against the law of my mind, and bringing me into captivity under the law of sin which is in my members. 24 Wretched man that I am! who shall deliver me out of the body of this death? 25 I thank God through Jesus Christ our Lord. So then I of myself with the mind, indeed, serve the law of God; but with the flesh the law of sin. 8:1 There is therefore now no condemnation to them that are in Christ Jesus. 2 For the law of the Spirit of life in Christ Jesus made me free from the law of sin and of death. 3 For what the law could not do, in that it was weak through the flesh, God, sending his own Son in the likeness of sinful flesh and for sin, condemned sin in the flesh. Romans 7:14-8:3 (ASV)

These important things are too often overlooked or ignored. The consenting to sin did not leave Paul bound (he said that if he did things that he did not want to do, it was not Paul that did them). If these were the words of a teenager trying to get out of trouble, we could laugh at such a simple interpretation of these Scriptures. However, these are not the words of a man but the words of God. How could sin dwelling in Paul's flesh not make him a sinner? Paul saw a law in his members—when he willed to do good, evil was present with him. What did he do? He delighted in the law of God after the inward man. Inward man, outward man...sound familiar? Paul separated them. How many Christians find that same law but only become discouraged by it?

Paul asked the question, "Oh wretched man that I am, who shall deliver me out of this body of death?" Did he stop there or is there a solution to all this twisting and turning? In the next verse, it says, "I thank God through Jesus Christ my Lord." He continued, "So with my mind I serve the law of God, but with the flesh the law of sin and death." The revelation of God's Spirit made all the difference to Paul! For us, too, Romans 8:1-3 finishes the point and delivers the soul.

The knowledge of good and evil does not allow us to understand salvation God's way because it prevents us from grasping the concept of two different men in man. This lesson bears repeating: the danger in knowing good and evil became clear when Cain, under its influence, offered God his best instead of what God required. Cain believed that his sacrifice was good. He ended up hating his brother because Abel's sacrifice was acceptable to God. Out of jealousy, Cain killed him. Evil judgments come instantaneously when our "good" behavior is not acknowledged as such.

To admonish the Church not to follow after the knowledge of good and evil, I can think of no better example than Jesus and His life here on earth. The priesthood of God, using the pure Word of God, but interpreting it according to the knowledge of good and evil, judged God (Jesus is God). He was found guilty—not perfect—and sentenced to death for His "sins."

Christianity, operating according to the knowledge of good and evil, will do the same thing. The fruit of this tree is destructive to faith because it accuses us and insists that God is angry without a remedy. This mindset is destructive to the Church because it rejects the perimeters established by God and establishes its own. It is destructive to the Body of Christ because it denies that the power of God is able to finish the workmanship of man. Instead, man crowns himself as potter over his own life.

Summary

The misconception that we must earn God's love by right actions is lethal to the soul. Nothing we have done or will ever do in the flesh can buy God's grace—it is free! God created man because He wanted a friend. After man fell into sin, God undertook the most massive rescue operation the universe has ever seen. Man's history since the fall has been the story of God reconciling us to Himself, so that He might once again have a friend to walk and talk with in the cool of the evening. Through Christ, God finished the work of reconciling us back to Himself by not imputing our trespasses to us (2 Cor. 5:19). Jesus took upon Himself the penalty for all of our sins, making Christ our only justification. In Him alone, there is life. That is good news!

A God who would condescend to reach down in to the muck and mire of our depravity, scoop us out, and cleanse us with His own blood most certainly is a God whose ways are much higher than our own. Only God has the infallible judgment, authority, and wisdom to declare what is good and what is evil. Our own finite, fallible, gullible sensibilities are useless to us when we pridefully judge anything after the flesh. Jesus warned us, "Judge not according to the appearance, but judge righteous judgment" (John 7:24). Righteousness is in God alone and our flesh has no ability to judge righteously. Our only place of safety is in eating from the tree of life and forsaking the tree of knowledge of good and evil.

The Ten Commandments were not given to man so that he could earn God's favor by keeping them and completely negate the need for unmerited favor. The law was given so that we might have easily understood parameters to rein in our arbitrary sense of right and wrong. In the New Covenant, God writes His laws upon our hearts, freeing us completely from having to determine right and wrong, no matter the circumstance. This means that God is the Potter, the Artisan who makes us and molds us into what He wants us to be. We are the clay, the lump with no ability to make itself into anything! Clay simply must yield to the hand of the Potter.

Let us yield to His loving hand, allowing Him to take us through trials and tribulations so that we, too, can learn to hold unwaveringly to His promise to make something beautiful out of our lives. In Christ, our past is redeemed, our present makes sense, and our future is secure. We please Him with our faith, so let us believe that nothing can possibly separate us from His love!

Study Questions

25. *Why didn't God want Adam and Eve to eat of the tree of the knowledge of good and evil*

26. *What was the certain outcome of their disobedience?*

27. *What was missing from the fruit of the tree of the knowledge of good and evil?*

28. *What did man lose when he began judging himself as evil? What was the result of that loss?*

29. *What does the tree of life represent? The tree of the knowledge of good and evil?*

30. *Why was Cain's sacrifice unacceptable to God?*

31. *How do we attain the righteousness of God? How does that differ from works?*

32. *Was God saying that he didn't want man to know the difference between good and evil? How could we be good and not do evil?*

33. *What are the two keys to doing right?*

34. *Why are trials so important to our walk with God?*

35. *What does it mean to be reconciled to God? To be justified?*

36. *What does Christ mean when He describes himself as the Potter?*

37. *Explain the difference between the way God's commandments were intended to be used and what man did with them. Why does it matter?*

38. *Explain why the fruit of the tree of knowledge of good and evil is so destructive to the Church.*

THREE

The Natural Man Does Not Receive the Things of God

12 Now we have received, not the spirit of the world, but the spirit, which is of God; that we might know the things that are freely given to us of God. 13 Which things also we speak, not in the words which man's wisdom teacheth, but which the Holy Ghost teacheth; comparing spiritual things with spiritual. 14 But the natural man receiveth not the things of the Spirit of God: for they are foolishness unto him: neither can he know them, because they are spiritually discerned. 15 But he that is spiritual judgeth all things, yet he himself is judged of no man. 1 Corinthians 2:12-15 (KJS)

These words are taken from Paul's first letter to the Christian assembly at Corinth. The concept is a necessary building block of the Church because it addresses the difference between the natural man and the spirit man. God knew that the carnal mind of man, with its power to reason and its disastrous view of good and evil (plucked by disobedience from the forbidden tree), would assert itself as guide in spiritual matters whether it really understood what God wanted or not.

Accepting God's final word on this subject would free the Church from much that troubles her. Led by the natural man, she has found herself in a most inconceivable place—earthbound and lost. God gave her His Spirit, the wings of a great eagle. Those wings are powerful enough to soar above the tempest of lies. The Church is meant to fly! God gave His Spirit of Truth to keep the Church in every matter of importance so that she can make right decisions and know the truth.

Christianity has the reputation of being in confusion. Not even ministers within the same denominations agree on scriptural interpretation. If that's not a perfect description of lost, I don't know what is. The Bible is proclaimed as the pilgrim's map, and it certainly is. However, the natural mind has no map-reading skills!

By taking a closer look at Paul's words, we see that verse 12 describes a "world spirit" and a "spirit which is of God." God gives us His Spirit so that we can know the things that are freely given to us of God. There are two spirits. Not only does God operate by means of a spirit, the world does too. They are not the same.

The world's spirit can influence us, and we should consider that a warning. We must try the spirits to see if they are of God (1 John 4:1). God's Spirit can teach us the things freely given to us by God, the world's spirit cannot. However, the world's spirit can manifest itself as being very religious. In fact, it has gods of its own. The Church must look for truth, not just religious experiences. God commands us to forsake the gods of the world.

Paul went on to say that believers speak of the things freely given by God, but not by the words that man's wisdom teaches. Man's wisdom *cannot* teach us these things. This is not a call for Christians to be ignorant or a sign that being stupid is holy. On the contrary, God commanded His disciples to study, to seek wisdom, and to value knowledge. Being ignorant of the difference between the two realms of the spirit is ignorance no matter how intelligent one may be in the natural realm!

Paul said that we speak the things that the Holy Ghost teaches, and by them, we compare spiritual things with spiritual. The understanding we lack in the Church comes from refusing to allow the Holy Ghost to be the only one to teach the absolutes of truth. Without the Holy Ghost, we cannot judge between two differing opinions concerning Scripture and determine which one is true. This has stripped the Church of a foundation upon which to build, making every opinion become as valid as the next. Confusion naturally results when our ignorance tries to bluff its way into a place of credibility on any subject. How could a gathering of God's children accept something so obviously earthly when our lineage is so evidently divine?

The Natural Man Can Be Very Religious, Can't He?

1 There was a man of the Pharisees, named Nicodemus, a ruler of the Jews: 2 The same came to Jesus by night, and said unto him, Rabbi, we know that thou art a teacher come from God: for no man can do these miracles that thou doest, except God be with him. 3 Jesus answered and said unto him, Verily, verily, I say unto thee, Except a man be born again, he cannot see the kingdom of God. {again: or, from above} 4 Nicodemus saith unto him, How can a man be born when he is old? can he enter the second time into his mother's womb, and be born? 5 Jesus answered, Verily, verily, I say unto thee, Except a man be born of water and [of] the Spirit, he cannot enter into the kingdom of God. 6 That which is born of the flesh is flesh; and that which is born of the Spirit is spirit. 7 Marvel not that I said unto thee, Ye must be born again. {again: or, from above} 8 The wind bloweth where it listeth, and thou hearest the sound thereof, but canst not tell whence it cometh, and whither it goeth: so is every one that is born of the Spirit. 9 Nicodemus answered and said unto him, How can these things be? 10 Jesus answered and said unto him, Art thou a master of Israel, and knowest not these things? 11 Verily, verily, I say unto thee, We speak that we do know, and testify that we have seen; and ye receive not our witness. 12 If I have told you earthly things, and ye believe not, how shall ye believe, if I tell you [of] heavenly things? 13 And no man hath ascended up to heaven, but he that came down from heaven, [even] the Son of man which is in heaven. 14 And as Moses lifted up the serpent in the wilderness, even so must the Son of man be lifted up: 15 That whosoever believeth in him should not perish, but have eternal life. 16 For God so loved the world, that he gave his only begotten Son, that whosoever believeth in him should not perish, but have everlasting life. 17 For God sent not his Son into the world to condemn the world; but that the world through him might be saved. 18 He that believeth on him is not condemned: but he that believeth not is condemned already, because he hath not believed in the name of the only begotten Son of God. 19 And this is the condemnation, that light is come into the world, and men loved darkness rather than light, because their deeds were evil. 20 For every one that doeth evil hateth the light, neither cometh to the light, lest his deeds should be reproved. {reproved: or, discovered} 21 But he that doeth truth cometh to the light, that his deeds may be made manifest, that they are wrought in God. John 3:1-21

All false religion is conceived in the carnal mind. The mind of man stood its ground in the days of Jesus. The high priest of the natural mind confronted the High Priest sent by God (under the true covenant that God gave Abraham and Moses). The kingdom of the natural man, filled with serious believers, collided with the Kingdom of truth (the very Kingdom on which they claimed to be waiting), rejected God, and crucified Him. How did this happen? It was the natural result of looking in the wrong realm. To the natural mind, the priestly obligation was to the external and temporal, not the invisible and eternal.

In John 3, we have a clear picture of the gulf that exists between the natural mind and the mind taught by the Holy Ghost. Nicodemus, who came to see Jesus, is the quintessential example of the natural man. First, he was serious about his religion. His attention was arrested by the powerful miracles in Jesus' ministry. He sought to explain these gigantic anomalies by attributing them to the sovereignty of God. His natural mind grappled with things too vague to grasp, but Nicodemus had no hostility to vent against this young minister, even though he seemed to be from the wrong tribe (under God's command, the tribe of Levi was the tribe of ministry but Jesus was from the tribe of Judah).

When Paul said that the natural man does not receive the things of the Spirit, he did not mean that the natural man is always hostile. He did not say that the natural man would not want to understand the things of God; he just said that the natural man could not understand.

For that very reason, God opened a door for the Holy Ghost when He started His Church. The Holy Ghost was poured out on the day of Pentecost, poured out to dwell in the heart of every believer. From inside of a man or woman, God the Teacher would bring forth truth—His plan,

His people, His glory! With the open door that God has provided, why stay within the limitations of the natural mind?

Nicodemus said some astounding things in his greeting to Jesus. He called Him "rabbi," which means master, and he called Him "teacher." Nicodemus also realized that no man could do what Jesus was doing unless God was with Him. Sounds perceptive for the natural mind, doesn't it? However, calling Jesus "master," "teacher," and "sent from God" meant that Nicodemus was ignorant of some very important truths. Jesus confronted him, saying, "Verily, verily, I say unto you, except a man be born again, he cannot see the Kingdom of God." Abrupt, isn't it? "Verily, verily" was a confrontational phrase used to command attention. As a religious leader, Nicodemus should have recognized that Jesus was the Eternal King, the Messiah. How far is "rabbi" from God? That's how far Nicodemus was from recognizing who Jesus was!

The wise men that saw the star knew the King had been born and found Bethlehem by inquiring of the Scriptures. Remember, they didn't "follow the star" to Bethlehem, they went to Herod, who called all the chief priests and scribes and demanded they tell him where Christ should be born. They said, "It is written, and thou Bethlehem in the land of Judah..." (Matt. 2:1-12). The old prophet Simeon knew the baby whom Mary and Joseph brought to the temple for dedication. He lifted Jesus and said, "Lord, now let thy servant depart in peace according to thy word, for my eyes have seen your salvation" (Luke 2:25-35).

Nicodemus was himself a rabbi, a master in Israel, but he didn't know that Jesus was the Lamb of God who takes away the sins of the world. He should have known that. Because of the revelation of the Holy Ghost, John the Baptist knew, and he spoke those words the first time he saw Jesus. Zacharias, the priest and father of John the Baptist, prophesied that John would go before the face of the Lord to prepare a way for Him (Luke 1:76). Nicodemus should have been aware of those things.

Nicodemus should have said, "I know you. You are Christ the Lord, born in the city of David, Savior of the world. The shepherds told us about the angels proclaiming these things in the heavens. You are the fulfillment of Isaiah's prophecies, You are the one born of a virgin, Emmanuel, Counselor, Prince of peace, Mighty God, Everlasting Father!"

Nicodemus' natural mind was not hostile but it was far from acknowledging who Jesus truly was. He was so far off that he appeared neither religious nor familiar with the Hebrew Scriptures, both of which he thought he was. Jesus told Nicodemus that he must be born again to see the Kingdom. His response is a perfect example of the natural mind believing that spiritual truths are foolishness. How can we be born again when we are old? How do I get back inside my mother?

Without Jesus as his guide, Nicodemus would have gone away feeling uncertain about what Jesus said. Any discussion with his religious friends would have digressed into mocking what none of them understood. What else could the natural mind do with such a statement? After what Jesus said, Nicodemus, who thought he understood everything he needed to, suddenly had questions. What a great example of shepherding: asking questions that lead to a desire to understand more. Jesus answered the questions that He generated, and the discussion took a spiritual turn. Nicodemus would not have asked those questions otherwise. Though his life revolved around the Hebrew religion, his understanding of that religion and its God were limited to what he could see and touch and understand with his natural mind, but God is a Spirit!

Except a Man Be Born of Water and of the Spirit, He Cannot Enter the Kingdom of God

To Nicodemus, this statement made even less sense than the first one! He believed he was in the Kingdom of God because he was a descendant of Abraham. The only way into the Kingdom that he understood was birth, and he felt a part of it because of who he was. Now, this Jesus was teaching him something unthinkable, saying that he was outside the Kingdom and that he must be "born again" to enter in.

With his natural mind in control, everything looked splendid up to that point—he had come by to visit this preacher and, in less than a minute, found out that he was not even in the Kingdom! Jesus, we know, was right in His assessment. Being a minister isn't enough, we must be born of the Spirit.

Jesus went on to say, "That which is born of the flesh is flesh, and that which is born of the Spirit is spirit." Nicodemus was stunned by what Jesus said. He marveled at the words, "You must be born again."

Knowing this, Jesus used the wind as an example to help him understand the meaning of the Spirit. "The wind bloweth where it listeth, and you hear the sound thereof, but you cannot tell where it comes from, and where it goes: so is every one that is born of the Spirit."

What was Nicodemus' answer to all of this? He asked Jesus, "How can these things be?" Jesus answered him by asking another question: "You are a master in Israel and you don't know these things?" He meant: You are a leader among My people...the kingdom of Israel is defined by *fellowship* with God through sacrificial offerings and the temple service, and you don't know Me?

Jesus repeated, "Verily, verily, I say unto you..." (For a young preacher with seemingly only miracles for authority, such words were very confrontational.) The words that followed were like hammer blows of accusation, thundering with power. "We speak that we do know, and testify that we have seen; and ye receive not our witness. If I have told you earthly things, and ye believe not, how shall ye believe if I tell you of heavenly things?"

Are these not the very words that Paul wrote for all the earth in his letter to the Church at Corinth? Jesus said, I'm telling you things about the Kingdom of God and its spiritual vistas unseen by the natural eye. In reading these verses for their full impact, we can see that Nicodemus was told some incredible spiritual truths! Look at John 3:12-15; it is some of the most confrontational doctrine in the Gospels.

The natural man and his carnal mind are lost in this maze of spiritual truth. What we easily understand when taught by the Holy Ghost is impossible to grasp by human reasoning, no matter how intelligent a person may be.

What would the statement in verse 13 mean to Nicodemus...up to heaven, down from heaven, in heaven? John 3:16 is one of the most beloved and oft-memorized statements in the Bible, yet it is a conclusion of verses 14 and 15. Those verses explain everything that Jesus told Nicodemus about God's salvation plan. Using the Hebrews' exodus from Egypt, Jesus explained salvation God's way.

4 And they journeyed from Mount Hor by the way to the Red Sea, to compass the land of Edom: and the soul of the people was much discouraged because of the way. 5 And the people spake against God, and against Moses, Wherefore have ye brought us up out of Egypt to die in the wilderness? for there is no bread, and there is no water; and our soul loatheth this light bread. 6 And Jehovah sent fiery serpents among the people, and they bit the people; and much people of Israel died. 7 And the people came to Moses, and said, We have sinned, because we have spoken against Jehovah, and against thee; pray unto Jehovah, that he take away the serpents from us. And Moses prayed for the people. 8 And Jehovah said unto Moses, Make thee a fiery serpent, and set it upon a standard: and it shall come to pass, that every one that is bitten, when he seeth it, shall live. 9 And Moses made a serpent of brass and set it upon the standard: and it came to pass that if a serpent had bitten any man, when he looked unto the serpent of brass, he lived. Numbers 21:4-9 (ASV)

Sin and the Cross of Calvary

Jesus used an historical event as an illustration. Nothing in the Old Testament Scriptures implies anything more being in this story. The natural man certainly could not see the promise of eternal life, but there it is. Jesus saw His own substitutionary death and the victory over sin that faith in His atoning sacrifice brings. The wages of sin is death. God finished sin off at the cross. As we see in this example, God's salvation plan is simple—obey God. When you are bitten, look to the cross—do not struggle, do not promise to do better if you get another chance, do not look at yourself, do not focus on the problem. Faith in Jesus is the answer!

The Israelites had every reason to understand the merciful and loving God that led them from Egypt's bondage. After Moses arrived, they saw nothing but God's intervening power and faithfulness to His promises. Tragically, their carnal minds accused God of not being a good God, an accusation that came from Satan in the garden. When they came to God in repentance, He mercifully provided a remedy every time.

There is no way the carnal mind or natural man could see the Son of God in the serpent hung on the pole. How could the perfect, sinless, obedient Son be pictured as a snake? Nicodemus got a lesson on the cross and did not even know it. God, in His faithfulness, shared His heart and desires with one of His children, and the inability of the natural man to assimilate the information is patently evident.

This exchange between Jesus and Nicodemus is clear to us as we read it from a vantage point of two thousand years of Christian experience, but the Church needs to understand God's will for her in these end times. The confusion that exists (because of conflicting views among believers) can be resolved by going to Jesus, as Nicodemus did. After all, Jesus said, "My sheep hear my voice, and I will lead them." The natural man thinks that this is foolishness: Go to Jesus now, as if we could just walk up to Him and ask Him questions? The truth is that we can!

The Church has an open door to God through prayer, and the Holy Ghost indwells every believer who has invited Him in. In the Book of Revelation, we see Jesus *in the midst* of the seven Churches. In fact, the Bible tells us that the Church is His Body and He is the Head. The reason that God would symbolize the relationship between Christ and His Bride in such terms is to show us the closeness and perfect dependence He intends.

A human body cannot function without a head. The entire body has nerve connections to the head that operate all the time. If a body part reports pain, the head rescues that part. If the toe on the right foot is on something sharp, the head does not send a message to move the left foot. The heel's line of communication is as direct as the ear's. The Church has a heavenly Father who really cares. Jesus lives to make intercession for us, and the Holy Ghost is sent to lead us into all truth. Notice, the carnal mind is not even in the equation!

Saul of Tarsus Met Jesus of Heaven and Became Paul of Revelation Knowledge

Paul wrote a heavenly declaration to the Church at Corinth, which tells us that the natural man does not receive the things of the Spirit of God. We can learn a lot from looking at the miraculous change that God wrought in Paul's life. This is clearly a "before and after" story! In Acts 9, Saul of Tarsus, the serious religious leader, met the very Jesus he was persecuting.

> *1 And Saul, yet breathing out threatenings and slaughter against the disciples of the Lord, went unto the high priest, 2 And desired of him letters to Damascus to the synagogues that if he found any of this way, whether they were men or women he might bring them bound into*

Jerusalem 3 And as he journeyed, he came near Damascus: and suddenly there shined round about him a light from heaven: 4 And he fell to the earth, and heard a voice saying unto him, Saul, Saul, why persecutest thou me? 5 And he said, Who art thou Lord? And the Lord said, I am Jesus whom thou persecutest: (it is) hard for thee to kick against the pricks. 6 And he trembling and astonished said, Lord, what wilt thou have me to do? And the Lord (said) unto him, Arise, and go into the city, and it shall be told thee what thou must do. 7 And the men which journeyed with him stood speechless, hearing a voice, but seeing no man. 8 And Saul arose from the earth; and when his eyes were opened, he saw no man: but they led him by the hand, and brought (him) into Damascus 9 And he was three days without sight, and neither did eat nor drink. 10 And there was a certain disciple at Damascus, named Ananias; and to him said the Lord in a vision, Ananias. And he said, Behold, I (am here), Lord 11 And the Lord (said) unto him, Arise, and go into the street which is called Straight, and inquire in the house of Judas for (one) called Saul, of Tarsus: for, behold, he prayeth, 12 And hath seen in a vision a man named Ananias coming in, and putting (his) hand on him, that he might receive his sight. 13 Then Ananias answered, Lord, I have heard by many of this man, how much evil he hath done to thy saints at Jerusalem: 14 And here he hath authority from the chief priests to bind all that call on they name. 15 But the Lord said unto him, Go thy way: for he is a chosen vessel unto me, to bear my name before the Gentiles, and kings, and the children of Israel: 16 For I will show him how great things he must suffer for my name's sake. Acts 9:1-16 (KJS)

This story is similar to the one about Nicodemus, only this time the man *was* hostile to the Christian faith. However, Saul was not trying to fight God. On the contrary, he thought that he was fighting *for* God. He knew the Old Testament very well, but only in the physical, historical sense.

The natural man has an adversary that he cannot see—Satan—whose power to manipulate is well documented in the Bible. Satan uses our emotions and our power to reason to prod us into doing things that are religious, but not godly. Saul of Tarsus bound Christians and tortured them until they blasphemed Jesus' name. He hauled them to prison and consented to their deaths. He did those horrible things to please God, not knowing that God would do none of those things. Saul's desire to serve God led his natural man to fight Him instead.

Understanding how Satan wages this war is important to the Church. Satan knows that he can manipulate man's desire to serve God by using false information to challenge him. Because man was created without the ability to know truth from lies, he naturally relies on human reasoning to decide what is the truth. Then, based on his own misinformation, he strikes out to defend the faith. Saul is a perfect example of such devilish manipulation. But after God changed him, the man who appeared to be totally evil was actually a precious builder in the Kingdom of God.

God could have easily created us with an ability to discern truth from lies. A blue vapor could surround someone's face if he lies or a voice from heaven could announce boldly, "That is a lie." Instead, God left man vulnerable to lies because He declares that He (God) is Truth. In coming to Him, we need only believe that He is telling the truth. That, of course, requires faith, and faith pleases God.

The day God started the Church in that upper room in Jerusalem, He gave her the Holy Ghost to indwell every believer. The Holy Ghost is the Spirit of Truth! Jesus said that the world could not receive this "Spirit of Truth" because it cannot see Him. The natural man cannot receive the Spirit of Truth because the natural man is limited to the realm of what he can see and touch. The natural man, operating by the power of the carnal mind, is like a storm brewing in the spirit realm. We can see this storm building again and again in the Bible. The goodness or wickedness of man is not the issue, but rather these two forces converging into collisions of colossal proportions.

Religious fervor clears our conscience of guilty feelings because we act in defense of what we believe (even if our actions are contrary to God's will). This removes God's voice from the matter. When God's input is shut out, human reasoning asserts itself as the judge, appoints emotions as the jury, and hands a win to the devil. Millions have died in these storms, which are not acts of God. God, inside a man named Ananias, brought peace to the storm we call Saul of Tarsus, giving the entire Church rest.

> *Then had the churches rest throughout all Judaea and Galilee and Samaria, and were edified; and walking in the fear of the Lord, and in the comfort of the Holy Ghost, were multiplied.* Acts 9:31 (KJS)

Indisputably, Paul was a good man. His love for God is beyond question. What we see in him, after the Holy Ghost taught him, is the wisdom and understanding the Christian faith hinges on. We have a clear example of just how different Paul the Christian was (with God's leading inside of him) than Saul the Jew (intellectually interpreting God's wishes and will) when Paul met Agrippa.

> *28 Then Agrippa said unto Paul, Almost thou persuadest me to be a*
> *Christian. 29 And Paul said, I would to God, that not only thou, but*
> *also all that hear me this day, were both almost, and altogether such*
> *as I am, except these bonds.* Acts 26:28-29 (KJS)

Agrippa was not a Christian, but Paul almost persuaded him to convert—two different ideals, two opposing beliefs. When human reasoning was the judge, Saul did not tolerate disagreement because he had no confidence in the ability of God's Spirit to influence an individual and change him later. He had no fatherly love to temper anger's fire. When emotions were his jury, he became enraged by rejection and found the offender guilty of death.

Converted, Paul said, "I wish you were altogether persuaded, just like I am today, except that I wouldn't want you to be bound." Saul, who had letters giving him permission to bind Christians, sought the opportunity to bind any who did not agree with his understanding of God. By God's transforming power, he became the man who said to the one in opposition, "I would not want you to be bound." In Christ, he found fatherly love and a living hope for the redemption of the lost. "For God so loved the world..."

When God decided to calm the storm created by Saul's desire to help Him, God stopped him on the road to Damascus and rendered him helpless. God instructed him in the truth and then called Ananias, who knew of the terrible things Saul had done to the Church. God asked Ananias to represent heaven's mercy extended to an offender—love, peace, and healing. What religion could love and pray for and heal an adversary of such immensely destructive proportions? No man is capable of this kind of love. Only God can love so much as that. What better argument could there be against the natural man ruling the Church?

Summary

As a religious leader in Israel, Nicodemus should have recognized Jesus as the Messiah. However, Nicodemus did not look upon Jesus with the eyes of the Spirit, but with the eyes of the natural mind. He was blind to the most fundamental truths about the Messiah and His Kingdom because the natural mind has no way of apprehending spiritual things. Jesus told Nicodemus that only those born of water and of the Spirit can see the Kingdom of God. Unless we are born again, we cannot see Jesus as the Messiah any better than Nicodemus.

Religious exercises do not enable us to see the Kingdom or make us a part of the Kingdom. False religion is a product of the natural mind. They that want to worship God must worship Him in Spirit and in truth, or they are not truly worshipping Him (John 4:23). If we ask Him to, God will use the Word as a two-edged sword to show us the difference between self-will worship and worship according to the will of the Spirit (Heb. 4:12-13). Only the Word can divide between our soul and our spirit man, enabling us to apprehend the truth and find rest.

Saul of Tarsus was a very religious man, but he didn't know God or see the Kingdom. He lived according to the natural mind and operated on intellect. After He met Jesus, Paul was transformed by the renewing of his mind—he was a new creature. Only the new creature can worship God and fellowship with Him according to the will of the Father. Trying to serve God by way of the natural man is futile.

Study Questions

39. *Why is the Church earthbound and lost?*
40. *Why did God give the Spirit of Truth to the Church?*
41. *What are the two spirits that Paul reveals to us in 1 Corinthians 2:12-15?*
42. *How can we tell the difference between the two spirits?*
43. *Where does this lack of understanding in the Church come from?*
44. *Why did Nicodemus have so much trouble understanding what Jesus talked to him about in John 3?*
45. *Why should Nicodemus have recognized Jesus as the Messiah?*
46. *What did Nicodemus believe qualified him to be in the Kingdom of God? What is the answer Jesus gave him?*
47. *How are we protected from our reasoning?*
48. *What happened to Saul of Tarsus on the road to Damascus?*

49. *Why is it important to the Church to understand how Satan wages war?*
50. *Why did God leave man vulnerable to lies?*
51. *What prevents the world from receiving the Holy Ghost?*
52. *How was Paul the Christian different from Saul of Tarsus?*
53. *What did God use Ananias to represent and why is that significant to us?*
54. *What does the natural man need to receive the things of God and how does he get it?*

FOUR

Every Believer Must Know the Voice of Jesus

1 After six days Jesus took Peter, James, and John his brother, and brought them up into a high mountain apart, and was transfigured before them: and his face did shine as the sun, and his raiment was white as the light. And behold, there appeared unto them Moses and Elijah talking with him. Then answered Peter, and said unto Jesus, Lord, it is good for us to be here: if thou wilt, let us make here three tabernacles; one for thee, and one for Moses, and one for Elijah. While he yet spoke, behold, a bright cloud overshadowed them: and behold a voice out of the cloud, which said, This is my beloved Son, in whom I'm well pleased; hear ye him. Matthew 17:1-5 (KJS)

"This Is My Son; HEAR YE HIM"

On the mountain of the transfiguration, the disciples awoke to find Moses and Elijah talking with Jesus. Moses representing the law and Elijah representing the prophets. These two ministries had been the major voices of the Hebrew economy, two facets of the Defining Covenant, adding light to the revelation of the Son. But on this day, the transcendent glory of the Transfigured Man outshone the combined glory and power of everything these men represent. Moses turned the river into blood and Elijah transfigured the sacrifice with fire from heaven, yet these great events were mere shadows foretelling coming events. Here now is the Son, the Source of redemption's blood and baptism's fire. Hear ye Him!

The Voice of Truth

The distinguishing dynamic of the voice of Jesus Christ is truth. Whatever He spoke to whomever He spoke was always absolute truth. Truth spoken in a time of religious confusion always seems confrontational. The words of Jesus were Spirit and life and they were true to the revelations all Scriptures held. When Jesus spoke of Abraham, the words that Moses wrote in Genesis became a part of the revelation about Him and also from Him! He could say, "Before Abraham was, I am" and it was true of Him. God standing in a physical body less than thirty-five years old did not dim the truth that Scripture was revealing.

The Voices of the First Covenant—Moses and Elijah

The Law Speaks Through Moses

Under the ministry of Moses, the law of God broke like a sunrise on the horizon of darkened humanity, and with its light, man beheld mercy's river of blood. The law of God condemned sin, demanded justice, and there, for the repentant, provided the blood of sacrificial cleansing. Under God's legal system, there would be a river of blood (water represents outward cleansing, blood represents total redemption before God). Moses' first miracle in Egypt was turning the water into blood.

Man's view of God as judgmental misses the truth completely. The law of God established truth-based criteria for man to judge by, thus defeating the power of the knowledge of good and evil with its relativity-based criteria. The Ten Commandments returned judgment to God and freed man from the condemnation conjured up by his own intellect. The law condemned sin, but God provided a way of escape from the punishment. He substituted the death of an animal for the death of man for his sins. It has always been God's mercy and God's grace that brings salvation to man.

Jesus looked at the law and saw the truth. The law is weak because it depends upon the flesh to obey it. The spirit man can obey the commands of God. Man must be reconciled to God by Christ's blood and indwelt by the Holy Spirit. Jesus not only preached His message, He lived it.

Satan's Twofold Battle

Not only must God's children be rescued from sin, they must also be rescued from false religion and its lie-based theology. Both Moses and Jesus were rejected because the system of judgment used by the children of Israel was not truth-based—the leaders no longer heard the voice of God. The warning in this picture is for the people of God throughout all ages.

Satan has two lines of warfare against humanity. Sin is the first line, with its wages of death. The second line is religion, which is based on human reasoning and human effort and has man as its head. Satan's warfare of religious deception is a most insidious plan. Under the guise of God's own Church, man falls prey to lies and ends up rejecting God. The Bible defines God by His own words; any lie attached to that Word changes the definition of God and invents another deity. Jesus lived the revelation of all that the Scriptures declared. Not only His words were true, His life was also true to God's perfect definition.

Knowing the voice of Jesus is knowing the truth!

While God's people were living enslaved in Egypt, the seeds of false religion were sown in their hearts. Abraham's God seemed distant and vague. God promised Abraham that his descendents would go into bondage but He also promised to send a deliverer after four hundred years. Though the Hebrews were living the reality of that word, there seemed to be no correlation between it and their having faith in God or His promises. God spoke *to* Moses and then *through* Moses. From Mount Sinai, God brought forth the law to be a schoolmaster that He might exalt the real victory, the blood (Gal. 3:24).

Moses the deliverer brought these descendents of Abraham out of the bondage of religion to the mountain set on fire by the very presence of God. Moses' voice became the voice of God for these people. His words were true and full of power, but he could not bring the children of Israel into the promised land. He could lead them out but he could not lead them in. The law and its limitations were all part of the plan of God.

As Moses' first miracle was turning the water into blood, Jesus' first miracle was turning water into wine (the wine is symbolic of blood). The parallel here is very instructive. Both covenants of God are based on the blood.

The water that Jesus turned into wine is described in John 2 as being "cleansed after the manner of the purifying of the Jews." (The water had to settle in order to allow the cleaner water to be drawn off the top.) The deeper truth, however, is that "purifying after the manner of the Jews" meant purifying after the law, or only outwardly. Jesus changed the water into wine with just His Word and joy replaced duty at the wedding!

Prophetic Intervention: The Voice of God Through Elijah

Elijah showed the intended use of the law by first washing the sacrifice but also showed that God would not be limited by man's inability to obey the law (1 Kings 17). God always had a plan that included Holy Ghost intervention—"what the law could not do in that it was weak through the flesh, God, sending his own Son..."

> 3 For what the law could not do, in that it was weak through the flesh, God, sending his own Son in the likeness of sinful flesh and for sin, condemned sin in the flesh: 4 that the ordinance of the law might be fulfilled in us, who walk not after the flesh, but after the Spirit. Romans 8:3-4 (ASV)

The conviction brought on by the voice of the law is merely a diagnosis intended to point the sin-sick soul to the Great Physician. The law was never intended to heal the disease, it was sent to glorify the Physician.

Outward cleansing should reveal the need in us for further cleansing. Being "good" by a legal standard will never satisfy one's soul. The blood of Jesus flowed from the cross a greater river and the Holy

Ghost, called down by Jesus as the baptism of fire, finishes the will of God in every believer into which it comes.

Elijah came to the children of Abraham with the voice of God at another period of bondage for them. Religion had become voice upon voice and confusion upon confusion. No one knew who was telling the truth and the land was full of idols.

Elijah's words stopped the rain and brought the fire from heaven that consumed the flesh of the sacrifice. The prophets of God are the eyes of the nation and the voice of God. Under the calling of God, they see the direction God intends to lead his people. They are also the voice of God of restoration. The voice of the prophet is linked to the presence of God and thereby ministers to the exact need of the hour. They bring judgment when judgment is needed in order to reinstate truth. They bring mercy to rejoice against judgment when repentance comes, reflecting the merciful nature of God. Prophets are the voice of truth, thundering across the pages of history and restoring the path of righteousness to the pilgrims who are homeward bound.

The Voice of the New Covenant—Jesus

"This is my beloved Son, hear ye him." Above the highest expectation demanded by the voice of the law, even with its river of blood. Above the highest vision of the prophetic voice, even with its consuming fire.

The voices that had been the vehicles of God in the Defining Testament were silenced before the Son. A Christian is not measured by the voice of the law or the vision of the prophets. He is measured by Christ!

The Church is to become a perfect man, the full stature of the man Christ Jesus. The law can bring us out but it can never take us into the full stature of Christ. The fire of Elijah's confrontation and restoration was but a promise of the indwelling fire of the Holy Ghost. The voice of Jesus is a consuming fire!

> *1 God Who at sundry times and in divers manners spake in times past unto the fathers by the prophets, 2 hath in these last days spoken unto us by His Son, whom he hath appointed heir of all things and by whom also he made the worlds...* Hebrews 1:1-2 (KJS)

God, who created all things, chose to reveal Himself by His voice—an intimate connection that is intended to reassure, not frighten. This God, who is Spirit, who fills the heavens, and who is too vast for the finite mind of man, reveals Himself in such a closeness that we hear His voice. He is beautiful, He is wonderful, and He is tender and merciful, but He would frighten us by His sheer magnitude, so He speaks. The voice that created the universe whispers to us, "Peace, be still," and darkness turns to light. There is a miracle of revelation in the written Word. We can read the Bible and the Spirit of His presence catches us up into this realm where He dwells, and we behold Him as He is.

My Sheep Know My Voice

1 Verily, verily, I say unto you, He that entereth not by the door into the fold of the sheep, but climbeth up some other way, the same is a thief and a robber. 2 But he that entereth in by the door is the shepherd of the sheep. 3 To him the porter openeth; and the sheep hear his voice: and he calleth his own sheep by name, and leadeth them out. 4 When he hath put forth all his own, he goeth before them, and the sheep follow him: for they know his voice. 5 And a stranger will they not follow, but will flee from him: for they know not the voice of strangers. John 10:1-5 (ASV)

My sheep hear my voice, and I know them, and they follow me... John 10:27 (KJS)

The Church must know the voice of her Shepherd in order to be led by Him and to enter in at the Door. He tells us that we will know His voice and follow Him only. Every pastor of a Christian church in the world today can say that he hears and follows that voice, but the voice of Jesus is absolute truth. The conflicts that exist in the Church because of differing interpretations of Scriptures are glaring evidence that the leadership of the Church as a whole is not hearing the voice of Jesus. Doctrine and dogma are long-winded, but not necessarily truth. There are many voices, but not all belong to the Shepherd.

In the Old Testament, God's voice was evident in every life connected to Him. Noah built the ark—not in answer to a flood—but in obedience to God, who knew that one was on the way. Abraham knew that his barren wife would have a son years in advance; he knew that his descendants would be slaves in Egypt for four hundred years; he knew that a deliverer would come and that his offspring would eventually possess the land of Canaan. She did, they did, and he did: just like God said! The God of the Bible is a Spirit, and they that worship Him must worship Him in spirit and in truth (John 4:23-24).

It would be presumptuous indeed to assume that a Spirit God would share His mind and will and in doing so would write a book that is one-dimensional. The Bible expresses the thoughts of God without sound, and the Holy Spirit is the breath moving up through the symbols recorded, creating a heavenly syntax that flows from the very life of God like a river.

How wonderful that Jesus tells us His sheep will hear His voice! In an hour of confusion, the Church has the voice of Jesus to reassure her. The voice is an intimate point of contact, for no one knows precisely how we hear something. Today, a multitude of voices say, "Follow me, I'm right." Remember, Jesus said that His sheep *would* hear His voice. He did not say they could hear it or they should hear it, He said they would hear it. What a precious promise!

How many believers stumble through times of perplexity, uncertain about what to do, when they should be able to hear the voice of Jesus? We may be able to hear Him through a preacher or a religious profes-sional, but each of us should be able to hear the Shepherd Himself. His voice is personal and real. The Bible is His Word. By the Holy Spirit's anointing, we can experience something much deeper than just words on a page; we can actually hear His voice. Thank God, He offers a depth of communion that can tune the Bride's ear to the one voice of the beloved Bridegroom.

If ever the Church needed to hear God's voice, she needs to now. The human intellect cannot hear the voice of God by reading the Bible, but the spirit man can. The indwelling of the Holy Ghost is the magnif-icent fulfillment of the promise of the tabernacle: the candlestick does illuminate the table of shewbread and the glory of God illuminates the mercy seat. The indwelling Spirit is our only means of hearing God's voice in the written Word.

When Jesus said that His sheep would know His voice, He also said that He knows the sheep. The intimacy of this relationship is evident, and it is based on a confidence that He wants to instill in us. We are His to care for. When we begin our Christian walk, He assures us that we will be okay because we can hear Him talk. He did not say we would immediately understand and comply, for that would reduce the relationship to one of only servitude. He tells us we will hear His voice, but we may not comprehend the words right away.

Only as believers grow up do they come to understand the words. Babies learn to discern voices before they learn words. Infants link their mother or father's voice to actions of some sort. We always hope that the actions are nurturing and loving, and that the child comes to associate the voice with having his needs met. If the infant suffers repeated pain, the association he forms to the voice is one of fear or dread. Before a baby can even understand what mom or dad is saying, a correlation is drawn between the person and their known behavior.

Sheep certainly cannot understand what a shepherd says; they react to what a shepherd does. The brains behind the operation belong to the shepherd; therefore, the responsibility to build and maintain the relationship is his. Sheep are very fearful and can fall victim to any number of predators. In His merciful love, Jesus gives us a promise of true safety: I know My sheep and they follow Me.

This does not sound as difficult as some make a Christian's life seem. If we know His voice, we are not going to follow a stranger and that keeps us safe from deception! He knows us, so we are not going to be forsaken or lost if we wander off from the rest of the flock; He will seek us until He finds us. Jesus gives us a picture of contented followers who are unafraid because the Shepherd watches them night and day. When Jesus speaks to a disciple through His Word and bears witness to it by His Spirit, it should mean more to that follower than any other doctrine. No religion is higher than truth.

Fellowship Divine

God's promise to talk to us on an individual level is precious. In the Old and New Testaments, God communicated with His sons and daughters. He not only expected them to hear, but to obey and to talk to Him as well. A vast majority of the Christian Church has only a vague notion of what God really promises each believer.

The Greek word for divine communication is *koinonia*, which is defined as fellowship, association, community, and intercourse. In the New Testament, *koinonia* is translated to English as "fellowship" and "communion." We misunderstand this word if we think God only talks to man like thunder from on high. Rather, it is as a father and child interact—both listening, both talking.

Most believers pray, but their understanding of what actually takes place varies greatly. Today, God's simple invitation to fellowship is complicated by varied and conflicting teachings about prayer: how to, when to, whom God hears and why, ways to best manipulate Him, repetition, and even just recitation. All He really wants is for us to come and talk to Him. He will hear us and answer—that's it! Too easy, the booksellers scream!

We have seen the concept of communion (as the Bible described our daily fellowship with the Father) come to mean eating a wafer offered by a religious professional, a ritual replacing the voice of God! It is worth noting that no magnificent cathedrals were built until man replaced the Holy Spirit as leader of the Church. The natural man substitutes things that impress and empower him for things that impress and empower God!

The wafer as fellowship with God can be withheld from people by a priesthood in order to punish or excommunicate them. That is power in the hands of men! The Word of God as fellowship with God bypasses those corrupt ministries and brings man back to direct communication with Him.

Down through Church history, the Bible has been forbidden to God's people by religious leaders as well as by dictators. Today, confusion among Christian leaders makes the average Christian view the Bible as too complex to understand. This is just another angle in Satan's war with God—he means to hinder God's children by removing their faith and confidence in reading and understanding.

How is it that a ritual has replaced the fellowship that Jesus seeks with us? The Bible defines communion as our daily communication with the Father. In His daily intercourse with His disciples, Jesus taught and listened. They knew He cared about *them* and not just His ministry. When they did not understand what He said, they asked Him questions and He answered on the spot. When He was rejected they were also rejected—such was the depth of their association. Paul longed for and encouraged all believers to commune with Jesus in just this way. Communion as a ritual is violence done to the intent and reality of the original written Word.

10 That I may know him, and the power of his resurrection, and the fellowship of his sufferings, being made conformable unto his death; 11 If by any means I might attain unto the resurrection of the dead.
Philippians 3:10-11 (KJS)

The Church, whose birth is recorded in the book of Acts, operated under divine authority by listening to the leading of the Holy Ghost. Jesus promised His disciples that the Comforter would speak Jesus' words to them once He withdrew from the physical realm. The night He was to be betrayed, He repeated again and again those words of comfort. As they ate the Passover with Him, He also revealed Himself as the Passover Lamb by using the physical example set before them.

The modern use of the word "communion" comes from this setting as well. Jesus said, "This is My body." Where was He? He was at the table of the Passover lamb, not just holding a piece of bread but telling the disciples that He is the Lamb of Passover. The Holy Ghost gave them a revelation that explained the entire feast in terms of Jesus' life.

A ritual begins when the natural man tries to grasp a spiritual truth apart from the Spirit of God. The carnal mind stares at the piece of bread, totally focused on the physical, while all around a glory shines forth in revelation light.

Those Jewish disciples had eaten that feast and celebrated the Lamb all of their lives without understanding its significance. On that night, however, Jesus said, this is Me, I'm going to die today (remember, the Jewish day begins at sundown and lasts until the next sundown). He did die that day and the death angel has had to pass over every dwelling on which His precious blood is applied ever since that day.

In Exodus 12, God gave Moses directives for eating the flesh of the Passover lamb. We must remember that we fellowship with God through His Word, Jesus. In John 1, Jesus is described as the Word of God: the Word of God at creation, the Word of God that contained life, and the Word become flesh. There are several commands concerning this fellowship, this eating of His flesh:

8 And they shall eat the flesh in that night, roast with fire, and unleavened bread; with bitter herbs they shall eat it. 9 Eat not of it raw, nor boiled at all with water, but roast with fire; its head with its legs and with the inwards thereof. 10 And ye shall let nothing of it remain until the morning; but that which remaineth of it until the morning ye shall burn with fire. 11 And thus shall ye eat it: with your loins girded, your shoes on your feet, and your staff in your hand; and ye shall eat it in haste: it is Jehovah's Passover. Exodus 12:8-11 (ASV)

Jesus told His disciples that the lamb symbolized His Body, to take and eat. In John 6, Jesus said that He was the Bread that came down from heaven, that a man may eat thereof and not die. He said that His flesh was that bread. In Exodus 12:9, we are commanded to roast the flesh (Jesus, the Word) with fire (the Holy Ghost, the Spirit of truth), and not to eat it raw (using the carnal mind to try to understand the Word rather than Holy Spirit fire). On the day of Pentecost, the Spirit sat on those in the upper room like cloven tongues of fire. The Bible must be interpreted and taught by the Holy Spirit.

God also commanded that we eat the inward parts of the lamb as well as the flesh. The inward parts are the things not seen on the surface. The lamb must be opened to uncover the inward parts. The Bible is the same: the Holy Spirit opens the Word and we find truths not seen on the surface. God commands us to eat the "hidden manna" of the Bible—this is not optional (Rev. 2:17). We may think that we can eat only what we want at the Feast of Passover, but we must eat according to the commands of God.

The Church cannot continue down this road of intellectually inter-preting the Holy Scriptures. The natural man cannot receive the things of the Spirit because they are spiritually discerned and they are foolish-ness to him (1 Cor. 2:14). To deny that the Word is made flesh and dwells among us is foolishness indeed. Substituting a wafer for the flesh of Jesus—when we have the Word made flesh—is a practice that could only come from the natural man.

In his letter to the assembly at Ephesus, Paul quoted from this passage in Exodus. He said, "...having your loins girt about with truth...your feet shod with the preparation of the gospel of peace...and the sword of the Spirit in your hand..." (Eph. 6:14-17). The sword Paul referred to is the Word of God. King David said, "...thy rod and thy staff they comfort me" (Psalm 23:4). Both implements describe the Word of God—sometimes it corrects us (the rod) and sometimes it just draws us closer to Him (the staff). God has spoken to man down through the ages and it's time to listen. The Church finds herself in a strange place because many ministers have not been teaching God's children about the availability of the voice of Jesus, nor have they acted in ways consistent with men who hear the voice of God.

The voice of Jesus is the unveiling of truth on any subject. The doctrines of men demand that this voice be silenced when it negates their personally held theories. Men say that they want to hear the voice of Jesus…until it contradicts what they teach. When that happens, they call His voice a liar. This is Satan's doing. It works as well for him today as it did two thousand years ago.

Today, to have God Himself actually talk to just any member of a church would seem extraordinary at best. Mentioning it to anyone invites concern or, worse, the title of prophet. At the same time, thousands flock to any location where some kind of unexplained phenomenon reportedly occurs. Books are written about angelic visits not based on biblical truth and churchgoers buy them. Contradicting doctrines abound and when anyone questions the confusion emanating from Church leadership, we are assured that God is the author of it all!

When it comes to interpreting the Bible, it is now every Bible school for itself. Without God's voice leading ministry and leading the lives of believers, doubt assaults the natural man with questions the carnal mind cannot answer. When searching from church to church uncovers glaring contradictions, doubt, not faith, is fortified. This is the reason God assures us that He will talk to us! We have to believe that He will talk and observe others to whom He does talk. We also need a foundation in the written Word of God and the Holy Ghost indwelling us.

God's Word and Will, Done on Earth as in Heaven

The first time God spoke, there was no human ear to hear Him. His words were creative, not instructive. Man sees himself as being so important in the scheme of things that he imagines God wants us to fulfill those words, no matter what they say. There are commands for man in the Bible, but much of the revelation of God points to the power of His words. There is a problem with man believing that God wants him to do all of these wonderful things—man cannot do them!

72

God promises that He will have a Church without spot or wrinkle (Eph. 5:27). Men get together and tell themselves that they are the Church, but what they see is full of spots and wrinkles. Men try and try to get rid of the sins and fail. Failure destroys faith in our relationship with the Father, whom we want so much to please. To escape the burden of this failure, we reason that God did not actually mean a Church without sin or failure (so spots must mean something else).

In John's first epistle, it says, "He that is born of God does not commit sin." The carnal mind finds that statement to be foolish. Men go back to the original languages of the Scriptures, trying to find a cure for the strong words of God. We must ask: is God instructing or creating here? If He is instructing, we need to comply. If He is creating, this is a promise. We need to believe in God's promises as Abraham did, who received a son from an old, barren womb.

When Jesus spoke to the fig tree, He did not hope that the fig tree understood Hebrew and would obey by its own power. The disciples found the tree dried up from the root when they passed by a short time later (Matt. 21:19-20). We need to understand that God also brings to pass commands that pertain to us.

God made His words the door and faith the key that unlocks it. The more impossible the command, the more faith accesses it. He commands and promises so that we are a part of the equation. When we cannot produce what God asks for, we must accept by faith that He will bring His words to pass. If we sin, we must repent and ask for His forgiveness and help. We surrender as one who is taken in battle. To our relief, the inner man of the Spirit is strengthened. Only the flesh man suffers defeat. In Genesis, God showed us this dynamic over and over again.

When God told Abraham to leave his kindred and family and go to a place that God would show him, Abraham took his father and Lot along! He left the rest, including the land where he grew up, but he was not completely obedient, so God held him short of the promised land. His father died of old age in Haran. God blessed both Abraham and Lot until they were too wealthy to stay in the same place. The day Lot left for the lush valley below, God spoke to Abraham about the promise again.

This revelation of how God works with us is not meant to foster a disobedient attitude. Rather, it is to fortify our understanding. The worst thing that we can do is give up and lose faith in God's plan for us. Faith is the victory that overcomes the world. Without faith, it is impossible to please God. God's voice is faith's rock of anchor. Even in correction, God's voice is the assurance that God is not finished working with us yet.

Under the law, man was given a locator, a point of reference moving him closer to recovery from his self-inflicted wound in the Garden of Eden. Lost and unaware of it—such is the legacy of the knowledge of good and evil. The random criteria (based on human reasoning and exploited by Satan) that man had used to judge good and reject evil were replaced by the law. With the law, God gave us absolutes for criteria—written instructions and divine intervention at the mercy seat. Thank God for the law! However, the law was only the first step toward salvation. It was to lead man away from the stranglehold his knowledge of good and evil placed him in, but it was not the tree of life. The law was the voice of God beckoning man down the road to recovery.

The law condemns sin and, under the divine direction of God, leads man to the mercy seat, where the blood makes peace. The carnal mind thinks that the law is all God wants—do's and don'ts. We think that keeping laws makes God happy. The real purpose of the law is to bring man to a place of repentance and then direct him back to God for cleansing. Man thinks that keeping the law cleanses him, yet his conscience still holds the residue of sin. Only faith in God works, but man's knowledge of good and evil causes him to believe that he must earn peace through good actions.

Paul showed us how far this misconception strays from God's plan, using Israel as an example:

> 1 Brethren, my heart's desire and prayer to God for Israel is, that they might be saved. 2 For I bear them record that they have a zeal of God, but not according to knowledge. 3 For they being ignorant of God's righteousness, and going about to establish their own righteousness, have not submitted themselves unto the righteousness of God. 4 For Christ [is] the end of the law for righteousness to every one that believeth. Romans 10:1-4 (KJS)

"Zeal without knowledge" means busily doing things that sound godly but never bothering to seek God's agenda. Christ is the end of the law for everyone that believes. We see, then, how important the voice of God is. His very being is revealed in His recorded words.

The historical dimension of the Bible entreats us to seek God for reconciliation. It does not reveal the mind of God beyond His desire for fallen man to repent of his sins and come back to the Father. There is a door of hope for the natural man to see. He can then repent if he wants to. The spiritual dimension of the Bible holds the revelation of God's secrets and is the anchor of truth. The fundamental building blocks of Christianity are encapsulated in the historical dimension; however, they are out of the sight range of the carnal mind.

In the natural realm, the number "1" is assigned a value that is an absolute. The same is true of all numbers, letters, colors, etc. The word "one" had no value until someone assigned it a value. Now, one apple or one car or one tree means the same thing to every Bible school student. The color red means the same throughout a culture. God's Spirit assigned values to the words of the Bible. The natural man can read the Bible but not necessarily understand what it says. We must have the Spirit of God reveal the meaning God intended. Wouldn't it be wonderful if Bible school students agreed on the absolutes of the Bible the way they agree on the natural absolutes?

Jesus is the Word ("...the Word became flesh and we beheld the only begotten of the Father, full of grace and truth..." (John 1:14)). In these last days, God has spoken to us by His Son (the written Word revealed). The Bible, God's Spirit, and a message that is of God, by God, and about God are all the heritage of the Church. The Word has been unsealed since Calvary's Lamb prevailed to open the Bible. The Church is now weeping like John on the Isle of Patmos, as confusion about God's words exists throughout Christendom.

We need the Book that Jesus opened and we need to repent for allowing the carnal mind to teach the things it cannot comprehend. Intellectual arguments will then fall like Korah and the men of renown, swallowed by the earth from whence they came. This will be to the glory of God and the true ministers of God.

The Solution: Heed the Warning of God

By the end of Israel's national independence, the people had mixed the religions of the neighboring nations with the truths of God. Confusion was rampant. No one knew who told the truth anymore, so God sent a prophet. Elijah stepped into this moment of historical dismay—a man of God sent to restore the absolutes of truth by signs and wonders (1 Kings 17). There was no rain or dew those years except by his command. Drought was the warning that God promised.

> *14 That I will give [you] the rain of your land in his due season, the first rain and the latter rain, that thou mayest gather in thy corn, and thy wine, and thine oil. 15 And I will send grass in thy fields for thy cattle, that thou mayest eat and be full. 16 Take heed to yourselves, that your heart be not deceived, and ye turn aside, and serve other gods, and worship them; 17 And [then] the LORD'S wrath be kindled against you, and he shut up the heaven, that there be no rain, and that the land yield not her fruit; and [lest] ye perish quickly from off the good land which the LORD giveth you.* Deuteronomy 11:14-17 (KJS)

Israel doubted the warning because it came through the words of a man. In the confusion of the hour, Israel forgot God and hunted Elijah. When Israel assembled at Mount Carmel, Elijah asked, "How long do you halt between opinions?"

How could the people of God give credibility to the prophets of Baal? It happened because the worship of God was polluted a little bit at a time over a long period of time. The falsehood that one generation received was passed to the next. The next generation, in turn, ingested even more corruption and passed it to their children, and so on, and so on… The question that Elijah asked Israel is just as valid today. How long do you halt between opinions, Church?

Let's look at what Elijah did on the mountain. In front of the confused congregation, he erected the altar of the evening sacrifice, which symbolizes fellowship with God (1 Kings 18). The people of God had stopped spending time with Him and listening for His instructions. The priesthood was also guilty in that day. Today, under the New Covenant, all believers are priests. "We are a royal priesthood, a holy nation…" (1 Peter 2:9). We cannot neglect fellowship with God in prayer and in the Word.

After he finished the altar, Elijah put the wood in order. The sacrifice that we offer to God (ourselves) must be consumed by fire. Wood is the starting point, the place where the flame must start. Wood is symbolic of the life of the natural man, made flammable by the desire to follow examples of obedience. What Abraham was for Isaac and all of his descendants, what all the men and women of the Bible are, and especially what Jesus was in His surrender to total obedience, become a flash point for our own obedience and surrender. When we want to be like Jesus because of His example, the Spirit of God is empowered to burn the dross out of us.

When Elijah called for the ox, which is symbolic of us as believers, it was dead already. There is no record of him wrestling with the ox. Our flesh was dealt with on Calvary (we are dead and our life is hid with Christ in God (Col. 3:3)). We must hold onto that by faith until it comes to pass in us, because faith is the substance of things hoped for and the evidence of things not seen (Heb. 11:1). Elijah laid the ox on the altar that he had raised up in the sight of all the people.

Next, Elijah called for four barrels of water. The four barrels were filled and then poured out on the sacrifice three successive times. Four is the number of revelation and three is the number of divine completeness. We see, then, that God was revealing Himself as the true God to all of Israel. The number twelve is symbolic of divine government. The revelation of God brings divine government. The water is symbolic of the Word of God, and it is through His Word that He reveals Himself. The water of the Word also washes the sacrifice. Jesus is going to have a Church without spot or wrinkle. He is going to wash her by the washing of the water of the Word (Eph. 5). A true man of God preaches the Word, realizing that he is washing the congregation according to God's will. He knows that he will then have to call the fire of God to consume the flesh of the flock.

Jesus is the High Priest who has the power to burn out of us all that must go. The Bible describes three ways that God deals with dead flesh—resurrecting it, burning it, or sending the fowls to eat it. When He burns the flesh, it is pleasing to Him, a sacrifice of a sweet-smelling savor. When the fowls eat the flesh, it means that it is rejected, judged.

The letter of the Bible can only kill us. Men think that killing the flesh is all that God wants, but they have never smelled rotting flesh! Without fire, dead flesh is a terrible problem. John the Baptist (expressing the spirit of Elijah) washed the last sacrifice—Jesus, the Lamb of God—as the law demanded. John, being the son of a priest and a Levite, met the required criteria. Jesus, being the Sacrifice, said that His washing was necessary to fulfill the law. He persuaded John to baptize Him (or wash Him, as the Greek word *baptizo* means). Thus, the story of Elijah was played out in the New Covenant!

After he poured the water, Elijah prayed. His petition asked three important things, all of which confront confusion:

1. All of God's people can return to knowing that He is the true God in Israel.
2. They can know there are true servants of God among all of the voices claiming to be.
3. Elijah, God's true servant, had done all of these things at God's word.

> *36 And it came to pass at [the time of] the offering of the [evening] sacrifice, that Elijah the prophet came near, and said, Lord God of Abraham, Isaac, and of Israel, let it be known this day that thou [art] God in Israel, and [that] I [am] thy servant, and [that] I have done all these things at thy word. 37 Hear me, O Lord, hear me, that this people may know that thou [art] the Lord God, and [that] thou hast turned their heart back again. 38 Then the fire of the Lord fell, and consumed the burnt sacrifice, and the wood, and the stones, and the dust, and licked up the water that [was] in the trench.* 1 Kings 18:36-38 (KJS)

That event marked the end of confusion! The voice of God was heard and seen. Truth confronted lies and the fire fell. John the Baptist said, "I baptize you with water, but there is one coming after me who was before me. He shall baptize you with the Holy Ghost and fire." The water is only part of the plan of salvation. When the fire of God is finished, a believer is changed in a way that only God can change him. The new man of the Spirit lives through the fire (like the three Hebrew children—Shadrach, Meshach and Abed-nego) and the old man of the flesh becomes ashes in the economy of God.

When Israel refused to repent after the warning of Elijah's day, God moved them to Babylon. Babylon gets its name from the Tower of Babel, which means "confusion of tongue." When Nebuchadnezzer conquered Judah (ending the national independence of Israel), he carried the royal seed to Babylon but the remainder of God's people were scattered throughout the nations. This was how invading kings stopped nations from rising again after being defeated. Moving to a nation where a different language was spoken made it necessary for the subjugated people to learn a new language. After a few generations in the new land, the old language was forgotten. With the people scattered about in many nations, the new languages became a barrier to reunification if ever they returned to their native land.

God used such a barrier to stop the people from accomplishing great things in their flesh for a carnal religion. The Tower of Babel was a warning from God that if His people ordained the flesh as their head He would send confusion of languages, thereby ending their unity.

After Israel would not receive His correction and stop its fleshly, carnal approach to religion, He had no choice but to scatter her language again. The Tower of Babel was revisited. God will not let the flesh man mount up and create a religion of carnal origins in His name. When the Church was born on the day of Pentecost, God broke the power of confusion of languages by His Holy Ghost. Let's look at Acts 2:

> 4 And they were all filled with the Holy Ghost, and began to speak with other tongues, as the Spirit gave them utterance. 5 And there were dwelling at Jerusalem Jews, devout men, out of every nation under heaven. 6 Now when this was noised abroad, the multitude came together, and were confounded, because that every man heard them speak in his own language. 7 And they were all amazed and marveled, saying one to another, Behold, are not all these which speak Galileans? 8 And how hear we every man in our own tongue, wherein we were born? 9 Parthians, and Medes, and Elamites, and the dwellers in Mesopotamia, and in Judaea, and Cappadocia, in Pontus, and Asia, 10 Phrygia, and Pamphylia, in Egypt, and in the parts of Libya about Cyrene, and strangers of Rome, Jews and proselytes, 11 Cretes and Arabians, we do hear them speak in our tongues the wonderful works of God. 12 And they were all amazed, and were in doubt, saying one to another, What meaneth this? Acts 2:4-12 (KJS)

These witnesses were all Jews, devout men out of every nation under heaven. Why were these Jews out of every nation under heaven? Nebuchadnezzer had scattered Israel. In this picture, we see that the Holy Ghost breaks Babylon's power! The confusion of tongues is abolished when the Teacher sent from God arrives! Hallelujah! When God speaks, we comprehend His person and His will more clearly than we do at any other time. The voice of Jesus, indwelling every believer, whispers, "This is the way, walk ye in it!" (Isa. 30:21).

Summary

In the picture of the Shepherd and His sheep, Jesus gives us every reason to trust and obey Him. He promises that we will hear His voice. He promises that He will seek us and find us if we get lost. In Psalm 23, He promises that His sheep shall not lack anything they need. In Isaiah 40:11, Jesus says that He will gather His lambs and carry them close to His heart. We often complicate our relationship to Christ, but this illustration reminds us how very simple it is meant to be.

Communion rituals are one example of the way we complicate our walk to our own hurt. Communion with the Most High God is meant to be a very simple time of talking and listening to the Friend who sticks closer than a brother. We can go to Him as a child goes to a father, confident that He accepts us as we are and corrects us when we need it. His desire is that we become one with Him, that we fellowship with Him in a fullness and an intimacy that only a Bride and Bridegroom can know.

God gave the law in order to lead us to a place of repentance. He intended for the law to show us that we are unrighteous and that we need to go to Him for cleansing. Understanding the true purpose of the law helps us understand God's heart and His voice. God speaks to us now through His Son. The Comforter is come, the Bible Teacher is sent to live in the heart of every believer! With Christ living inside of us, we have every provision we need—His presence keeps us.

Moses' ministry was the provision God gave Israel as a covering authority for them—he was the voice of God to those people because he led them according to the cloud by day and the pillar of fire by night. He also interceded for them before God. If they stepped out from underneath that covering through rebellion, they forsook the canopy of God's protection and direction. Through the leadership of the fivefold ministry, the Church is meant to operate in the same way under the New Covenant (1 Cor. 10:1-14; Eph. 4).

In the story of Elijah and the prophets of Baal, God gives us many precious pictures of His heart and His promises. Offering ourselves as a living sacrifice and allowing God to cleanse us with the water of the Word and consume our flesh with the fire of the Holy Ghost will lead us ever closer to Him. Spending time in the Word and in prayer are so important to us and to God. He grieves when we forget Him days without number. When we know Him as the indwelling Christ, we long for time with Him just as passionately as He longs for us!

Study Questions

55. What is the dynamic of the voice of Jesus that makes it stand out from all other voices?
56. What does water represent in the Bible? What does blood represent? How is this significant in Moses' first miracle?
57. What was the purpose of the Law?
58. What is wrong with man's view of God as judgmental? What is the truth?
59. What do God's children have to be rescued from and why?
60. Why couldn't Moses take the children of Israel into the Promised Land?
61. What is the parallel between Moses' first miracle and Jesus' first miracle?
62. What does the story of Elijah teach us?
63. What is the function of the prophets of God?
64. What is God teaching us through the Transfiguration of Jesus on the mountain where he appeared with Moses and Elijah and heard God say, "This is my Son, hear ye Him"?
65. What did Jesus say about His voice?
66. What is our only means of hearing God's voice in His written Word?
67. Besides our knowing His voice, what additional assurance does Christ give us that ensures an intimate relationship between us and Him?
68. What is the simple truth about prayer?
69. How is communion as a ritual offensive to God?
70. What is the spiritual significance of the Last Supper?
71. What is revealed to us about communion through the word God gave Moses in Exodus 12 about how to eat the Passover Lamb?
72. How and why does Satan try to keep us out of the Bible and what is God's provision that protects us from Satan's lies?
73. Why is it important for us to know the difference between when God's word is creative and when it is instructive?
74. What is the difference between the historical and spiritual dimensions of the Bible?
75. What is the heritage of the Church?
76. What was the result of Israel's mixing truth with religion and what did God do about it?
77. How does the story of Elijah from 1 Kings 18 compare with God's ministry today?
78. What was the significance of John the Baptist baptizing Jesus?

79. Water (washing of the Word) is only part of the plan of salvation. What is the rest of it?

80. Why did God demolish the common language of man in the descendants of Noah and how is this significant today?

81. What is God's plan for ending the confusion of tongues?

FIVE

The Holy Ghost Is the Teacher Sent from God to Indwell Every Believer

If we do not learn from mistakes of the past, we repeat them. The nation of Israel was the first church that God ordained. The New Testament Church is a holy nation, and the Old Testament holy nation was a church. The nation of Israel made mistakes. They incorporated the most dynamic parts of pagan religious services into their own temple worship of God, bringing abominations into their ritualistic fellowship with the true God. They also worshiped other gods.

God called idolatry "adultery" when He talked of His people being unfaithful to the truth. False theology is the same as a false god, and the Church cannot ignore the comparison. Satan knows that lies are an abomination to God. It was through lies that he separated Adam and Eve from the tree of life.

Lies grow and multiply—the Israelites eventually believed that their idolatrous practices came from God! They were surprised when God called them idolatrous, just as many Christians today are insulted by the suggestion that lies are being taught as truth within the Christian

Church. Lies still constitute sin in the eyes of God. Sadly, most church-goers do not know what is true and what is false in what they believe. Thankfully, most preachers would not knowingly teach falsehoods. The problem is that when a lie is thought to be the truth, no one thinks it is a lie.

The first question is, "Who is to say what is truth? Just because we don't agree doesn't mean that you are right and I am wrong." Satan knows that lies are a vicious weapon because they are passed off as truth when they are actually very far from it. When a lie is taught for hundreds of years, longevity alone makes it sacred. The problem we have when we discover that lies have been sown throughout the Church is then knowing whom we can turn to that all the Church could safely believe.

Think of the day that the Church was born in Jerusalem: around a hundred and twenty disciples, gathered by the Lord's command, were transformed by the baptism with the Holy Ghost. Our answer is that we need faith in the Teacher sent from God! We need to go back to the one Teacher who teaches absolute truth, the Holy Ghost! God promises that He will lead and guide us into all truth. Peace comes from knowing God's will and seeing it come to pass in our lives. Under the kingship of Jesus, the Church is transformed into New Jerusalem. In the book of Revelation, John saw New Jerusalem coming down out of heaven as a Bride adorned for her Husband.

Jesus is the Head of His Body, the Church. He told the apostles that He would send another Comforter, even the Holy Ghost, to dwell in the heart of every believer, to lead and guide them into all truth (John 16:13). Here, we have another absolute: Christ the Head sent the Teacher whom He chose; the Church will either submit to or reject that Teacher. That Teacher is the Holy Ghost.

Leaven and the Teacher Sent from Heaven

Leaven is a substance added to dough that causes it to rise. Leaven is a picture of something that has life. Jesus said, "…The kingdom of heaven is like leaven that a woman hides in three measures of flour until the whole is leavened" (Matt. 13:33).

To teach about the New Testament without using the foundation laid in the Old Testament is like trying to build a third story on a building before the first and second stories are there. God knew that His adversary, Satan, would try to twist His words of truth into lies that could deceive mankind. To assure that truth would be preserved, God used historical events to portray spiritual truths.

After Adam sinned, God took Adam's covering of leaves and replaced it with a flesh covering by substitution—a living animal died in Adam's place. Later, the Bible would tell us that without the shedding of blood there is no remission of sin, thereby revealing the death of Jesus in our place (Hebrews 9:22). As the flesh of another covered Adam's flesh, so does Jesus' flesh cover us when we accept Him. Christians understand that we need the blood of Jesus to wash away our sins. This is why being a "good person" does not satisfy the righteous requirements of God. The life-giving promises of the death and resurrection of Jesus were foretold in the first pages of the Old Testament!

Remember, God hid the true meanings of these historical events in the same way that governments at war encode their messages. God knew that He was at war with Satan and knew Satan to be a liar. He also knew that Satan would use God's own words to give himself credibility. God sent His messages of comfort and promise, but much of it was hidden. It was sealed off from man's understanding until God deemed it appropriate to open it. No human understanding can break the code. It is not a code a computer can break, it is a code only God can unseal. This "life of understanding" from God is the leaven of the Bible.

> 1 And I saw in the right hand of him that sat on the throne a book written within and on the backside, sealed with seven seals. 2 And I saw a strong angel proclaiming with a loud voice, Who is worthy to open the book, and to loose the seals thereof? 3 And no man in heaven, nor in earth, neither under the earth, was able to open the book, neither to look thereon. 4 And I wept much, because no man was found worthy to open and to read the book, neither to look thereon. 5 And one of the elders saith unto me, Weep not: behold, the Lion of the tribe of Juda, the Root of David, hath prevailed to open the book, and to loose the seven seals thereof. Revelation 5:1-5 (KJS)

> The secret [things belong] unto the Lord our God: but those [things which are] revealed [belong] unto us and to our children forever, that [we] may do all the words of this law. Deuteronomy 29:29 (KJS)

To our natural understanding, the story of Jonah is about a prophet of God sent to call a Gentile nation to repentance. We need the Holy Ghost to put "life," or leaven, into the story if we are to understand it spiritually. By God's Spirit of revelation, we can see that it describes Jesus being in the earth three days and three nights (as Jonah was in the belly of the whale). Jesus quoted the story of Jonah, saying it told of His time in the tomb (Matt. 12:40).

Jesus talked about the Scriptures from a spiritual view and few received it. No matter what the flesh saw, the Holy Ghost revealed the truth. In a nation filled with rejecting hearts, it was evident that the Holy Ghost was the one to trust. The only people who knew that Jesus was the Son of God were the people told so by the Holy Ghost. It is the same today (1 Cor. 12:3).

25 And, behold, there was a man in Jerusalem, whose name [was] Simeon; and the same man [was] just and devout, waiting for the consolation of Israel: and the Holy Ghost was upon him. 26 And it was revealed unto him by the Holy Ghost, that he should not see death, before he had seen the Lord's Christ. 27 And he came by the Spirit into the temple: and when the parents brought in the child Jesus, to do for him after the custom of the law, 28 Then took he him up in his arms, and blessed God, and said, 29 Lord, now lettest thou thy servant depart in peace, according to thy word: 30 For mine eyes have seen thy salvation, 31 Which thou hast prepared before the face of all people; 32 A light to lighten the Gentiles, and the glory of thy people Israel.
Luke 2:25-32 (KJS)

16 And Simon Peter answered and said, Thou art the Christ, the Son of the living God. 17 And Jesus answered and said unto him, Blessed art thou, Simon Bar-jona: for flesh and blood hath not revealed [it] unto thee, but my Father which is in heaven. 18 And I say also unto thee, That thou art Peter, and upon this rock I will build my church; and the gates of hell shall not prevail against it. 19 And I will give unto thee the keys of the kingdom of heaven: and whatsoever thou shalt bind on earth shall be bound in heaven: and whatsoever thou shalt loose on earth shall be loosed in heaven. 20 Then charged he his disciples that they should tell no man that he was Jesus the Christ.
Matthew 16:16-20 (KJS)

Man has added his intellectualized interpretation to the Bible with appalling results. Man's leaven, or "interpretation," of the Bible is malice against God's Kingdom.

5 And when his disciples were come to the other side, they had forgotten to take bread. 6 Then Jesus said unto them, Take heed and beware of the leaven of the Pharisees and of the Sadducees. 7 And they reasoned among themselves, saying, [It is] because we have taken no bread. 8 [Which] when Jesus perceived, he said unto them, O ye of little faith, why reason ye among yourselves, because ye have brought no bread? 9 Do ye not yet understand, neither remember the five loaves of the five thousand, and how many baskets ye took up? 10 Neither the seven loaves of the four thousand, and how many baskets ye took up? 11 How is it that ye do not understand that I spake [it] not to you concerning bread, that ye should beware of the leaven of the Pharisees and of the Sadducees? 12 Then understood they how that he bade [them] not beware of the leaven of bread, but of the doctrine of the Pharisees and of the Sadducees. Matthew 16:5-12 (KJS)

When Jesus told His disciples to beware of the "leaven" of the Pharisees and of the Sadducees, they tried to understand what He said with their human intellect. They were not able to. Jesus, seeing that they did not understand, asked them, "Do you not yet understand neither remember the five loaves of the five thousand, and how many baskets you took up? Neither the seven loaves and the four thousand and how many you took up?" Jesus was concerned about the way in which the two religious denominations of His day had added their own interpretation ("leaven" as He called it) to His Word. He used the number of baskets that were gathered after He broke the bread to feed the multitudes as a revelation of truth. Understand—twelve and seven? Oh, You are talking about doctrine, they said. Most ministers don't even allude to this conversation because it means nothing without the understanding of the Old Testament foundation.

The carnal mind is lost right about now! Using those numbers, the Holy Ghost made them understand a message about the doctrine of Jesus. It's true! God has assigned symbolic, spiritual meanings to numbers in the Bible and the Spirit teaches us their meanings. We know that the number "12" symbolizes the revelation of God and that the number "7" symbolizes perfection. Knowing what the numbers symbolized, the disciples were able to comprehend that Jesus had come as the perfect revelation of God and as the power of God that perfects us. His ministry was a sharp contrast to the religious activity of the Pharisees and Sadducees.

Those two groups of ministries had added their own "teachings" to the Scriptures, things that they used to condemn Jesus and His disciples. Their accusations, using *their* traditional teachings, seemed right and the people were confused. Does that sound like today? The Bible tells us that Jesus is the Bread from heaven and the Word of God. According to God's plan, the Bible is our bread and teachings about its content is the leaven. The teaching must be truth.

In the Old Testament, God gave seven feasts for His people to enjoy. They were times of great national unity and each had a secret meaning. The full understanding of those feasts did not come until Jesus arrived to fulfill all Scriptures. The seven feasts told of future events and provided startling details about the life of Jesus and His Church.

The seven feasts are:

1. *The Feast of Passover*
2. *The Feast of Unleavened Bread*
3. *The Feast of First Fruits*
4. ***The Feast of Pentecost***
5. *The Feast of Trumpets*
6. *The Feast of Atonement*
7. *The Feast of Tabernacles*

> 18 In the first [month], on the fourteenth day of the month at even, ye shall eat unleavened bread, until the one and twentieth day of the month at even. 19 Seven days shall there be no leaven found in your houses: for whosoever eateth that which is leavened, even that soul shall be cut off from the congregation of Israel, whether he be a stranger, or born in the land. 20 Ye shall eat nothing leavened; in all your habitations shall ye eat unleavened bread. Exodus 12:18-20 (KJS)

This passage gives a strong warning about leaven—if there was any in their houses, they were out of the Kingdom.

In the first three feasts, the Israelites could not have leaven. If leaven is a picture of sin, as some teach, why would God forbid it in the first three feasts (they represent the law, which God knew was weak through the flesh) and then demand it in the New Covenant Church, where Christ's blood justifies, sanctifies, and purifies? "Who shall lay anything to the charge of God's elect? It is God that justifieth."

> *33 Who shall lay any thing to the charge of God's elect ? [It is] God that justifieth. 34 Who [is] he that condemneth? [It is] Christ that died, yea rather, that is risen again, who is even at the right hand of God, who also maketh intercession for us.* Romans 8:33-34 (KJS)

God commanded leaven to be in the feast that symbolizes the birth of the Church (Pentecost)! Leaven could be in that feast because Jesus sent the Teacher of truth, the Holy Ghost, on that day. God forbade leaven prior to that because He wasn't going to teach the revelations of His Bible until after His sacrifice had been crucified by His priesthood. It is easy to see why, knowing the implications. Forbidding man to teach about the Bible without God's interpretation would have kept out lies, lies that accused Jesus falsely. Leaven could be there once Jesus had been crucified and the Bible was unsealed. Jesus was slain and He redeemed us by His blood, which made Him worthy to open the Book. No other is found worthy. "The Lion of the tribe of Judah hath prevailed to open the book..." (Rev. 5:5). On that feast day, the Holy Ghost was poured out upon all flesh and the Teacher sent from God arrived! With God indwelling every believer and teaching truth from the inside, the Church was on her way to winning the lost of the world.

The True Church: Christ's Body, Bride, and Building

In the book of Revelation, John saw a Church system that was the Bride of Christ. She was pure, holy, and undefiled, and she had made herself ready to meet the Bridegroom. She was depicted in many different ways throughout the book. In the beginning, she was pictured by the seven golden candlesticks; in the end, she was the city celestial, New Jerusalem. The Bride grows from being seven lamps that shed light on a limited basis to the greatest city the world will ever see. This is revelation, it is prophecy—it is not a plea from God, asking man to make this divine promise come to pass. God is going to have a Church without spot or wrinkle, one the gates of Hell will not prevail against, and He is the Author and Finisher of her faith.

The Church defined as the "Body of Christ" is a declaration of the Word of God made manifest in the flesh in every generation. The Church defined as the "Bride of Christ" is a declaration of the work of God perfected in the Spirit in every generation. The Church defined as the "Building of Christ" is a declaration of the will of God uniting in vision and purpose the saints of every generation. If we can understand God's view of the Church, we can also understand the Holy Spirit's role in our lives, both individually and corporately.

The Church as His Body: The Promise of Christ in Us

Christ's Body is the Word of God. We need the Holy Ghost to teach us the Word of God. If He teaches us, we can see Jesus as He is. The Church is His Body and His Body is the Word. When Jesus walked on earth two thousand years ago, men could see God manifested through His Church. The same will happen today.

In the New Testament, it says that we are "of His flesh and of His bones" (Eph. 5:30). We are told: "as He is, so are we in this world" (1 John 4:17). Again, in another place, we are reminded of "the mystery of godliness: God was manifest in the flesh..." (1 Tim. 3:16). Speaking of Jesus, we read: "...He is the Head of the Body, the Church" (Col. 1:18). John started his Gospel by declaring: "In the beginning was the Word and the Word was with God and the Word was God... and the Word became flesh and dwelt among us." Jesus is the Word become flesh. In the Book of Revelation, it says that Jesus was given a name that no one knew but He Himself, and His name is Word of God.

The Word of God (Jesus) is the Bible. The Bible is our sword. "The weapons of our warfare are not carnal, but mighty through God to the pulling down of strongholds..." (2 Cor. 10:4).

> *13 Wherefore take unto you the whole armor of God, that ye may be able to withstand in the evil day, and having done all, to stand. 14 Stand therefore, having your loins girt about with truth, and having on the breastplate of righteousness; 15 And your feet shod with the preparation of the gospel of peace; 16 Above all, taking the shield of faith, wherewith ye shall be able to quench all the fiery darts of the*

wicked. 17 And take the helmet of salvation, and the sword of the Spirit, which is the word of God: 18 Praying always with all prayer and supplication in the Spirit, and watching thereunto with all perseverance and supplication for all saints... Ephesians 6:13-18 (KJS)

The Church's weapon is the sword of the Spirit. When twisted by Satan, however, the sword becomes a weapon used against us. Jesus used "It is written..." as a sword to defeat the father of lies on the mountain of testing. The Word in us has the power to do the same. The Church must come back to knowing all truth in order for the Word of God to crush Satan. Half-truths will not stop his assault of lies. Our sword (the Bible) must not be dull; it will not be when the Holy Ghost is allowed to sharpen it.

The Church is described as the Body of Jesus. We must believe His words and, through the power of the Holy Spirit, obey them as He obeyed them. As members of His Church, we are to live His word every day, so plainly that the world sees Christ and is converted. The Word is truth; they that are part of Him know the truth and walk in it.

The Church will be one with the Word and that Word is absolute truth. The Body of Jesus is the will of God made manifest, the desire of God realized, and the power of God incarnate. Jesus' flesh was in subjection to the Spirit of God, and obedience was the recognizable outcome of subjection. Christ's flesh lived what the Word of God spoke and surrendered to the Spirit's dominion. When the Church lives the Word of God as the Spirit of God teaches her to, the world will see God. Emmanuel!

23 For the husband is the head of the wife, even as Christ is the head of the church: and he is the savior of the body. 24 Therefore as the church is subject unto Christ, so [let] the wives [be] to their own husbands in every thing. 25 Husbands, love your wives, even as Christ also loved the church, and gave himself for it; 26 That he might sanctify and cleanse it with the washing of water by the word, 27 That he might present it to himself a glorious church, not having spot, or wrinkle, or any such thing; but that it should be holy and without blemish. 28 So ought men to love their wives as their own bodies. He that loveth his wife loveth himself. 29 For no man ever yet hated his own flesh; but nourisheth and cherisheth it, even as the Lord the church: 30 For we are members of his body, of his flesh, and of his bones. 31 For this cause shall a man leave his father and mother, and shall be joined unto his wife, and they two shall be one flesh. 32 This is a great mystery: but I speak concerning Christ and the church. 33 Nevertheless let every one of you in particular so love his wife even as himself; and the wife [see] that she reverence [her] husband. Ephesians 5:23-33 (KJS)

Christ is the "Head of the Church" and "Savior of the Body." He gives Himself for her, that He might sanctify and cleanse her. Jesus washes her with His words so that He might present to Himself a glorious Church without spot or wrinkle—a holy Church without blemish. Because we are part of Him, the standard applied to the Church (which calls itself the Body of Christ) cannot be less than the standard Jesus applied to His own flesh when He walked in it on the earth. Look at Ephesians 5:30: "For we are members of His body, of His flesh, and of His bones!" His flesh! We are members of His flesh, which was brought to total defeat by the Spirit of God. The same victory belongs to us.

While Christ walked among His people in Israel, thousands thronged Him everywhere He went. Many times, He had to move on to escape the crowds. The needs were more than one man could possibly meet, so He sent the twelve apostles out in His name. In those Galileans, the world beheld the same splendor that it saw in Jesus. At any moment, Christ could be in more than a dozen places, and that was only the beginning! The Church is supposed to provide physical hands and feet while God provides the Spirit's power and wisdom. As I mentioned before, every believer in the Church is a priest—yes, a priest. Not just a priest, a *royal priest!* Under the New Testament covenant, every born-again believer is part of a royal priesthood.

9 But ye [are] a chosen generation, a royal priesthood, a holy nation, a peculiar people; that ye should shew forth the praises of him who hath called you out of darkness into his marvellous light: 10 Which in time past [were] not a people, but [are] now the people of God: which had not obtained mercy, but now have obtained mercy. 1 Peter 2:9-10 (KJS)

After His resurrection, Jesus was not recognized by the world or even by His friends. Mary Magdalene thought that He was a gardener when He appeared to her the first time! It was not until He spoke her name that she knew the man was Jesus. In Mark 16:12, it says, "After that He appeared in another form unto two of them, as they walked into the country." The men on the way to Emmaus were talking about the events of Jesus' crucifixion and resurrection and the tragedy of it all. Their interpretations were according to their natural understanding. Even though the men were disciples, they tried to understand these astounding events according to their carnal minds. From such a perspective, the truth was impossible for them to see. Look at this story from Luke's Gospel:

> 25 Then he said unto them, O fools, and slow of heart to believe all that the prophets have spoken: 26 Ought not Christ to have suffered these things, and to enter into his glory? 27 And beginning at Moses and all the prophets, he expounded unto them in all the Scriptures the things concerning himself. 28 And they drew nigh unto the village, whither they went: and he made as though he would have gone further. 29 But they constrained him, saying, Abide with us: for it is toward evening, and the day is far spent. And he went in to tarry with them. 30 And it came to pass, as he sat at meat with them, he took bread, and blessed [it], and broke, and gave to them. 31 And their eyes were opened, and they knew him; and he vanished out of their sight.
> Luke 24:25-31 (KJS)

It was only when their sight was elevated to the spiritual realm that those men recognized their Friend. The natural man cannot recognize Christ, for He is spiritually discerned.

Remember, Jesus said that His sheep would know His voice, and the voice of a stranger they will not follow (John 10:4-5). The voice of Jesus is the Word of God. All through the Bible, God says, "Obey my voice." The voice of God is a constant part of a believer's life. God would not have written that statement if we were not to hear and understand His voice. If the people of the Old Testament should have heard God's voice and obeyed it, how much more should we, who have the Spirit indwelling us, hear and obey it?

Let's look at another example, this one taken from John's Gospel:

> 4 But when the morning was now come, Jesus stood on the shore: but the disciples knew not that it was Jesus. 5 Then Jesus saith unto them,

Children, have ye any meat? They answered him, No. 6 And he said unto them, Cast the net on the right side of the ship, and ye shall find. They cast therefore, and now they were not able to draw it for the multitude of fishes. 7 Therefore that disciple whom Jesus loved saith unto Peter, It is the Lord. Now when Simon Peter heard that it was the Lord, he girt [his] fisher's coat [unto him], (for he was naked,) and did cast himself into the sea. 8 And the other disciples came in a little ship; (for they were not far from land, but as it were two hundred cubits,) dragging the net with fishes. 9 As soon then as they were come to land, they saw a fire of coals there, and fish laid thereon, and bread. 10 Jesus saith unto them, Bring of the fish which ye have now caught. 11 Simon Peter went up, and drew the net to land full of great fishes, an hundred and fifty and three: and for all there were so many, yet was not the net broken. 12 Jesus saith unto them, Come [and] dine. And none of the disciples durst ask him, Who art thou? knowing that it was the Lord. 13 Jesus then cometh, and taketh bread, and giveth them, and fish likewise. 14 This is now the third time that Jesus showed himself to his disciples, after that he was risen from the dead.
John 21:4-14 (KJS)

Jesus was less than a hundred yards from the disciples. Yet, in verse 4 it says that they did not know Him. In verse 6, Christ spoke and the fish obeyed His command to fill the nets! John finally recognized Jesus after He spoke. Jesus did this to send a message to both His disciples and us: stop looking at the flesh, I am a many-membered Body! The Church is "bone of His bone and flesh of His flesh"—His Body!

Jesus could only minister in one location until He sent out His disciples. Now, anywhere two or three of His disciples are gathered, He is in the midst. This is the promise of the Church being His Body. The world is waiting for it to come to pass.

I would like to share with you the reason Jesus wanted each of His followers to "preach the gospel to every creature," using myself as an example. I was born again in 1962, at the age of twelve. Using 1962 as a starting point, let's say there were only twelve Christians in the world— eleven other believers and myself. If each of us won just one person to Christ that year, there would have been twenty-four Christians in the entire world by 1963. An entire year to win one convert does not sound too hard. If every believer would win one person each year, our numbers would double. Surely, God could lead us to one hungry, hurting sinner in a year. Let's look at the math:

1962 = 12
1963 = 24
1964 = 48
1965 = 96
1966 = 192
1967 = 384
1968 = 768
1969 = 1,536
1970 = 3,072
1971 = 6,144
1972 = 12,288
1973 = 24,576
1974 = 49,152
1975 = 98,304
1976 = 196,608
1977 = 393,216
1978 = 786,432
1979 = 1,572,864
1980 = 3,145,728
1981 = 6,291,456
1982 = 12,582,912
1983 = 25,165,824
1984 = 50,331,648
1985 = 100,663,296
1986 = 201,326,592
1987 = 402,653,184
1988 = 805,306,368
1989 = 1,610,612,736
1990 = 3,221,225,472
1991 = 6,442,450,944

The whole world would have been won before the end of 1991, and the first group of twelve would have only needed to win twenty-nine souls to Christ in those twenty-nine years—one per year. However, each new believer would also win one a year. Think about it—we would have won the world's souls in just under twenty-nine years—not starting with the millions that called themselves Christians in 1962, but starting with the same number of disciples that Jesus had, twelve!

The Church is His Body! It is not comprised of just a few great ministers, but of all the saints (born-again believers). We are the Body of Christ on the earth. Jesus told His followers, including us, that we would do greater things than He did because He was going to the Father. God's Word in each believer glorifies God. His creative power demonstrates His will done on earth as it is in heaven. The Bible, written to declare victory over the adversary, Satan, is a weapon in the hands of the faithful—a Body seen by all who seek truth. Jesus truly is "God with us."

The Church as His Bride: The Promise of the Sinless One

Christ's Bride is the work of God perfected. In Genesis 24, Abraham sent his oldest servant, Eliezer (whose name means "God is help"), to find a bride for Isaac in Abraham's homeland. This is a picture of God sending the Holy Spirit to find and return a Bride for Jesus. Within this picture, we see the kind of woman God seeks for His Son.

Eliezer waited at the well, praying that God would verify the woman of His choice, not Eliezer's. He prayed for a sign: "The damsel that I ask a drink from and she not only gives me drink but offers to draw for my camels is the one." Rebecca came and fulfilled that sign.

Watering ten camels was a large task for a young woman who also had to gather water for her family. Such an act bespeaks a true heart of service. She sought nothing in return for her kindness, gave willingly, and took care of strangers as well as her own. She was willing to work hard and asked for nothing in return.

Rebecca was God's choice for Isaac…and she was barren! She needed a miracle from God to bring forth life. The fruit of her womb was not of the flesh. The flesh could not make her fertile, but God could. The Kingdom of God is a Kingdom of barren wombs and virgins! Nothing of the flesh will do here. God wants us to see that human effort cannot fulfill His promises. Even Abraham, father of the Kingdom, could not produce the promised son in his flesh. He could make an Ishmael, but that nation has only been a lasting problem for the seed of promise.

As we learned earlier, the promise God gives concerning the Church is perfection. He promises something so impossible to the flesh that all the glory will be His upon its completion. Man takes one look at the promise, makes a boast in his sincerity, overrates his ability, tries in the flesh, and fails. Humiliated by his impotence but unwilling to admit failure, man claims that Satan can conquer the flesh, but not God. Today, most ministers refuse to preach the perfection of the Church, except as some intellectualized concept of "maturity."

Paul, in his letter to the assembly at Ephesus, described the impact on the Church that God-ordained ministries would have:

> 11 And he gave some, apostles; and some, prophets; and some, evangelists; and some, pastors and teachers; 12 For the perfecting of the saints, for the work of the ministry, for the edifying of the body of Christ: 13 Till we all come in the unity of the faith, and of the knowledge of the Son of God, unto a perfect man, unto the measure of the stature of the fulness of Christ: 14 That we [henceforth] be no more children, tossed to and fro, and carried about with every wind of doctrine, by the sleight of men, [and] cunning craftiness, whereby they lie in wait to deceive; 15 But speaking the truth in love, may grow up into him in all things, which is the head, [even] Christ: 16 From whom the whole body fitly joined together and compacted by that which every joint supplieth, according to the effectual working in the measure of every part, maketh increase of the body unto the edifying of itself in love. Ephesians 4:11-16 (KJS)

In this small book, the Spirit of God defines the job that God expects His ministers to do. Anyone who claims to be in a position of leadership in the Church must be doing this job and nothing else. (I am talking about the true assembly, where Jesus is the Head, when I say the Church leaders will be doing what God wants.)

God is the "He" that gave "some apostles, and some prophets...for the perfecting of the saints." This entire concept pivots around God: He spoke it, He ordained the ministers, and He decreed the perfection of the saints. If the God for whom nothing is impossible declares this as His desire for His people, who can question the outcome? It is accomplished by His ability, which is why He starts with His provision of ministries. It was the same way in the book of Genesis:

> And when Abram was ninety years old and nine, the Lord appeared to Abram, and said unto him, I [am] the Almighty God; walk before me, and be thou perfect. Genesis 17:1 (KJS)

God's command to Abraham was, "Walk before me and be thou perfect." Notice how He started the conversation: "I AM THE ALMIGHTY GOD...I AM!" When we start with the right information, we come to the right conclusions. God did not say, "You are almighty man, walk before me and be thou perfect." We need the Holy Ghost to teach us what the will of God is.

Ministry is the Holy Spirit's work. His ministers are God-called, God-ordained, and Spirit-filled. Wanting to be a minister is not enough—God has to call us. Men whom God never called are leading churches all over the world. Ministers taught and ordained by men rather than by God lead many churches. There are men in the ministry who want to help their fellow man, but who should have become doctors or policemen instead. A true call to ministry does not originate with man—it only originates with God!

God gave ministries to the Church in order to do specific things. Doing something other than what He wants is unacceptable. What of ministers who teach that the Church will not come to perfection on earth, contrary to God's own Word? We see whom a preacher counts on to do the perfecting in light of how he views the potter and the clay. If he sees that Christians are God's workmanship, created in Christ Jesus, he agrees that the Church will come to perfection on the earth because God will bring it to pass. If he believes that his flesh is the potter and that his soul is the clay, he says that man cannot be perfect on the earth. Ignorance concerning God's will for the Church and concerning the identity of the Potter is inexcusable for a man who owns a Bible.

Paul, under the unction of the Holy Ghost, told us the three things that God defines as His will for the Church (verse 12).

1. The perfecting of the saints
2. The work of the ministry
3. The edifying of the Body of Christ

Immediately, the Spirit goes on to define what He means by these words. The external ministry is given "until we all come in the unity of the faith, and of the knowledge of the Son of God, unto a perfect man, unto the measure of the stature of the fullness of Christ." The Church will be in unity; she will know the Son of God. More than know of Him, she will know Him. That word "know" is the same as "Adam knew

Eve and they conceived a son" (Hebrew *yada*, Strong's #3045; Greek *ginosko*, Strong's #1097).

The Church will not only come to perfection, she will come to be a perfect man. How's that for glory? The Church will become one with Jesus. On the earth, the world will behold the Lamb of God. The Bible says that we are bone of His bone and flesh of His flesh. The perfected Church will attain the full stature of Jesus! That is what "measure of the stature" means: the full stature. The Church is to become "one with the Word of God" until she is transformed and the world sees Jesus. Is that a bad plan?

How can God's utmost desire cause so much debate? He is not asking man to do this, He is declaring His intent and assuring us of His will in this matter. Jesus instructed His disciples to pray that God's will be done on earth as it is in heaven. If God's will is for His Church to be perfect in heaven, which no one doubts, our prayers ask that His will be done on earth just as it is in heaven. We must not only believe when we pray in order to receive, we must also listen to what we are praying. Some say that Jesus only prayed for these things to happen when the "Kingdom comes," but John the Baptist and Jesus both taught that the Kingdom of God had come in the days of John's ministry. In fact, Jesus said, "The kingdom of God comes not with observation...for, behold, the kingdom of God is within you" (Luke 17:20-21).

Let's look more closely at the "until" in Ephesians 4:13. God gives the ministries until the Church comes to the full stature of Christ. What happens then? The Body, once edified from the outside, will edify itself from the inside. It will edify itself in love and by that which every joint supplies. The use of the word "joint" here is wonderful in its beauty. Joints allow movement between two solid bones. They are lubricated, so there is no friction as the two bones move in different directions.

More importantly, this means that the Church will become a living organism—not an organization, but a life. The Church is to be a living Body building itself up in love as the Bible teaches. The Church began as saints acted upon by ministry from the outside; she will end up as a Body edifying itself in love. Man could not promise such a miracle and man cannot bring it to pass. True ministers of God understand this. They believe that *God* made the promise and *God* can fulfill it!

We are not startled when someone teaches that the Church is going to be without spot or wrinkle. Said that way, we accept it as truth.

However, if someone uses the word "perfection," as Jesus did, the flesh strangles trying to swallow it. The Holy Ghost teaches perfection; all who are taught by the Holy Ghost agree that God can do it.

A perfect Church will dwell on the earth...who can believe such a thing? Who could create such a thing? Only a God who started His Church by putting a new man inside of every believer could do it. Only a God whose creative power spoke, "Let there be light: and there was light" could do it. "We are His workmanship, created in Christ Jesus!" Only a God who died on a cross and took all flesh with Him (corporately) could do it. We read of these things in the Scriptures and we receive them by faith.

When the Passover lamb died on the night God brought His people out of Egypt, the firstborn of every living thing in Egypt died. Every firstborn creature not underneath the blood covering died that night. Our flesh man is the firstborn! First the flesh, then the Spirit—this is a promise. Jesus' death on the cross means that our flesh man died on the cross. Receive it by faith.

How could a man taught by the carnal mind grasp such things? Impossible! God's ministers do not just preach, they edify the Body of Christ! They build up the very Body of Christ on the earth. Notice, the Scripture does not say that the ministers should starve the Body of Christ, or kill it; it says they must edify the Body.

It seems strange that so many people believe Jesus walked on the earth and was without sin in His Body, but also believe that sin must be a part of the Church, Christ's Body! In Romans 8:1, it says, "There is therefore now no condemnation to them which are in Christ Jesus, who walk not after the flesh, but after the Spirit..." Is that true? Can we walk after the Spirit and not after the flesh? Paul went on to say that the "law of the Spirit of life, in Christ Jesus, has made us free from the law of sin and death."

The Church of the twenty-first century is like Martha at the tomb of her brother Lazarus. We tell Jesus that the Father will give Him anything that He asks, but when He says to roll away the stone, we say that the flesh stinks! The Church perfected is a miracle out of the tombs of the flesh man. It is proof that a God exists who can do anything.

Before we go back to Ephesians 4, I want to point out Romans 8:3-4.

3 For what the law could not do, in that it was weak through the flesh,
God sending his own Son in the likeness of sinful flesh, and for sin,

condemned sin in the flesh: 4 That the righteousness of the law might be fulfilled in us, who walk not after the flesh, but after the Spirit.

This is also a great place to include Hebrews 7:11-19.

11 If therefore perfection were by the Levitical priesthood, (for under it the people received the law,) what further need [was there] that another priest should rise after the order of Melchisedec, and not be called after the order of Aaron? 12 For the priesthood being changed, there is made of necessity a change also of the law. 13 For he of whom these things are spoken pertaineth to another tribe, of which no man gave attendance at the altar. 14 For [it is] evident that our Lord sprang out of Juda; of which tribe Moses spake nothing concerning priesthood. 15 And it is yet far more evident: for that after the similitude of Melchisedec there ariseth another priest, 16 Who is made, not after the law of a carnal commandment, but after the power of an endless life. 17 For he testifieth, Thou [art] a priest forever after the order of Melchisedec. 18 For there is verily a disannulling of the commandment going before for the weakness and unprofitableness thereof. 19 For the law made nothing perfect, but the bringing in of a better hope [did]; by the which we draw nigh unto God.

This word "perfection," which causes so much fear in the hearts of the unbelieving and so much anger in the minds of the fearful, promises to give the Church a spotless robe of pure white here on the earth, where Satan says God cannot do it.

Returning to Ephesians 4, we read that the ministries are to bring us to "a perfect man" and to the "full stature of the man Christ Jesus." As we read on, it says when the Church comes to this place of perfection, she will no longer be "tossed to and fro by every wind of doctrine." Next, we see the Church being transformed into a Body that is not edified by the fivefold ministry from the outside, but rather by the "joints" within. That is the Church perfected. By the Holy Ghost's teaching and leading, Christians will come to the place where they are no longer children, tossed to and fro by every wind of doctrine.

The confusion of Babylon is not in the true Church. Such Christians know what is truth and what is not. It is very easy to pass a lie off to a child. How would they know what is truth and what is a lie? God gives us a great promise—the Holy Ghost will bring the Church to such a place where she will no longer wonder who is telling the truth. All arguments will cease because ministries will agree, having the same mind and the same judgment. Only the indwelling Spirit of God leads and guides us into all truth, and truth unifies.

The fivefold ministry is parental over the Bride. These parents of the Bride keep her and prepare her for her marriage to the Lamb.

> *2 For I am jealous over you with godly jealousy: for I have espoused you to one husband, that I may present [you as] a chaste virgin to Christ. 3 But I fear, lest by any means, as the serpent beguiled Eve through his subtlety, so your minds should be corrupted from the simplicity that is in Christ. 4 For if he that cometh preacheth another Jesus, whom we have not preached, or [if] ye receive another spirit, which ye have not received, or another gospel, which ye have not accepted, ye might well bear with [him].* 2 Corinthians 11:2-4 (KJS)

God, knowing the war Satan would wage against this truth, defined it in terms that are impossible to ignore. His ministries edify the Body of Christ. Under the direction of the Holy Ghost, they "build up" the Body of Christ. The body of Christ, as we observed in the Gospels, was led by the Spirit, defeated the flesh by that same Spirit, and obeyed the same Spirit unto death. In His Word, God says that the Church is that same Body! What an assurance of victory!

By saying that ministers edify the Body of Christ, God's reveals the power invested in His apostles, prophets, evangelists, pastors, and teachers and defines the perfection He promises. Jesus was perfect because He overcame sin in the flesh. He was tempted in all points as we are. Yet, Jesus never sinned (Heb. 4:15). When we accept Him as our Savior, He impregnates our spirit with His own Spirit and a new man forms inside of us, a spiritual baby. God doesn't hope that Christians will try hard enough to live right, He gives us new life! The new man does not sin. In fact, the Bible says he cannot sin (1 John 3:9-10). The new man is just a baby to start with, so the old man wins many of the early battles for supremacy. However, by the nurturing and protection of the Holy Ghost, he grows into a strong spirit man who turns defeats into victories.

Perfection has been taught in every generation since the Church began. Perfection is not a new revelation, just a neglected revelation.

Instead of following the Bible's plan, the Church has been busy writing "how-to" books for the past two thousand years. We have tried to live holy lives and failed. We have tried to do better and failed, but God's promise has always been to give us the land! The "better promises" of the New Testament are based on faith, not works. Martin Luther stood on that truth and we must stand on that truth as well.

John tells us that the new man, who is born of God, does not sin. We Christians read that and wonder what it means. We have been born again, yet our flesh still sins. What is wrong with us? Why isn't that Scripture fulfilled in us? When we look at the flesh-born man while we read about the spirit-born man, the promise never appears true, nor can it. We must compare spiritual things with spiritual! We must receive the revelation that there is an inside man and an outside man. In doing so, we can see, like Joshua and Caleb, that the Promised Land is ours. Every giant in the land will fall and the land is ours!

Paul confronted this misunderstanding in his letter to the Galatians:

> 1 O foolish Galatians, who hath bewitched you, that ye should not obey the truth, before whose eyes Jesus Christ hath been evidently set forth, crucified among you? 2 This only would I learn of you, Received ye the Spirit by the works of the law, or by the hearing of faith? 3 Are ye so foolish? having begun in the Spirit, are ye now made perfect by the flesh? 4 Have ye suffered so many things in vain? if [it be] yet in vain. 5 He therefore that ministereth to you the Spirit, and worketh miracles among you, [doeth he it] by the works of the law, or by the hearing of faith? Galatians 3:1-5 (KJS)

Look at verse 3: **"Are you so foolish? Having begun in the Spirit, are ye now made perfect by the flesh?"** What God has begun in the Spirit can never be made perfect by the flesh. The Holy Ghost leads us to faith. Faith holds to God and His words. This faith is what leads us to victory over sin. Paul wrote about Christians who went back to keeping the letter of the law in order to attain victory over sin. The same thing happens today—the natural man feels like he must "do" something worthy of God's love in order to have it. Nothing could be further from the truth.

Without faith, it is impossible to please God. Our righteousness is by faith, our sanctification is by faith, our redemption is by faith, and our victory that overcomes the world is by faith. We know that it is "not of works lest any man should boast," yet we still preach as though man is both the potter and the clay.

We must constantly ask ourselves whether we are trying to make ourselves perfect by fleshly means or by spiritual means. The book of Hebrews discusses entering the land of promise. It says that the first people who came to the Jordan River did not enter in because of unbelief. God promised them victory over the land of Canaan. **He chose to bring forth victory by fighting their battles for them.** God commanded, "Rest in me." They were unable to rest. The Promised Land is a picture of our flesh. There are giants dwelling in each of us, but Jesus defeated them at the cross. The Holy Ghost will teach us these things if we will listen.

The Church is chosen by God to be the Bride of Christ. His glory is to transform her on the earth, where Satan says that He cannot do such a thing. We cannot transform ourselves by keeping laws. Our only hope for change is in letting God change us.

Nowhere is the natural man's teaching more evident than in the matter of sinless perfection. In the days of Moses, the natural man came to the Jordan River and sent out his spies. Trusting in their own understanding and ignoring God's promise, they received an evil report and believed that God could not (or would not) give them the land. They believed that the God who gave a miracle son to Abraham (whom they were all descendants of) could not defeat those giants!

Thanks to the mercy and faithfulness of God, the story didn't end there. Under the ministry of Moses (a picture of the fivefold ministry), God led Israel through the wilderness until the old man died (those who died were the older generation) and the new man went in. The old man did not have the faith to believe that God would fight and win all the battles. The new man did believe. In Hebrews, it says that they could not enter into the "rest" that God had promised them. A promised land filled with nations and armies...and God called it a rest? With faith in God, it is a rest! If we trust in our own abilities, we certainly have no rest! In Hebrews 4, it says that all who have entered into rest have **ceased from their own labors.**

> 18 And to whom sware he that they should not enter into his rest, but to them that believed not? 19 So we see that they could not enter in because of unbelief. 1Let us therefore fear, lest, a promise being left

[us] of entering into his rest, any of you should seem to come short of it. 2 For unto us was the gospel preached, as well as unto them: but the word preached did not profit them, not being mixed with faith in them that heard [it]. 3 For we which have believed do enter into rest, as he said, As I have sworn in my wrath, if they shall enter into my rest: although the works were finished from the foundation of the world. 4 For he spake in a certain place of the seventh [day] on this wise, And God did rest the seventh day from all his works. 5 And in this [place] again, If they shall enter into my rest. 6 Seeing therefore it remaineth that some must enter therein, and they to whom it was first preached entered not in because of unbelief: 7 Again, he limiteth a certain day, saying in David, Today, after so long a time; as it is said, Today if ye will hear his voice, harden not your hearts. 8 For if Jesus had given them rest, then would he not afterward have spoken of another day. 9 There remaineth therefore a rest to the people of God. 10 For he that is entered into his rest, he also hath ceased from his own works, as God [did] from his. Hebrews 3:18–4:10 (KJS)

The perfected Church is a place of rest because the works were finished by God from the foundations of the world. The Church is being warned: "Let us fear, lest, a promise being left us of entering into His rest, any of you should seem to come short of it." Notice, this warning is to the New Testament Church. There remains, therefore, a rest to the people of God.

Let us look closely at verse 10: "For he that is entered into His rest, he also hath ceased from his own works, as God did from His." **Grace is a place of rest!** When the Spirit of God reveals to us that our work is to believe in the Son, we can rest from our own labors. When we see that we are His workmanship, not our own, we will be able to rest in His promise of victory.

The Church as His Building: The Promise of Unity

9 For we are laborers together with God: ye are God's husbandry, [ye are] God's building. 10 According to the grace of God which is given unto me, as a wise masterbuilder, I have laid the foundation, and another buildeth thereon. But let every man take heed how he buildeth thereupon. 11 For other foundation can no man lay than that is laid, which is Jesus Christ. 12 Now if any man build upon this foundation

gold, silver, precious stones, wood, hay, stubble; 13 Every man's work shall be made manifest: for the day shall declare it, because it shall be revealed by fire; and the fire shall try every man's work of what sort it is. 14 If any man's work abide which he hath built thereupon, he shall receive a reward. 15 If any man's work shall be burned, he shall suffer loss: but he himself shall be saved; yet so as by fire. 16 Know ye not that ye are the temple of God, and [that] the Spirit of God dwelleth in you?
1 Corinthians 3:9-16 (KJS)

The Church is not just a building, it is God's Temple. God places every believer into the habitation of God. We are His Temple—what joy! In verse 9, Paul said that we are laborers together with God. Start a project with the Almighty and miracles happen! In this passage, we see the fivefold ministries of Ephesians 4 working on the Temple. Ministers must take heed concerning how they build. They can build gold, silver, and precious stones or hay, wood, and stubble—incorruptible or corruptible.

The Bible tells us that the true Church will be built up into a unity of incorruptible faith and belief. However, there is another church system in the world, foretold of by God and described in the Book of Revelation: a people gathered and building in the name of Christ who are harlots by nature. There are recognizable differences between the two groups: the group's head, or leadership (man or Christ), what each group is being taught (truth or lies), and where each group is being led (one is named Jerusalem, the other is Babylon). The word "Jerusalem" means peace, the word "Babylon" means confusion.

The false church (or harlot, as she is called in Revelation) will continue under differing doctrines and beliefs until she is consumed. God is not the author of confusion. Denying that there is confusion in all of the differing beliefs of Christendom is lying. Remember, Jesus said that a house or a kingdom divided against itself will not stand (Mark 3:25).

As we learned in the previous chapter, God always gives His people signs to show them when they are going astray. When man sets his own agenda and his flesh starts to build the Temple, God scatters the work with confusion of language. The Church has never noticed that God sent this sign of confusion of languages! We see that the Baptists do not understand the Pentecostals and the Methodists do not understand the Lutherans, but we ignore the confusion and hope it will just go away.

Remember, confusion of languages began at the Tower of Babel. The descendants of Noah, building a tower to God, had to stop when God confused their languages. When Israel incorporated false gods into the temple worship, God sent them into Babylon. The Babylonians scattered them all over the known world. Their languages became as scattered as they were. When God started the Church, scattered Jews had come to Jerusalem from all over the world to celebrate the Feast of Pentecost. After the Holy Ghost fell, those Jews heard the disciples preaching in their own languages. God wants us to understand that He restores a common language to His people through the power of the Holy Ghost. We need the Holy Ghost to come now and restore us to the truth spoken in the days of Jesus and His disciples.

We must not forget why the Jews were scattered in the first place. In the Old Testament, God told them that if they strayed from Him the rain would stop. When God's signs were heeded, repentance brought forgiveness and rain. Eventually, the Jews stopped repenting. God not only stopped the rain, but also warned them that they would go into captivity if they kept worshipping false gods. The people did not repent or put away their idols, so God sent them into Babylon.

False doctrines are the same as false gods. When man leads the Church instead of the Holy Ghost, truth becomes mingled with carnal teaching. Anyone can claim to be an expert because there is no way to discern false doctrines without the Holy Ghost. One man's teachings are no better than the next man's. When no one knows who is telling the truth, it's time for man to admit that he's lost! It's not easy to get an entire organization to admit that it's lost. It's easier to attack challengers than lose face. In our selfishness, we say, "I'm not even going to examine what I believe." We also suffer from pride. Even in the face of proof, pride prevents us from admitting we're wrong.

In the days of Jesus, the Church received a strong warning about this very thing. Jesus raised the dead, opened the eyes of the blind, cleansed lepers…and was crucified by the leaders. There were men and women who knew that Jesus was the Son of God, but most of the leaders did not. That same disaster is at the door of the Church today. If a Christian is taught a lie about something in the Bible, he is likely to reject the truth when he hears it, thus rejecting Jesus. Satan knows that we tend to believe whatever we are taught first. If we hear a lie first, it is difficult for us to depart from the lie and receive the truth when we hear it. Thankfully, we have God's promise that if we seek we shall find (Matt. 7:7-8, Luke 11:9-13).

We must submit to the Holy Ghost so that He can protect us from our inability to discern the truth. The Holy Ghost is the only authority who has all truth. When every pastor hears from the Spirit of God, unity is the only possible outcome. The promise of the Church triumphant is the promise of the Holy Spirit's success. God ordained this for us, and it is up to His Spirit to perform, perfect, and protect. The story of the Church is the story of the Spirit. God sent Him to find her, gather her, and bring her home to Himself. The Holy Ghost has become a doctrine when, in reality, He is the Doctor. While men have argued about His attributes as though they are mere theology, He has always been the indwelling God, Theologian to the Church. The Holy Ghost is God! Mention the Feast of Pentecost, and most Church leaders do not think about the birth of the Church. Instead, they think about speaking in other tongues. To many preachers, the Holy Ghost is a past-tense phenomenon rather than an ever-active continuum. Without the Teacher, we turn to man for answers. The Church must believe the truth. Praise God, He sent His Spirit to dwell inside of us and to lead us and guide us into all truth!

Summary

As the Head of the Church, Jesus sent the Holy Ghost to the Church to be her Comforter, her Teacher, and the indwelling Spirit of God. The Church can either submit to Christ as the Head or reject Him. Submission requires yielding to the Holy Spirit and forsaking the ways of the flesh.

Jesus told His disciples to beware the leaven of the Pharisees and Sadducees, wanting them to be watchful of letting man's doctrines and intellectual interpretations of Scripture infiltrate the Church. The only leaven that is acceptable in spiritual matters is the "life of understanding" of the Holy Ghost.

God describes the Church as His Body, His Bride, and His Building. In each picture, we see a different facet of what it means to have the Holy Ghost dwelling within us. The Church as the Body of Christ speaks of His indwelling, the Church as the Bride of Christ speaks of the promise of the sinless one, and the Church as the Building of Christ speaks of the promise of unity. As long as man rejects the headship of Christ and the teaching of the Holy Ghost, these wonderful promises go unfulfilled. As we surrender and submit, we experience life in abundance, knowing undoubtedly that the Comforter is come!

Study Questions

82. *Why did Christ send us the Holy Ghost?*
83. *What did God do in His word to assure that truth would be revealed?*
84. *What is the spiritual significance of leaven? What is the difference between the Holy Ghost's leaven and man's leaven?*
85. *Name the seven Jewish feasts. Which was the first to allow leaven? Why?*
86. *Define the church as the Body, Bride, and Building of Christ.*
87. *Why does the Church need to come back to knowing all truth?*
88. *How does God plan to reveal Jesus to the world?*
89. *What is our assurance of victory over flesh?*
90. *Why did Jesus need the Apostles? What significance does that have for us today?*
91. *What is God's promise concerning His Church?*
92. *What is the fivefold ministry and what is its purpose?*
93. *What is God's plan for His Church?*
94. *Will we know when the Church has reached perfection?*
95. *How are we made perfect?*
96. *What tool does God give us that enables us to rest in His promises?*
97. *What is the only work God requires of us?*
98. *How does Christ's true Church differ from the Church lead by man?*
99. *Why did God bring Jews from all over the world to Jerusalem when He started His Church?*
100. *Why must we submit to the Holy Ghost?*

Absolute

SIX

Once We Repent of Our Sins, We Become His Workmanship, Created in Christ Jesus

The Bible explains God's salvation plan in clear, simple language. Yet after two thousand years of Church history, the Christian community remains largely ignorant of a very important truth: God continues to intervene in our lives *after* repentance and conversion. We are saved by grace through faith and we must remember that faith is not of ourselves; it is a gift of God. **Salvation is a gift from God!**

Most believers understand that just joining a church is not what Jesus meant when He talked about being born again. Most Christians also understand that sinners do not have to get their lives straightened out before they go to Jesus, repent, and ask to be saved. However, many unfortunately do believe that *we* become responsible for our salvation after our initial conversion.

Teachings on Christian living often ignore the second half of Paul's revelation on salvation. Christianity has become a "self-help" religion. Men mistake the moment of conversion for salvation. In doing so, they cut short the work that God has promised to do in us. Neglecting to heed

God's promises, we struggle with failure as we seek to please Him. God says that we are "His workmanship, created in Christ Jesus" after our conversion. What does being His workmanship mean? It means that Christianity is not a "self-help" religion. God did not tell man to make himself in the image of God. A believer will not achieve God's will for his life by reciting creeds or following formulas. Trying hard is not enough.

The Christian faith is based on God's power. God's power is unleashed by faith in the promises of the Bible. Only Christianity proclaims that man will become what God desires through God's own sacrifice and power. While the power is available to all, only those who believe receive it. Christian salvation means that God gives unmerited favor to the undeserving for the purpose of reconciliation. It begins with a simple act of contrition based on faith. The contrite person is then impregnated with the living seed of God's own Word and a new creature is born within his soul. Accepting Jesus' death on the cross as the substitute payment for sins is not only the beginning of salvation, it is the end of salvation.

Once we are born again of the Spirit, we become the workmanship of God. Victorious living depends upon His ability, not upon ours. Obedience to God's Word is a very important part of a Christian's life, but sadly, many trust in their own flesh to achieve that obedience. Training the carnal mind to lead the natural man until the flesh resembles Christ is an impossible task, putting believers on a religious treadmill made by Satan—it takes us nowhere. God addresses this quandary by telling us to believe in His Word! Satan wants us to believe that God's demands are too high for us to obey. This is a lie, but Christians everywhere are burdened with laws that have no importance to God. While millions labor to please God, the Bible says that only faith pleases Him.

Not of Works...

> ...*for by grace have ye been saved through faith; and that not of yourselves, [it is] the gift of God: not of works that no man should glory. For we are his workmanship, created in Christ Jesus for good works, which God afore prepared that we should walk in them.* Ephesians 2:8 (ASV)

We are saved by faith in God's favor, a favor we do not deserve. We are saved by a faith not even our own, but given to us as a gift from God.

That is good news! Today, the biblical account of salvation is not what most churchgoers hear. Depending on who we listen to, salvation may be described as a by-product of human actions, such as how people are baptized or even what people wear. Most churches agree that our initial forgiveness is free…we don't have to start "saving" ourselves until after Jesus saves us! Obviously, such teaching confuses believers. If the Bible teaches that salvation is by "grace through faith," faith must stop right there and hold on. If salvation is not of works in the beginning, it never will be. It is tragic to believe that sinful flesh is responsible for making a man's soul acceptable to God.

The only work God authorizes us to do in the Bible is believe. Out of believing comes an understanding of the Word; understanding leads to obedience. The seriously religious, who want to serve and honor God, are prone to mistakenly attempt to do the work themselves.

Let's look closely at these Scriptures in Ephesians 2. They happen to be the most quoted Scriptures on salvation in the entire Bible, and for good reason. They are a perfect encapsulation of the thoughts of God on the subject.

We want to study four words in this text:

Salvation, Grace, Workmanship, and Created

In one phrase, the Holy Spirit clarifies and simplifies God's will concerning man's salvation. He used four words that couldn't ever have appeared together in all the preceding years of man's existence. This passage shows man's need of a Savior, God's willingness to forgive, and the miracle God promises. Leave out any one of these four words and the meaning changes completely!

What other subject deserves more scrutiny? Of all the things man deems important, of all the subjects man dwells upon, I cannot think of even one that is more important than God's Word on the salvation of a man's soul. The entire Bible is one story—salvation's story.

Salvation:

The word "salvation" is defined as: 1. Preservation or deliverance from destruction, difficulty, or evil. 2. (*theological*) Deliverance from the power or penalty of sin; redemption. a. The agent or means of such deliverance.

Man did not need salvation in the Garden of Eden. Adam and Eve ate of the tree of life and walked with God in a full relationship of family. Jealous of such bliss, Satan entered the garden and tempted Eve, drawing her and Adam into disobedience. Adam and Eve had only one commandment to obey but they still got into trouble!

The Book of Genesis is the story of man's failure. There are actually three geneses, or beginnings, in this book: Adam, a perfect man; Noah, a perfect man; and Abraham, an idol worshiper. Through their stories, God shows us that a perfect man could not carry the hopes of the human race on the shoulders of his own abilities even though he was perfect. Abraham's success came from his belief in and obedience to God. Faith became his righteousness and faith sustained his righteousness. Because of his faith, Abraham became the father of Israel.

The book of Exodus is the story of God's success. God sent a ministry to lead His people, a ministry under the leadership of the Holy Ghost (the pillar of fire by night and the pillar of cloud by day). The combination of God's ministry and God's presence took the children of Israel out of religious bondage and into the promised land of God. Moses represents the fivefold ministry outlined in Ephesians 4, which God ordains to do the same thing today.

In Exodus, God's chosen people were taken out of religion, not sin. They were in God's Kingdom because they were born into the lineage of Abraham (faith). They were in Egypt because they had followed Joseph (Jesus) into the land for bread. As long as Egypt's leaders were in subjection to Joseph's (Jesus') wisdom and presence, the people were free; when the leaders of this religious environment lost their personal relationship with Joseph (Jesus), God's people were enslaved (religion vs. relationship).

Satan has two plans for mankind. If he can keep people in bondage to sin, he does. However, he knows that the hearts of men cry out for a relationship with God the Father, so he has also started religions all over the world. They are based on truth and use God's Word, but are filled with lies. Satan defeated Eve that way.

Remember, bowing to a lie is the same as idolatry. We can love a lie more than the truth. We think our belief is truth and we love the lie as we should love Jesus. Christianity has Jesus Christ as her Head. He is alive and He speaks to those who will listen so that He might overcome every lie. The carnal mind can never produce the will of God, nor can the human intellect define the will of God or aspire to it. Under God's amnesty, only Jesus is the fulfillment of God's will—the way, the truth, and the life.

Salvation is actually a three-part work. God says that death is the penalty for sin, which is why man cannot accomplish his own salvation. Death reigned until God gave the law. Under the law, obedience to God's commands and the shedding of blood in the prescribed manner gave salvation from the guilt of sin. In God's three-part plan, He provided the necessary obedience and sacrifice.

1. He paid the debt incurred by the disobedience of man on the cross of Calvary.
2. He shed the blood for cleansing.
3. He covered the guilty with the flesh of the Sacrifice.

We remember and celebrate the death of Jesus, our Passover Lamb, and His blood. Once we accept Him by faith, the blood cleanses us. We forget that He also covers us with His own flesh. Not only are we washed in the blood of Jesus; we are also clothed with His flesh, which never sinned. God sees the flesh of Jesus when He looks at a believer. We wear His righteousness by faith! Christians spend lifetimes trying to fix what is already covered by Jesus' flesh. This is another place where faith must hold to an unseen promise.

The world rejects both the absolutes of truth and God's voice. The Age of Enlightenment placed man in the center of the universe, denying God's existence and exalting doubt. God calls us to come out of the world and be separate from its poisonous unbelief. Salvation is an act of God upon the soul of man and it requires faith; the Bible calls anyone who has not repented to Jesus for his sins a sinner.

We must go back to the Bible for our example of how man is converted. In Acts 10, God sent an angel to the house of Cornelius. This man's story is the quintessential example of salvation God's way. Let's look at each step closely because this entire circumstance was orchestrated by God and written down for our benefit.

Cornelius was a man who prayed to God, fasted, and gave alms to the poor. He sounds like a great leader for the men's Bible study, right? The Bible says that he was not even born again at that point! The angel of the Lord told Cornelius to send for a Christian minister. The minister would tell him what he needed to do to gain eternal life. This shows us that being good and doing righteous things do not satisfy God's requirement for repentance.

Notice, the angel did not tell Cornelius about salvation because God gave the Church this wonderful commission. God entrusted the news of His amnesty to the Church. Her joy is telling the whole world the Good News—Jesus is risen and the debt for sin has been paid!

When Peter arrived, he focused on Jesus and His life, not on the failures of Cornelius. Peter told of the death and resurrection of Jesus and how Jesus showed Himself to chosen witnesses after His resurrection. Peter said that he was one of those chosen witnesses. In verse 42, he continued with these words:

> 42 And he commanded us to preach unto the people, and to testify that it is he which was ordained of God [to be] the Judge of quick and dead. 43 To him give all the prophets witness, that through his name whosoever believeth in him shall receive remission of sins. Acts 10:42-43 (KJS)

For Cornelius, salvation was not about praying, fasting, giving alms, or hearing the teachings of Jesus. He did all of those things without being saved. Instead, it was about Cornelius *believing* that what Jesus did and said was for him personally. "Whosoever *believeth* on Him..." When Cornelius and his family were changed, there was no doubting that something dynamic had happened to all of them—the Holy Ghost fell on them and they began to speak in other tongues.

One cause of the Church's drift away from the truth about salvation is the knowledge of good and evil, our heritage from Adam. When the Church goes back to teaching only biblical truths about what is good and what is evil, salvation will not be based on men's works or rituals, but based only on faith in the grace of Jesus Christ.

Faith starts the process and faith finishes the work. As wonderful as it *feels* to do something very religious, we need to separate the things we do in our own strength to celebrate God and His love from the unction of the Holy Ghost. We also need to separate what God truly requires from what man says He requires.

The Gospels contain many sad examples of religious leaders confusing their own traditions and laws with the true laws of God. Today, we do that (and more) a thousand times over! The religious outcry today has the same results as it did two thousand years ago—men hate each other because of things they think are doctrinally important and miss God. Have we forgotten that we are His workmanship?

Grace:

The word "grace" is defined as: (theological) 1. a. A divine love and protection bestowed freely on people. b. The state of being protected or sanctified by the favor of God. c. An excellence or power granted by God. d. A favor rendered by one who need not do so. e. Mercy; clemency.

Salvation is the greatest act of love and protection ever freely bestowed on mankind. It is divine love and mercy. How sublime a sound went forth into the entire world when Paul wrote to the Ephesians about grace! Grace—what other word is like that? Its true meaning is so unsettling that two thousand years (and one reformation) after the birth of the Church, the natural man is still trying to *earn* salvation.

Who enjoys giving a gift if the recipient boasts of paying for it himself? Religion has done immeasurable harm to humanity by selling heaven for a price—sometimes for money, sometimes for acts of self-development too lofty to reach. Mankind, willing to pay any price, extracts the demanded bounty from every resource as long as he possibly can, only to find the cost continually rises. Man without God has never shown or known grace.

Only once did heaven come at a high cost and it was borne by God Himself, Jesus Christ. Satan hates the very word "grace," for it negates the trauma inflicted by the knowledge of good and evil. A man under grace accepts God's final word on his debt for sin and rejoices.

Jesus' first miracle took place at a wedding, a joyous occasion (John 2:1-12). The Son of God turned water into wine. Grace is the wine made from the water of the Word! The celebration symbolizes the union of the Bride (the Church) and the Bridegroom (Jesus).

> *7 And the Lord said, I will destroy man whom I have created from the face of the earth; both man, and beast, and the creeping thing, and the fowls of the air; for it repenteth me that I have made them. 8 But Noah found grace in the eyes of the Lord.* Genesis 6:7-8 (KJS)

7 And when there had been much disputing, Peter rose up, and said unto them, Men [and] brethren, ye know how that a good while ago God made choice among us, that the Gentiles by my mouth should hear the word of the gospel, and believe. 8 And God, which knoweth the hearts, bare them witness, giving them the Holy Ghost, even as [he did] unto us; 9 And put no difference between us and them, purifying their hearts by faith. 10 Now therefore why tempt ye God, to put a yoke upon the neck of the disciples, which neither our fathers nor we were able to bear? 11 But we believe that through the grace of the Lord Jesus Christ we shall be saved, even as they. 12 Then all the multitude kept silence, and gave audience to Barnabas and Paul, declaring what miracles and wonders God had wrought among the Gentiles by them. Acts 15:7-12 (KJS)

Peter said in verse 9 that God knew their hearts and their hearts were purified by faith. Their hearts were not purified by actions or by obedience to a doctrine, but by faith. Peter went on to say that the struggle to do the law was a burden neither their fathers nor the disciples were able to bear. They did not find pleasure in the failure; they found a burden in the failure. The alternative he put forth is belief in the **grace** of the Lord Jesus Christ.

1 What shall we say then that Abraham our father, as pertaining to the flesh, hath found? 2 For if Abraham were justified by works, he hath [whereof] to glory; but not before God. 3 For what saith the Scripture? Abraham believed God, and it was counted unto him for righteousness. 4 Now to him that worketh is the reward not reckoned of grace, but of debt. 5 But to him that worketh not, but believeth on him that justifieth the ungodly, his faith is counted for righteousness. 6 Even as David also describeth the blessedness of the man, unto whom God imputeth righteousness without works, 7 [Saying], Blessed [are] they whose iniquities are forgiven, and whose sins are covered. Romans 4:1-7 (KJS)

Too much of the Church is taught "self-help" theology. Psychologists venture a guess at our problems and theologians buy into the latest motivating techniques, hoping to rev up the discouraged. They have missed the problem all along: honest seekers feel inadequate. The peace that accompanies victory eludes them and they know it. Faith in the work of God, grace, and mercy comprise the only way for believers to overcome sin. We will overcome the world, but it will not be by works of the religious kind.

> 3 For this is the love of God, that we keep his commandments: and his commandments are not grievous. 4 For whatsoever is born of God overcometh the world: and this is the victory that overcometh the world, [even] our faith. 5 Who is he that overcometh the world, but he that believeth that Jesus is the Son of God? 1 John 5:3-5 (KJS)

> 19 For I through the law am dead to the law, that I might live unto God. 20 I am crucified with Christ: nevertheless I live; yet not I, but Christ liveth in me: and the life which I now live in the flesh I live by the faith of the Son of God, who loved me, and gave himself for me. 21 I do not frustrate the grace of God: for if righteousness [come] by the law, then Christ is dead in vain. 1 O foolish Galatians, who hath bewitched you, that ye should not obey the truth, before whose eyes Jesus Christ hath been evidently set forth, crucified among you? 2 This only would I learn of you, Received ye the Spirit by the works of the law, or by the hearing of faith? 3 Are ye so foolish? having begun in the Spirit, are ye now made perfect by the flesh? 4 Have ye suffered so many things in vain? if [it be] yet in vain. 5 He therefore that ministereth to you the Spirit, and worketh miracles among you, [doeth he it] by the works of the law, or by the hearing of faith? Galatians 2:19-3:5 (KJS)

Here is a question we need to constantly ask ourselves: having begun in the Spirit, are we now made perfect by the flesh? God promises to have a people who are not servants of sin. He promises to have a people of faith, belonging to an Assembly without spots or wrinkles. When the Church stands on the revelation of who Jesus is, the gates of Hell will not prevail against her.

In 1 John, it says "if we sin" (not when we sin) we have an advocate with the Father, Jesus Christ the Righteous. Under the direction of the Holy Ghost, John said, "I write these things that ye sin not." God would not tell us to do something that is impossible to do through Him. For man, sinlessness is indeed impossible, but for a Church that is "reborn," a new creation in Christ, it is altogether possible! Christ dwelling in us overcomes the weakness of the flesh. When I am weak, then am I strong. His strength is made perfect in weakness (2 Cor. 12:9).

Jesus told the woman caught in adultery, "Go and sin no more." He told the fig tree to dry up from the roots and the power of His words made it so. He said, "Peace be still," and the wind ceased blowing, the waves calmed. He commanded a dead man to come from the tomb and life returned to him so that the body could obey the Master. He said the word "go" and the demons went. If He really told that woman, "By your own power, sin no more," she must have been some woman!

5 This then is the message which we have heard of him, and declare unto you, that God is light, and in him is no darkness at all. 6 If we say that we have fellowship with him, and walk in darkness, we lie, and do not the truth: 7 But if we walk in the light, as he is in the light, we have fellowship one with another, and the blood of Jesus Christ his Son cleanseth us from all sin. 8 If we say that we have no sin, we deceive ourselves, and the truth is not in us. 9 If we confess our sins, he is faithful and just to forgive us [our] sins, and to cleanse us from all unrighteousness. 10 If we say that we have not sinned, we make him a liar, and his word is not in us. 1 John 1:5-10 (KJS)

The perfected Church understands that we have sin in our flesh, but she also knows what happens when we confess it. In verse 9, it says that Jesus is faithful not only to forgive our sins but also to cleanse us from *all* unrighteousness. We do not cleanse ourselves. He cleanses us. Misunderstanding who cleanses us is what feeds religion's fires.

When Jesus sees our repentant hearts and hears our mourning cries, He comforts us with words of forgiveness. Jesus knows what He is up against when He comes into the heart of a believer—He brought His own flesh into total surrender. His indwelling is the glory of the plan. When He indwells us, we do not want sin to reign in our mortal bodies. Show me a man who is filled with the Holy Spirit and I will show you a man who wants to be holy.

The Sermon on the Mount is the best example I can think of to provide God's explanation of why grace not only saves, but also changes the heart of man.

3 Blessed [are] the poor in spirit: for theirs is the kingdom of heaven. 4 Blessed [are] they that mourn: for they shall be comforted. 5 Blessed [are] the meek: for they shall inherit the earth. 6 Blessed [are] they which do hunger and thirst after righteousness: for they shall be filled. 7 Blessed [are] the merciful: for they shall obtain mercy. 8 Blessed [are] the pure in heart: for they shall see God. 9 Blessed [are] the peacemakers: for they shall be called the children of God. 10 Blessed [are] they which are persecuted for righteousness' sake: for theirs is the kingdom of heaven. 11 Blessed are ye, when [men] shall revile you, and persecute [you], and shall say all manner of evil against you falsely, for my sake. 12 Rejoice, and be exceeding glad: for great [is] your reward in heaven: for so persecuted they the prophets which were before you. Matthew 5:3-12 (KJS)

Individually, each statement about the blessed says a great deal. As a group, they form a judgment revealing a progression in the heart of a believer. God wants to see that progression in us, not by effort but by yielding to Him. Jesus started His sermon by proclaiming that those who had tried to serve Him and failed are blessed! The poor in Spirit are blessed? Everyone knows He should condemn them and demand they try harder...

Jesus' ministry was a declaration of what God originally intended for man at Creation. His ministry was a Testament, stating His intention to leave His followers *all* that He possessed, including His victories over flesh, Satan, and sin. In His Testament, Jesus left us His faith, His mind, and His Spirit. Jesus gave His life for us; upon His death, His Testament became our inheritance.

16 For where a testament [is], there must also of necessity be the death of the testator. 17 For a testament [is] of force after men are dead: otherwise it is of no strength at all while the testator liveth. 18 Whereupon neither the first [testament] was dedicated without blood. 19 For when Moses had spoken every precept to all the people according to the law, he took the blood of calves and of goats, with water, and scarlet wool, and hyssop, and sprinkled both the book, and all the people, 20 Saying, This [is] the blood of the testament which God hath enjoined unto you. 21 Moreover he sprinkled with blood both the tabernacle, and all the vessels of the ministry. 22 And almost all things are by the law purged with blood; and without shedding of blood is no remission. Hebrews 9:16-22 (KJS)

Based on this glorious Testament, Jesus declared that the religious failures in His Kingdom were blessed because He was among them. He was not only their New Hope, He was their Salvation. The spiritually poor now had help. By acknowledging their poverty and confessing their sins, they could be forgiven and cleansed.

How many ministers tell us that those in debt to God are the blessed? The implication is clear—we must admit our need for God's salvation. This is grace at its conception. The phrase "blessed are they that mourn" shows us the sin-sick soul weeping over failures instead of accepting them or making excuses for them. There are people who admit poverty in spiritual things but do not mourn over their sins. God says that if a man admits his poverty and weeps over his wrong, he is blessed.

> *20 Moreover the law entered, that the offence might abound. But where sin abounded, grace did much more abound: 21 That as sin hath reigned unto death, even so might grace reign through right-eousness unto eternal life by Jesus Christ our Lord. 1 What shall we say then? Shall we continue in sin, that grace may abound? 2 God forbid. How shall we, that are dead to sin, live any longer therein? 3 Know ye not, that so many of us as were baptized into Jesus Christ were baptized into his death? 4 Therefore we are buried with him by baptism into death: that like as Christ was raised up from the dead by the glory of the Father, even so we also should walk in newness of life.*
> Romans 5:20-6:4 (KJS)

The next indicator of the blessed man is one who is meek, a man who allows God to deal with him as He sees fit. A blessed man is one whose will surrenders readily to the sovereign will of God. Knowing this, Jesus instructed His disciples to pray that God's will be done in us as it is in heaven. We can see that if we admit our need for Jesus as our Savior, mourn because of our sin, see ourselves as servant to God and His working, and are pliable in His hands, it means grace is doing the final work inside of us.

Next, Jesus said that we will hunger and thirst after righteousness, the natural result of the other things He mentioned. These truths defeat the argument that salvation by grace alone leads to fleshly excess. Jesus said that a forgiven man who is not boastful or self-righteous, but remembers that God gave him his forgiveness, will treat sinners with the same love he receives from God. He is blessed! Such a man is merciful. A wise man sows mercy, knowing that he reaps what he sows. This man will have a pure heart because God will be his heart's desire. He will always repent when God convicts him, he will surrender to God's will in spite of his own will, hunger for righteousness, and reap mercy from God because he sows mercy to others.

The man indwelt by God does not laugh at sin or congratulate himself when no one catches him sinning—he knows that God is real. His chief desire is to please his Lord. Faith holds to God's promise of holiness from day one of a believer's life. If God promises to save a soul, He will save that soul!

Workmanship:

The word "workmanship" is defined as: 1. The skill of a craftsperson or an artisan. 2. The quality of something made, as by an artisan. 3. Something made or produced by a workman. 4. The product of effort or endeavor.

"For we are His workmanship, created in Christ Jesus..." Ephesians 2:10 (KJS)

Though quoted often, this is the most neglected phrase in the Bible. **Believing that we are products of the workmanship of Christ is the most important thing we can believe.** If He is doing the work on us, then we must trust Him to do it. Too many sermons describe God as doing little more than sitting in heaven waiting for His children to fix themselves up. If we are His workmanship, then He does the work that turns us into what He desires.

1 Give ear, O ye heavens, and I will speak; and hear, O earth, the words of my mouth. 2 My doctrine shall drop as the rain, my speech shall distil as the dew, as the small rain upon the tender herb, and as the showers upon the grass: 3 Because I will publish the name of the Lord: ascribe ye greatness unto our God. 4 [He is] the Rock, his work [is] perfect: for all his ways [are] judgment: a God of truth and without iniquity, just and right [is] he. Deuteronomy 32:1-4 (KJS)

20 Now the God of peace, that brought again from the dead our Lord Jesus, that great shepherd of the sheep, through the blood of the everlasting covenant, 21 Make you perfect in every good work to do his will, working in you that which is wellpleasing in his sight, through Jesus Christ; to whom [be] glory for ever and ever. Amen. Hebrews 13:20-21 (KJS)

God's work is *perfect*! "Now the God of peace…make you perfect in every good work to do His will…!" This God of peace is the Craftsman who has to do with our souls!

[It is] God that girdeth me with strength, and maketh my way perfect. Psalms 18:32 (KJS)

7 Though I walk in the midst of trouble, thou wilt revive me: thou shalt stretch forth thine hand against the wrath of mine enemies, and thy right hand shall save me. 8 The Lord will perfect [that which] concerneth me: thy mercy, O Lord, [endureth] forever: forsake not the works of thine own hands. Psalms 138:7-8 (KJS)

God will perfect that which concerns us! In all of these Scriptures, God is the one doing the work. If we believe this, we will be able to understand His plan for our salvation.

When Paul used the word "workmanship," he borrowed it from the Old Testament. It was used solely in connection to the tabernacle. The tabernacle was the workmanship of men who were chosen by God to work on it. God gave them the ability and wisdom to do the work.

The New Testament tells us that Christians are the Tabernacle, the dwelling place of God. Jesus told His disciples: "In my Father's house are many dwellings…I go to prepare a place for you…that where I am, there you may be also" (John 14:2-3). Later He prayed, "That they all may be one; as thou, Father, art in me, and I in thee, that they also may be one in us…" (John 17:21). We are His Temple. Once we understand that Jesus is the Builder ordained by God to do this work, we can enter into His rest.

Now I beseech you, brethren, by the name of our Lord Jesus Christ, that ye all speak the same thing, and [that] there be no divisions among you; but [that] ye be perfectly joined together in the same mind and in the same judgment. 1 Corinthians 1:10 (KJS)

16 Know ye not that ye are the temple of God, and [that] the Spirit of God dwelleth in you? 17 If any man defile the temple of God, him shall God destroy; for the temple of God is holy, which [temple] ye are. 1 Corinthians 3:16-17 (KJS)

14 Be ye not unequally yoked together with unbelievers: for what fellowship hath righteousness with unrighteousness? and what communion hath light with darkness? 15 And what concord hath Christ with Belial? or what part hath he that believeth with an infidel? 16 And what agreement hath the temple of God with idols? for ye are the temple of the living God; as God hath said, I will dwell in them, and walk in [them]; and I will be their God, and they shall be my people. 17 Wherefore come out from among them, and be ye separate, saith the Lord, and touch not the unclean [thing]; and I will receive you, 18 And will be a Father unto you, and ye shall be my sons and daughters, saith the Lord Almighty. f2 Corinthians 6:14-18 (KJS)

3 And I have filled him with the spirit of God, in wisdom, and in understanding, and in knowledge, and in all manner of workmanship, 4 To devise cunning works, to work in gold, and in silver, and in brass, 5 And in cutting of stones, to set [them], and in carving of timber, to work in all manner of workmanship. 6 And I, behold, I have given with him Aholiab, the son of Ahisamach, of the tribe of Dan: and in the hearts of all that are wise hearted I have put wisdom, that they may make all that I have commanded thee; 7 The tabernacle of the congregation, and the ark of the testimony, and the mercy seat that [is] thereupon, and all the furniture of the tabernacle... Exodus 31:3-7 (KJS)

The tabernacle of the Old Testament economy is a picture of God's people fellowshipping with Him in a full communion. Every board and curtain had a special meaning known only to God. He knew that one day He would open the revelation of the tabernacle so that man could understand the mysteries of the Kingdom. Four times in the Old Testament, God revealed the tabernacle and the spiritual dimensions, or patterns, for the unity of His Church. More of the Old Testament is devoted to this one subject than to any other, and the importance implied by that is evident. God has opened up a tremendous amount of revelation knowledge concerning the pattern of the tabernacle, but the Church of the twenty-first century is slow to receive it.

The final (and ultimate) understanding contained in the tabernacle picture is that the Church will come to unity and perfection just as simply and certainly as the tabernacle of Moses was built, because the Builder and Maker is God! The Church is New Jerusalem and Abraham is the father of the Kingdom. Again, faith is what frees God to execute His will. The Church is the glorious workmanship of the God who can do *all* things well. How can we doubt in the face of such evidence?

> *20 Neither pray I for these alone, but for them also which shall believe on me through their word; 21 That they all may be one; as thou, Father, [art] in me, and I in thee, that they also may be one in us: that the world may believe that thou hast sent me. 22 And the glory which thou gavest me I have given them; that they may be one, even as we are one: 23 I in them, and thou in me, that they may be made perfect in one; and that the world may know that thou hast sent me, and hast loved them, as thou hast loved me. 24 Father, I will that they also, whom thou hast given me, be with me where I am; that they may behold my glory, which thou hast given me: for thou lovedst me before the foundation of the world.* John 17:20-24 (KJS)

Jesus, as our great High Priest, prayed that we become one as He and the Father are one! More than that, He *is still* praying that we will be one in He and the Father. When He prayed that the wind might cease, it ceased, that the waves might calm, they calmed. When did He ever pray and not receive what He prayed for?

Remember, Jesus wants us to pray that the will of God be done on earth as it is in heaven. When we pray in faith, His will shall be done in us as it is in heaven (we are made of dust, meaning earth). Do you want God's will, desires, and promises accomplished in you as they are in heaven, where His will is supreme? He does not give us a thousand and one commandments, He instructs us to pray and believe. Faith is the key.

We read what Jesus prayed in the upper room and are astounded. He prayed that the many believers of the Church "may be made perfect in one" and that "the world may know that You have sent Me, and loved them." Is it possible that the world does not know that God loves the world and that He sent Jesus because the lively stones of the Church are not one in Him? According to Jesus' prayer, that is the case. While we have been fighting over doctrines, we should have been praying that His will would be done on earth as it is in heaven. We should have been praying that we would become one, or as He says, "…be made perfect in one."

> *1 Wherefore, holy brethren, partakers of the heavenly calling, consider the Apostle and High Priest of our profession, Christ Jesus; 2 Who was faithful to him that appointed him, as also Moses [was faithful] in all his house. 3 For this [man] was counted worthy of more glory than Moses, inasmuch as he who hath builded the house hath more honor than the house. 4 For every house is builded by some [man]; but he that built all things [is] God. 5 And Moses verily [was] faithful in all his house, as a servant, for a testimony of those things which were to be spoken after; 6 But Christ as a son over his own house; whose house are we, if we hold fast the confidence and the rejoicing of the hope firm unto the end.* Hebrews 3:1-6 (KJS)

We are the House that Jesus builds. Who builds the House? Jesus does!

If a pastor came into the sanctuary on Sunday morning and began to yell at the pulpit, berating it for not being tall enough or stained the correct color, the congregation would laugh. However, when the same pastor comes in on Sunday morning and begins admonishing the people to make themselves into Christ's image, no one laughs. The pulpit is the workmanship of men, and everyone understands that, yet the Bible declares that every believer is the workmanship of Christ and no one understands that!

Created:

The word "created" is defined as: 1. To cause to exist; bring into being.

In Jerusalem on the day of Pentecost, God turned the darkness of three thousand years of religious deterioration into light. He did so solely by His Spirit. The prophets of old foretold of that day in a multitude of ways. When the Lord spoke to Zerubbabel, He said: "Not by might, not by power, but by my Spirit, saith the Lord" (Zech. 4:6).

The failure of the law is not a reflection of the law itself or even of God's people, but a commentary on the inability of the natural man to obey God. In Romans 8, God said, "…What the law could not do, in that it was weak through the flesh, God sending His own Son in the likeness of sinful flesh and for sin condemned sin in the flesh. That the righteousness of the law might be fulfilled in us who walk not after the flesh but after the Spirit."

The law could not bring man to the righteousness that God demanded because the flesh of man had to obey. The flesh could not obey; the weakness is in the flesh. When the carnal mind does not want to do something, it makes up excuses. When the carnal mind cannot do something, it makes up excuses. Religion, in the hands of man, is the vehicle by which excuses become doctrines. Because the Bible stands guard against such abuses, truth is manipulated until it is impossible to determine what God says. The natural man hides his failures underneath the pages that he tears out of the Covenant he cannot understand.

When God was manifest in the flesh, He turned from the weakness of the flesh and relied on the power of the Spirit. Denying the flesh and elevating the will of God, Jesus sought to fulfill everything foretold about Him. The Word became the worker and the Spirit became the tutor. Through surrender to the revealed Word, Jesus pursued victory in order to restore the unaltered Word and the secured revelation to man. He secured all sixty-six books of the revelation of Jesus Christ. He did not make thirty-nine old, obscure books an appendix to twenty-seven new ones. The Lion of the tribe of Judah opened the thirty-nine books of the Old Testament, which completely supported the tremendous changes of the New Covenant. Jesus made the revelation complete.

The word "create" is a powerful word, on par with "let there be light." No religion has a word in its vocabulary with enough power behind it to make a saint out of a mere mortal. God is the only power in the universe able to create within us the ability to stop serving sin if we want to.

> *10 For in that he died, he died unto sin once: but in that he liveth, he liveth unto God. 11 Likewise reckon ye also yourselves to be dead indeed unto sin, but alive unto God through Jesus Christ our Lord. 12 Let not sin therefore reign in your mortal body, that ye should obey it in the lusts thereof. 13 Neither yield ye your members [as] instruments*

of unrighteousness unto sin: but yield yourselves unto God, as those that are alive from the dead, and your members [as] instruments of righteousness unto God. 14 For sin shall not have dominion over you: for ye are not under the law, but under grace. 15 What then? shall we sin, because we are not under the law, but under grace? God forbid. 16 Know ye not, that to whom ye yield yourselves servants to obey, his servants ye are to whom ye obey; whether of sin unto death, or of obedience unto righteousness? 17 But God be thanked, that ye were the servants of sin, but ye have obeyed from the heart that form of doctrine which was delivered you. 18 Being then made free from sin, ye became the servants of righteousness. Romans 6:10-18 (KJS)

Verse 14 states: "For sin shall not have dominion over you." Verse 16 states: "…His servants you are to whom you obey." Verse 17 states: "You were [past tense] the servants of sin, but you have obeyed…" Verse 18 states: "Being then *made free* from sin, you became the servants of righteousness."

In Psalm 51, David prayed a prayer that is a prophetic utterance describing the needs of the sin-sick soul (who may even be a member of the Church).

5 Behold, I was shapen in iniquity; and in sin did my mother conceive me. 6 Behold, thou desirest truth in the inward parts: and in the hidden [part] thou shalt make me to know wisdom. 7 Purge me with hyssop, and I shall be clean: wash me, and I shall be whiter than snow. 8 Make me to hear joy and gladness; [that] the bones [which] thou hast broken may rejoice. 9 Hide thy face from my sins, and blot out all mine iniquities. 10 Create in me a clean heart, O God; and renew a right spirit within me. 11 Cast me not away from thy presence; and take not thy holy spirit from me. 12 Restore unto me the joy of thy salvation; and uphold me [with thy] free spirit. 13 [Then] will I teach transgressors thy ways; and sinners shall be converted unto thee. Psalm 51:5-13 (KJS)

Only God's salvation can *create* a clean heart. Doing better and trying harder can never create a clean heart. David prayed for forgiveness, asking God to blot out all of his iniquities. But he went even further, asking the Creator God to put a new heart in him and to renew a right spirit within him. This is not about the outside man looking good, this is about the inside man made right in God's sight. That is what really matters, after all.

In the Sermon on the Mount, we know that Jesus said, "Be ye therefore perfect even as your Father which is in heaven is perfect" (Matthew 5:48). Can this command even be relevant without the creative Word of God? Be *perfect* as your Father in heaven is *perfect*? Is this where Jesus went too far or is this the Architect's conception and the blueprint's picture? Is the design for the New Testament Temple too bold? Does He really mean a Temple made holy by the presence of the Holy God, a light outshining the brightness of the noonday sun? Is the hand of God unable to create such a place for Him dwell in on earth? Didn't God have such a dwelling in Jesus? The theologies of man cannot even touch such things!

Summary

It is very important that we understand what salvation truly means. If we mistakenly believe that conversion is the same as salvation, we will miss out on the tremendous plan that God has in store for us. If we live as though Christianity is a "self-help" religion, we encounter failure, discouragement, and frustration as we try to make ourselves conform to the image of Christ. If we live instead as His workmanship, we can enjoy victory, peace, and rest regardless of our circumstances. Once we understand that we are not able to change ourselves and are not expected to, we can freely abide in Christ knowing that only He can change us.

Salvation begins at the cross and ends at the cross. Faith is what pleases God. Believing the Bible and the promises it contains unleashes God's power. God is the only power in the universe able to create within us the ability to stop serving sin if we want to.

Here is a question we need to constantly ask ourselves: having begun in the Spirit, are we now made perfect by the flesh? Christ dwelling in us overcomes the weakness of the flesh. The Beatitudes are a great example of the progression a believer goes through as God does His work of grace in the heart. As God brings to pass this progression inside of us individually, it impacts the entire Body of Christ by increasing unity.

Let us pray against fear, doubt, and unbelief in our hearts and in the Church. Let us pray for the unity in the Body that only comes from God. James 4:2 says that we have not because we ask not. If we want to live in a place of rest, knowing that we are His workmanship and not our own, we can ask and receive!

Study Questions

101. *How are we saved?*
102. *Once we've been converted to Christ, who is then to be trusted with the completion?*
103. *What is the one thing that we need in all that we do, that we might please God?*
104. *What were the three beginnings in Genesis and which one succeeded? Why?*
105. *What is the significance of the Book of Exodus for us?*
106. *What are Satan's two plans for mankind?*
107. *Describe the three-part work of salvation?*
108. *Why is it so important that we understand that we are covered with His flesh*
109. *What are the key points regarding salvation that God reveals to us in the story about Cornelius in the Book of Acts?*
110. *Why is the true meaning of the word "grace" so unsettling to man?*
111. *What is the only way believers overcome sin?*
112. *What is our inheritance through Christ?*
113. *What is the most important thing we can believe as followers of Christ? Why?*
114. *Why is it important that we understand the pictures God gave us in the Tabernacle?*
115. *What was the law unable to do? Why?*
116. *How did Jesus fulfill all prophecy about Himself?*
117. *How do we stop serving sin?*
118. *What is the most important dynamic of the Holy Ghost?*

SEVEN

The Bible Was Written Both Historically and Spiritually, Part 1

The carnal mind is confused by the spiritual dynamics of the Bible and it should be. The natural man, attempting to analyze the intimate message from God to His Bride, misunderstands the content because he lacks the insights that her personal relationship affords her.

The Bible contains the history of man as a means for God to reveal Himself. Among the multitude of gods in antiquity, there was a true God. By separating Abraham from his idol-worshipping family and making His voice known to him, God began a long process of self-revelation. The history recorded in the Bible is in direct correlation to the disclosure of God about Himself and His desire for man. Divine inspiration remained focused on God saving man and as such, it is really a history of the revelation of God. This is not to say that the history contained in the Bible is not valuable as secular history—it is.

The Book of Genesis contains an encapsulation of all that God would do on the earth, including the salvation of man by a sacrificial substitution. While it chronicled the failure of man, it also glorified the mercy and grace of God. It was necessary for God to conceal some of the promises because of their serious content. God's plan for one man to die for all of mankind was so complex that it had to be hidden and protected, lest man misunderstand God's plan for His own Son and conceive a religion that demanded human sacrifices.

The Bible itself tells us that God put a seal on its contents, denying access to the carnal mind to ensure the integrity of His signs and prophecies. Man is always eager to "help" God!

In addition to being sealed, the Bible contained mysteries, allegories, and parables along with the historical.

One Story, Two Views

> *18 Then answered the Jews and said unto him, What sign shewest thou unto us, seeing that thou doest these things? 19 Jesus answered and said unto them, Destroy this temple, and in three days I will raise it up. 20 Then said the Jews, Forty and six years was this temple in building, and wilt thou rear it up in three days? 21 But he spake of the temple of his body. 22 When therefore he was risen from the dead, his disciples remembered that he had said this unto them; and they believed the Scripture, and the word which Jesus had said.* John 2:18-22 (KJS)

The temple, the very center of Jewish identity, the meeting place between heaven and earth, and Jesus dared to say tear it down! This temple of stone was only a pattern of things to come and it appears that, at the time, no one understood that but Jesus. Jesus viewed the beautiful temple with the eyes of the Spirit, and those He spoke to viewed it with the eyes of the flesh. What a tragic difference it made for the people.

These Scriptures should be a warning sign for all ages. More than just the temple, all of the physical dynamics of the Old Testament were about to change. Jesus is the New Temple, a body for God to indwell. The old temple is a picture, a pattern of the new and the Bible is full of prophecies about this change.

This Latter House has more glory than the former because the stones of which it is made are lively stones. These lively stones have a mind of their own and because they must choose to be a part of this

House, the value of this Temple is increased immeasurably—there is no comparison between a house you only visit and the home you dwell in with your family!

This transition from "pattern" to "spiritual reality" would bring everything that the Jews knew into this different realm. If you stop and consider all of the things that changed, the list is staggering! Everything that God ordained in the physical pointed to a spiritual fulfillment. These children of Israel were at a most profound moment in history and were not even aware of it. Going back to examine these opposing realms (Spirit vs. flesh) moving toward a collision is not for the purpose of criticizing the Jewish people, but to draw a serious parallel between their view of the temple and Christianity's present view of itself.

Because their relationship with God was based on the historical and not the spiritual, they had lost contact with God. As long as the temple was standing, they assumed God was there. Doctors of theology replaced prophets as doctrines replaced the voice of God. The four hundred years of silence that preceded Jesus' earthly appearance was sent by God to amplify the voice of the Defining Covenant's last prophet, John the Baptist, and to create a hunger for the Bread of heaven.

The priesthood, preoccupied with their own voices, never noticed the silence from heaven. They always had something to say about God. It was not the same as God speaking through them, but who would notice? False hopes filled men's souls, dreams of food replaced spiritual nourishment, and darkness settled over the land. Keeping the people within the divided camps was all that mattered to them.

The Pharisees became a kingdom and the Sadducees became a kingdom…and the priests became the kings. The Christian community is moving down the same road, divided along denominational lines, kingdoms within the Kingdom, fighting constantly along doctrinal lines. Sermon "Twinkies" filled with fantasy teachings curb the people's appetite for real meat. Truth is spurned.

Because he tries to read the Bible as an ordinary book, man has come to conclusions about its content that simply show his ignorance of spiritual things. This God of creation, whose words brought light and order from darkness and chaos in six days, took the better part of two millennia to write this precious Book. He used something like forty writers from many different places and backgrounds to craft these sixty-six ornaments into one lampstand. (Exo. 25:31-37 tells us that there were sixty-six orna-ments on the candlestick in the temple of Moses, one for each book in the Bible.)

In Psalm 119, it says, "Thy Word is a lamp unto my feet and a light unto my pathway" (Psalms 119:105). When the Holy Spirit spoke those words through the psalmist, it is certain that he did not understand that the lampstand in the temple was a pattern of the Bible. The different writers, working independently of each other but under the leading of the Holy Spirit, nevertheless crafted a single book!

As a history book, the Bible is illuminating. As a spiritual point of intimacy, the Bible is impregnating. The historical aspect is important because it shows the consistency of God's love toward man, but the spir-itual aspect is more important because it introduces an intimacy that brings a familiarity to the reality of God.

As we discussed before, the problem with the spiritual aspect of the Bible is that the natural man cannot go there without being born again. This Kingdom of God is invisible to the carnal mind. Without the Holy Ghost as Teacher and Judge, the Spirit realm can be a haven for liars and religious con men. For too long, the Church has been living in the silence of God and no one has noticed. With all the religious meetings and power contests, most think God is really moving. The truth is, when the television cameras turn on somebody has to do something, even if it is just making noise. The Church should be hungry and expectant. Instead, she thinks she's full and has need of nothing.

The Church has been too long without a voice of absolute authority on issues of contention. Within the pages of the Bible, God has hidden truth to conceal it from all that would tamper with its message.

The Old Testament is a big part of the spiritual equation, a part that is most misunderstood. Written as allegorical absolutes within the historical context, God sealed the message to assure its purity. The Old Testament has been relegated to that place of "honored but no longer relevant," which is reserved for anything that begins with the word "old." It should be called the "Defining Testament" because it is the "thousand words" that a picture is said to be worth. The Gospels constitute the pictures but the Old Testament explains the details unseen by the natural eye. The New Testament truths illuminated by Old Testament parameters complete the revelation of Jesus Christ.

The Seven Feasts of the Defining Covenant

The seven feasts of Israel describe seven historical phenomena, events that would change the world and finish the very will of God in His people. The victory of God's will in Christ and in the Church resonate from the moment in history when God, in His magnificence of mystery, hid these prophetic declarations in the midst of joyous merriment. He concealed the most serious moments in history within the laughter of His people, Israel. These feasts were a description of not only the will of God, but of a chronological order as well. The first four of these feasts were more than memorials, they were allegories defining events in the four Gospels. These prisms break open the light so that we can see the full array of colors—they explain in depth what the Church must understand.

1. *Passover*: The Passover lamb was to be slain on the fourteenth day of the first month. When God told this to Moses, He spoke of the very day Jesus, the Lamb of God, would be slain. Even though the priests of Jesus' day did not believe that He was from God, they killed Him on precisely the day that God demanded.

Passover also described the death of Jesus and the application of His blood over the "doorpost" of the heart. The shedding of His blood became man's protection from God's judgment of sin. The angel of death cannot touch one of God's children, whose confession of sin and belief in Jesus has placed them underneath His blood. As we learned earlier, Passover also gives detailed instructions regarding how to eat the flesh of the Passover Lamb (the Word of God) because it is important to read the Bible in the way that God has prescribed (John 1:13,14).

2. *Unleavened Bread*: Leaven is life. It is an illustration used by God to show that once something comes to life, that life force will change what it is a part of and even what it comes into contact with in many ways. It can give life to either good or evil. Leaven is a good example of teaching. After you teach a man how to fish, he tries what he is taught. The application brings the teaching to life.

When Jesus said that the Kingdom of God was like leaven that a woman hid in three measures of flour, He meant that the Kingdom of God is a living truth and it will act upon the environment around it, giving life to that which is dead. Leaven is predictable. Given something to eat, something to drink, and something to act upon, it will bring forth action.

Grinding wheat seed separates the germ from the kernel of grain and therefore renders it lifeless in and of itself. You cannot plant flour and have it grow. If you add yeast to that same dead flour, put in some malt or sugar for food, and give it liquid to drink, you will see those life-less ingredients come to life and grow, rising up out of the pan.

When temptation comes and we turn away from it, we deny it life. Entertaining tempting thoughts is what moves temptation into sin. Those thoughts, which give the temptation its life in us, are leaven.

> *3 For though we walk in the flesh, we do not war after the flesh: 4 (For the weapons of our warfare [are] not carnal, but mighty through God to the pulling down of strong holds;) 5 Casting down imaginations, and every high thing that exalteth itself against the knowledge of God, and bringing into captivity every thought to the obedience of Christ; {imaginations: or, reasonings} 6 And having in a readiness to revenge all disobedience, when your obedience is fulfilled.* 2 Corinthians 10:3-6 (KJS)

The Bible is truth, but when man adds his interpretation to it, the application of that teaching gives life to the *teaching,* but not necessarily to the words of God. In the days of Jesus, the doctrines added by men to the Word of God were the very points that fought Him. He and His disciples were accused of being sinners because they plucked corn on the Sabbath day and ate it. God did command Israel not to harvest their crops on the Sabbath day, but the priesthood's leaven of malice and wickedness accused Jesus and His disciples of harvesting, and they were not (Mark 2:23-28).

At the time of the exodus, the bread came out of Egypt and leaven represented the doctrines of manmade religion. The truth that we see later in the story is that the false god (which the calf represented in Egypt) did, in fact, come with the people...in their hearts. The golden calf raised up by Aaron was raised up again at a later date in Israel's history by King Jeroboam. He called it the calf that delivered Israel from Egypt (1 Kings 12:25-33)! No wonder God commanded the people to remove all leaven from their houses!

God's battle down through the ages has been with the injection of theological corruption into the truth of His revelation. Under the Old Testament covenant, God commanded man to read His Word and obey it, not to interpret what He meant. God held back the understanding of the Old Testament until the appointed time. So you could obey the commandments and bring the sacrifices for the blood atonement and be caught up with Jesus on that great resurrection morning.

Leaven was the added ingredient that Satan was after. If men taught that you could not eat without first washing your hands, it would not have seemed like an important intrusion against the Word of God. After all, washing our hands after we have been to the market is a good idea. However, the day that teaching was used as a judgment against Jesus and His disciples, labeling them imposters, the "life" man added to the Bible was indeed malice and wickedness.

3. *Firstfruit*: The firstfruit of the harvest was waved by the high priest on the first day of the week after the harvest began. Jesus was the first of the harvest of human souls and He was resurrected on the first day of the week. As the High Priest, He waved the harvest sheaf of the firstfruit before the Father. This feast also declared the very day of His resurrection. Those people under the Blood Covenant of the Old Testament will be resurrected by God and protected by the blood of bulls and goats. Once Jesus died, however, He became the only door that exists to God. There is no other!

4. *Pentecost*: This feast is about the birth of the Church. Again, on the exact day of the Old Testament feast, God brought forth the Church by sending the Spirit of truth to indwell every believer. Two loaves of bread were baked and waved before God on this day. The flour was ground extra fine for those two loaves, a picture of the unity of the people of God—many people, one Body.

This is also the first feast where leaven was commanded to be put in the bread. **The day that God put His Holy Ghost in man was the day that man was allowed to have leaven.** The Holy Ghost is the Teacher of truth. In fact, as we have discussed, He is called the Spirit of truth. Once man had a Teacher who would teach the Bible in truth, God said that leaven was okay.

The Old Testament was supposed to be a leaven-free environment. Had it been so, the people would have received Jesus. Their doctrines were not what He was teaching, so their kingdom rose up and fought against Him and His Kingdom.

These four feasts were in the first part of the year. The next three feasts were in the seventh month, and they reveal things that will come to God's people in the last days just as surely as the first four feasts were fulfilled.

5. *Trumpets*: This feast is about the gathering of God's people in the last days. In 1948, the physical nation of Israel gathered because the trumpet of God sounded. The natural ear never heard the sound of it.

It was also at this time that the Church experienced the peak of her great healing revival. The message that God sent through His ministries during those dramatic years was, "Hear My voice." Those men and women through whom God moved so powerfully were not accepted by the denominational churches, not even the Pentecostal churches! Like Jesus, they were outside the camp.

Once the miracles swept people out of their dry, dead churches, Church leaders finally began to embrace the revival as true. The miracles were but a trumpet sound. So loudly did God sound this trumpet that people all over the world heard of it. Sadly, though, men focused on the miracles and failed to understand the portent of the message God gave. This revival, filled with Holy Ghost power, was the spiritual gathering of God's people.

Also in 1948, the World Council of Churches was formed. This was man's attempt at gathering. It was counterfeit.

The fact that Israel is a physical sign does not negate her important role in God's plan of unification. Remember, there were two loaves in the feast of Pentecost.

6. *Atonement*: This is the feast of rest or Sabbath. It describes a time of tribulation that will worry the carnal mind, but not the spirit man who is at rest. Both the Christian Church and Israel largely ignored the commandment of God to rest. It is one of the Ten Commandments, yet it is the only one that the Church teaches as irrelevant. Not one preacher would stand in a pulpit and preach the breaking of the other nine. This commandment means little because it makes no sense to the carnal

mind. It is a test of faith and the natural man does not find rest in trusting God. Preachers teach that we don't need to keep the Sabbath day because we are free from the law. If that is true as they are using it, then why are the other nine still commandments? If we are freed from one we are freed from all.

When the rich young ruler came to Jesus and asked what he had to do to have eternal life, Jesus answered him, saying, "Keep the commandments." There were a multitude of commandments in those days: the commandments of each religious division in Israel, the commandments of the law of Moses, the commandments of the elders, and so on. The rich young ruler asked Jesus which commandments He meant. Jesus described the Ten Commandments, written by the finger of God on the tables of stone. The young man replied, "I've kept those." Jesus then said to him: There's one you have not kept. You have not kept the Sabbath day. Actually, Jesus said, "Go, sell all that you have and give it to the poor, and come follow Me." The man left filled with sorrow because he would not or could not do that. You see, he could not rest in God as his provider. Money was his place of rest (Matt. 19:16-23).

When a Christian keeps the Sabbath day, he cannot carry a burden on that day, even in his heart. Every worry and doubt must be brought into captivity and put under the Word of God. Many men have learned to bring lust into captivity and thereby defeat adultery in the heart. Jesus said that anger was murder while it was within the heart, and He called lustful thoughts adultery (Matthew 5). Doubt and unbelief are also sins. The Sabbath commandment addresses these sins because we are forbidden to carry them on that day of rest. Once we practice bringing those things into captivity for twenty-four hours, we become very aware of their presence and are able to see them as sin every day.

God commanded a one-day Sabbath once a week and a one-year Sabbath every seven years. In addition, there was a year of Jubilee every fiftieth year. The entire nation was forbidden to grow food for one year out of every seven. That is rest? Not opening for business on the busiest day of the week and losing all that money is rest?

The Sabbath day is a commandment to rest in God. It is about faith and the application of God's Word to test our thoughts, find out which ones are sinful, and reject them. By keeping the Sabbath day, it becomes apparent that the spirit man can rest and the flesh man cannot.

9 There remaineth therefore a rest to the people of God. {rest: or, keeping of a sabbath} 10 For he that is entered into his rest, he also hath ceased from his own works, as God [did] from his. 11 Let us labor therefore to enter into that rest, lest any man fall after the same example of unbelief. 12 For the word of God [is] quick, and powerful, and sharper than any two-edged sword, piercing even to the dividing asunder of soul and spirit, and of the joints and marrow, and [is] a discerner of the thoughts and intents of the heart. 13 Neither is there any creature that is not manifest in his sight: but all things [are] naked and opened unto the eyes of him with whom we have to do. Hebrews 4:9-13 (KJS)*

5 Trust in the LORD with all thine heart; and lean not unto thine own understanding. 6 In all thy ways acknowledge him, and he shall direct thy paths. Proverbs 3:5-6 (KJS)

Physical Israel never kept the years of Sabbath she was commanded to. God carried her into Babylon until the land had kept Sabbath the number of years they owed Him. Israel was a nation for four hundred ninety years, so they owed God seventy years of Sabbath. In Second Chronicles, God explains what He did.

36 Therefore he brought upon them the king of the Chaldees, who slew their young men with the sword in the house of their sanctuary, and had no compassion upon young man or maiden, old man, or him that stooped for age: he gave [them] all into his hand. 18 And all the vessels of the house of God, great and small, and the treasures of the house of the LORD, and the treasures of the king, and of his princes; all [these] he brought to Babylon. 19 And they burnt the house of God, and brake down the wall of Jerusalem, and burnt all the palaces thereof with fire, and destroyed all the goodly vessels thereof. 20 And them that had escaped from the sword carried he away to Babylon; where they were servants to him and his sons until the reign of the kingdom of Persia: 21 To fulfil the word of the LORD by the mouth of Jeremiah, until the land had enjoyed her Sabbaths: [for] as long as she lay desolate she kept Sabbath, to fulfill threescore and ten years. 2 Chronicles 36:17-21 (KJS)

Israel's land had to lay desolate to keep the Sabbath. The Church cannot draw a parallel between this and the abomination that brings desolation that Daniel prophesied about (Dan. 9:27, 11:31, 12:11). And she should.

Now the Christian Church has ignored God's commandment to rest, and the Bible tells of a day under the beast system that the Church will be brought to a time of Sabbath. Under the beast system, man cannot buy, sell, or work without taking the image, name, or number of the beast. These are the three important dynamics of the Sabbath day (Rev. 13, 16:2, 19:20), you could not buy, sell or work.

The believer who can rest in God will not need to take the name or number to get by. There will not be torment to the true believer who has practiced resting in God's provisions. The natural man cannot rest in faith but the spirit man can. The natural man must be brought into subjection by obeying the commandment to rest, just as the natural man is brought into subjection about lust or anger.

In Matthew 24, Jesus told His disciples, "Pray that your flight is not in the winter time or on the Sabbath day." The doctrines of men dismiss God's words, but the true believer seeks God's interpretation and prays as he is instructed to. If the Church has no time of flight, why would Jesus include this in His teaching about the end times? If the flight of the Church means being caught up to Jesus in the sky, why would winter matter, or the Sabbath day?

The leaven of man will reject what God is saying to the Church, but he that hath ears let him hear what the Spirit says unto the Church. God is *not* going to pour His wrath out on His Church—that is why He tells her to rest in Him. During the feast of atonement, all work is forbidden and anyone who does not rest is taken from among God's people.

7. *Tabernacles*: The Feast of Tabernacles is a promise that God will finish His Tabernacle on the earth. We are the Tabernacle of God. The finished work is God dwelling in a Church that is unified and mature, having attained to the full stature of the man Christ Jesus. The world will then see Jesus in us! Man struggling in his own strength to do all that the Word of God declares will not stop God from bringing to pass His creative master-piece. **The world will see the manifestation of the Sons of God!** The mystery that has been hid down through the ages, but was revealed to Paul the apostle and now to us is "Christ in you the hope of glory" (Col. 1:27).

You can see how God put truth into these feasts and then sealed the revelation until the appointed time. This is not about man figuring out these mysteries by his intellect, it is about God breaking the seal and allowing man to see them. Look at what God said in the book of Isaiah:

> *10 For the LORD hath poured out upon you the spirit of deep sleep, and hath closed your eyes: the prophets and your rulers, the seers hath he covered. 11 And the vision of all is become unto you as the words of a book that is sealed, which [men] deliver to one that is learned, saying, Read this, I pray thee: and he saith, I cannot; for it [is] sealed: 12 And the book is delivered to him that is not learned, saying, Read this, I pray thee: and he saith, I am not learned. 13 Wherefore the Lord said, Forasmuch as this people draw near [me] with their mouth, and with their lips do honor me, but have removed their heart far from me, and their fear toward me is taught by the precept of men: 14 Therefore, behold, I will proceed to do a marvellous work among this people, [even] a marvellous work and a wonder: for the wisdom of their wise [men] shall perish, and the understanding of their prudent [men] shall be hid.* Isaiah 29:10-14 (KJS)

God poured out upon them the spirit of deep sleep and closed their eyes. This happened to the spiritual leaders as well as to the physical leaders. God says that "the vision of all [the writings of the Old Testament] were as the words of a book that was sealed." What does man do with that? He brings this sealed book to a man who can read. He wants the book to be read. The man who can read says, "I cannot read this book, it is sealed." Does man stop there or go back to God and ask Him to open the seal? No, he takes the book to someone who cannot read! He figures that maybe the solution is to bypass someone smart enough to read, thinking that the unlearned man may not notice the seal! The unlearned man is smart enough to say, "I am not learned." Would to God man had said just that, but at some point he began to pretend that he could read the sealed Book!

God went on to say that He would do a marvelous work and a wonder. What is it? The wisdom of the wise men will perish and the understanding of the prudent men shall be hid. Man and his intellect are helplessly in need of God to reveal the hidden things.

> *34 All these things spake Jesus unto the multitude in parables; and without a parable spake he not unto them: 35 That it might be*

fulfilled which was spoken by the prophet, saying, I will open my mouth in parables; I will utter things which have been kept secret from the foundation of the world. Matthew 13:34-35 (KJS)

We have discussed before that Jesus prevailed to open the Book (Rev. 5). Full of the Holy Ghost, His words were full of life and consequences. During His earthly ministry, He still preached in parables. His parables were divine disclosure, the things that had been kept secret from the foundation of the world were being revealed. The time of revealing was at hand, but it will be under His dominion. Right now He's teaching the ministers who will parent the children.

God was establishing a leadership that would be ready when the Church was born on the day of Pentecost. Each new convert is a baby, and babies need care. Jesus would not make disciples of the multitudes and leave them without a mature ministry to feed and protect them. New believers, described by God as babies, would not know if a preacher was lying to them. Just as natural babies cannot discern between who to trust and who not to, spiritual babies cannot discern either.

28 Take heed therefore unto yourselves, and to all the flock, over the which the Holy Ghost hath made you overseers, to feed the church of God, which he hath purchased with his own blood. 29 For I know this, that after my departing shall grievous wolves enter in among you, not sparing the flock. 30 Also of your own selves shall men arise, speaking perverse things, to draw away disciples after them. Acts 20:28-30 (KJS)

The ministries of God are a defense against such satanic assaults. If the apostle Paul spoke of his own presence as a protection against lies, there is an important implication for all ministries who are called by God to do the same thing. If ministries were doing what God commanded, there would be unity and we would all be speaking the same things. In each school of thought, men rally around their own creed. It was not so when Paul spoke what he did in the book of Acts. The Word of God claims that there is one faith, one hope, one baptism (Eph. 4:5). In John 17, Jesus prayed that we would be "one, as He and the Father were one." We cannot repeat the ideal of God for the Church laid out in First Corinthians without seeing how far we miss the mark. Our God commanded unity, yet we go on ignoring the dire consequences of division among us. A house or a kingdom divided will not stand (Mark 3:25).

> *Now I beseech you, brethren, by the name of our Lord Jesus Christ, that ye all speak the same thing, and [that] there be no divisions among you; but [that] ye be perfectly joined together in the same mind and in the same judgment.* 1Cor 1:10 (KJS)

Is there anyone left on earth who believes this will be so on the earth? The revealing and understanding of the mysteries in the Bible will bring us back to this.

The entire Old Testament contains messages about Jesus and His worldwide Church. From the blood and skins that covered Adam and Eve to the temple of Ezekiel's vision, Jesus is the theme throughout. These embedded messages were taught as historical facts and remained hidden for centuries. God knew that Satan, in his war against God's Word, would seek to twist its promises and deny its purity. These hidden truths have been given to us to restore God's truth to the Church.

Remember, when Jesus opened up the story of Jonah, He told of His own death and resurrection. This simple statement, "As Jonah was three days and three nights in the belly of the fish, so must the Son of man be three days and three nights in the bowels of the earth," was actually a great unsealing of Old Testament history. God knew that men could retell the events within this great story and never suspect it contained classified information from the Kingdom of God. At the appointed time, Jesus opened His orders and, by the Holy Spirit, understood the message! Jonah told the men aboard the ship: Unless I am sacrificed by being thrown overboard, you will all perish. If I die, you will live. Jesus knew that He would be in the bowels of the earth for a specific number of days and, just as the Old Testament story promised, it was so.

As we learned earlier, Jesus also opened up the story of Moses and the serpent on the pole.

> *14 And as Moses lifted up the serpent in the wilderness, even so must the Son of man be lifted up: 15 That whosoever believeth in him should not perish, but have eternal life.* John 3:14-15 (KJS)

These are but a couple of examples of the way in which the Old Testament was sealed. We have come upon Scriptures about mysteries, allegories, and parables in the New Testament as we have been discussing the spiritual dynamics and the unsealing of the Old Testament. Now, let's look more closely at these three important parts of the Word of God.

Mysteries, Allegories, and Parables

Mysteries

BDB/Thayers #3466 musterion moos-tay'-ree-on}; from a derivative of muo (to shut the mouth); TDNT - 4:802,615; n n AV - mystery 27; 27
1) Hidden thing, secret, mystery; 1a) Generally mysteries, religious secrets, confided only to the initiated and not to ordinary mortals; 1b) A hidden or secret thing, not obvious to the understanding; 1c) A hidden purpose or counsel; 1c1) Secret will;1c1a) of men; 1c1b) of God: the secret counsels which govern God in dealing with the righteous, which are hidden from ungodly and wicked men but plain to the godly; 3) in rabbinic writings, it denotes the mystic or hidden sense: of an OT saying, of an image or form seen in a vision, of a dream

Within this definition, we see that the Greek word *musterion* is a derivative of *muo* (to shut the mouth) and denotes "religious secrets confided only to the initiated and not to ordinary mortals" (a born-again believer is not an ordinary mortal). Do you remember Deuteronomy 29:29?

The secret [things belong] unto the LORD our God: but those [things which are] revealed [belong] unto us and to our children forever, that [we] may do all the words of this law.

The definition also says "**a hidden thing not obvious to the understanding.**" Notice how the word is defined in 1c1b: "**of God: the secret counsels which govern God in dealing with the righteous, which are hidden from ungodly and wicked men but plain to the godly. 3) in rabbinic writings, it denotes the mystic or hidden sense: of an Old Testament saying, of an image or form seen in a vision or dream.**"

As we touched on earlier, Jesus spoke in parables to the crowds, planting the seeds of truth in the hearts of those who would receive by faith without receiving the understanding.

He did explain the parables to the disciples because it was time for them to understand. The understanding brought forth life (leaven), and the disciples needed to grow in the truth and become mature before the multitudes received life. His words contined life, and that life produced spiritual babies. He would not bring babies to life without ministers in place first to feed them the spiritual food they needed. Once the one hundred twenty disciples came out of the upper room on the day of Pentecost, full of experience, full of the Holy Ghost, and full of His words, the same multitudes heard the unveiling of the mysteries for themselves. Before His ascension, Jesus confronted Peter about feeding His lambs.

> *15 So when they had dined, Jesus saith to Simon Peter, Simon, [son] of Jonas, lovest thou me more than these? He saith unto him, Yea, Lord; thou knowest that I love thee. He saith unto him, feed my lambs. 16 He saith to him again the second time, Simon, [son] of Jonas, lovest thou me? He saith unto him, Yea, Lord; thou knowest that I love thee. He saith unto him, feed my sheep. 17 He saith unto him the third time, Simon, [son] of Jonas, lovest thou me? Peter was grieved because he said unto him the third time, Lovest thou me? And he said unto him, Lord, thou knowest all things; thou knowest that I love thee. Jesus saith unto him, Feed my sheep.* John 21:15-17 (KJS)

He taught the men who would teach the people. When all things were ready, He opened the door of understanding and the water flooded out. This was not prejudicial exclusion, for God was creating a new race. He made a spiritual race out of every nation under heaven, and the bread they would need could only come from the seeds of truth Jesus sowed into the fertile soil of the heart. It was the same at creation: God created the food first. When everything was ready He created man.

Another mystery is the crucifixion of Jesus by the Jewish priesthood. God detailed the blood atonement in the Old Testament, with the Jewish priesthood being the method by which He would slay the Sacrifice. The Sacrifice had to be washed first by a priest. John the

Baptist, a Levite, did this. John wanted to be Spirit-baptized by Jesus, but the Lord forbade it, declaring that His own water baptism was a fulfillment of the law.

The Jewish high priest prophesied that it would be expedient for one man to die and not the whole nation (John 11:49-51). Though he spoke from a point of rejecting Jesus, the words were still from God through him. At last, God ordained that the priesthood should kill the sacrifice. Although the Roman government had the ultimate right of execution, it was the demands of the priests that produced the blood that sin's stains demanded. Salvation came by God through a priesthood hostile to the Sacrifice. Even so, they obeyed God to the letter. Their rejection of His teaching led the nation in the wrong direction, to their total confusion. They crucified the Lamb of God, as John declared Him, on the very day that the Passover Lamb was ordained to die in the Old Testament. That is a mystery unfolded!

We can also see the mystery of the Jews' blindness continuing until the fullness of the Gentile age.

> For I would not, brethren, that ye should be ignorant of this mystery, lest ye should be wise in your own conceits; that blindness in part is happened to Israel, until the fulness of the Gentiles be come in. 26 And so all Israel shall be saved: as it is written, There shall come out of Sion the Deliverer, and shall turn away ungodliness from Jacob.
> Romans 11:25 (KJS)

When the Church comes into unity (so that the Jewish nation does not become divided like the Christian Church is now), God will allow the Jews to see Christ as their Messiah, alive in the Church. The Church is a womb to birth Christ to the world, not a tomb to memorialize His past life. The Church is His Body.

Allegories

BDB/Thayers # 238 allegoreo al-lay-gor-eh'-o};from 243 and agoreo (to harangue, cf 58); TDNT - 1:260,42; v AV - be an allegory 1; 1

1) to speak allegorically or in a figure

American Heritage Dictionary: allegory—1a.) The use of characters or events to represent ideas or principles in a story, play, or picture. b.) A story, play, or picture in which such representation occurs. 2.) A symbolic representation.

The use of allegory is evident throughout Old Testament Scripture. God projected His will as a matter of fact within the historical context because His word contains the power to create and finish what He stated, even though it is hidden from the mind of man. Throughout the Bible, God has spoken His will that it might come to pass. The Kingdom of God is facilitated by His spoken Word. Jesus understood this when He said, "It is written of me." The things that were written about His death and resurrection were written as facts, just as the things written about His birth from a virgin womb.

When God substituted the animal (which He sacrificed) for Adam and Eve's death after their disobedience, the historical context contained a principle: death is the payment for sin. It also contained an idea: God's mercy provided a substitute and accepted the sacrificial death in place of Adam's. Adam's actions clearly placed him in debt to God and the debt had to be paid. The story also contained an allegory. God showed the death of Jesus on the cross, paying the debt for man through the sacrifice of His own life. More than just the blood shed for sin, man was covered by the flesh of the sacrifice so that man's life was to be hid in Christ. Man has been freed from the debt of sin and made flesh of His flesh!

In the story of Abraham, the apostle Paul saw the allegory of the two covenants. Paul, who served God with total commitment, persecuted the Church of Jesus Christ because his understanding of the Hebrew Scriptures was purely historical. It was the revelation of the Holy Ghost that opened the Scriptures up to him. Paul needed that revelation in order to answer the question as to how a man could know the Word of God and not know the God of that word. In the book of Galatians, Paul used the story of Abraham to explain the idea of the New Covenant and the principles on which it operates.

19 My little children, of whom I travail in birth again until Christ be formed in you, 20 I desire to be present with you now, and to change my voice; for I stand in doubt of you. 21 Tell me, ye that desire to be under the law, do ye not hear the law? 22 For it is written, that Abraham had two sons, the one by a bondmaid, the other by a freewoman. 23 But he [who was] of the bondwoman was born after the flesh; but he of the freewoman [was] by promise. 24 Which things are an allegory: for these are the two covenants; the one from the mount Sinai, which gendereth to bondage, which is Agar. 25 For this Agar is mount Sinai in Arabia, and answereth to Jerusalem which now is, and is in bondage with her children. 26 But Jerusalem which is above is free, which is the mother of us all. 27 For it is written, Rejoice, [thou] barren that bearest not; break forth and cry, thou that travailest not: for the desolate hath many more children than she which hath an husband. 28 Now we, brethren, as Isaac was, are the children of promise. 29 But as then he that was born after the flesh persecuted him [that was born] after the Spirit, even so [it is] now. 30 Nevertheless what saith the Scripture? Cast out the bondwoman and her son: for the son of the bondwoman shall not be heir with the son of the freewoman. 31 So then, brethren, we are not children of the bondwoman, but of the free. Galatians 4:19-31 (KJS)

Notice, Paul not only used the story of Abraham, Sarah, and Hagar, but quoted from Isaiah 54. The Spirit revealed the theme that Paul told the Galatians about throughout the Bible. When God placed something allegorically in the historical context, He reiterated it in the prophetical and lived it in the Gospels. There is no allegory that stands alone without witness in just this way. The entire Bible is a picture that defies intellectual interpretation, whose details are so divinely inspired that a single lamb laying slain across an altar encapsulates the unfathomable love of God, the desperate need of man, and the victory only grace could bring. Born in a stable as any lamb could be, crucified on Passover as the lamb should be, food for the hungry as the flesh of the lamb would be: Jesus the Lamb lived the allegory, revealed the mystery, taught the parable, and fulfilled the historical.

Parables

BDB/Thayers # 4912 mashal maw-shawl'}; apparently from 04910 in some original sense of superiority in mental action; TWOT - 1258a; n m AV - proverb 19, parable 18, byword 1, like 1; 39
1) proverb, parable;1a) proverb, proverbial saying, aphorism; 1b) byword; 1c) similitude, parable; 1d) poem; 1e) sentences of ethical wisdom, ethical maxims

BDB/Thayers # 4910 mashal maw-shal'}; a primitive root; TWOT
- 1259; v AV - rule 38, ruler 19, reign 8, dominion 7, governor 4,
ruled over 2, power 2, indeed 1; 81
1) to rule, have dominion, reign; 1a) (Qal) to rule, have dominion;
1b) (Hiphil); 1b1) to cause to rule; 1b2) to exercise dominion

These definitions from the Hebrew writings describe the parable as
God exercising dominion over His word. He alone holds the interpretation; man must come to Him for instruction. This is a safeguard to us
when we realize that God speaks to those He has chosen and they listen
to Him as well.

In the New Testament, the Greek word for parable is *parabole*.

BDB/Thayers # 3850 parabole par-ab-ol-ay'}; from 3846; TDNT -
5:744,773; n f AV - parable 46, figure 2, comparison 1, proverb 1;
50
1) a placing of one thing by the side of another, juxtaposition, as
of ships in battle; 2) metaph.; 2a) a comparing, comparison of
one thing with another, likeness, similitude; 2b) an example by
which a doctrine or precept is illustrated; 2c) a narrative, fictitious
but agreeable to the laws and usages of human life, by which
either the duties of men or the things of God, particularly the
nature and history of God's kingdom are figuratively portrayed;
2d) a parable: an earthly story with a heavenly meaning;3) a pithy
and instructive saying, involving some likeness or comparison and
having preceptive or admonitory force;3a) an aphorism, a maxim;
4) a proverb; 5) an act by which one exposes himself or his
possessions to danger, a venture, a risk

From the beginning, God used the parable to control the life that
His words brought forth. When Jesus taught His disciples, we know that
parables created a perimeter of dissemination, thereby ensuring that
only those chosen would understand. The parables did something
else—they created a desire to understand in the people who heard them,
just as riddles do. When Jesus was finished preaching, His words
impacted the uninitiated and fostered a lasting impression. The riddles
ran through their minds while they longed for the answer.

Historical

God reserved the right to use the history of His people to vouchsafe truth. The very foundations of His Kingdom were laid in the Christcentric history of Israel. From Abraham's binding of Isaac on the altar of sacrifice, to the Passover lamb and the shedding of blood for the remission of sin, Christ Jesus, and His role as High Priest and Sacrifice are described.

The tabernacle of Moses described Jesus and His salvation by grace: His Holy Spirit leading, His perpetual supply of bread for the soul, His fellowship with the saints, and the cross of Calvary. It also described the Bible, including the number of books it would contain when completed, the number of witnesses who would come out of the upper room filled with the Holy Ghost, and the greatest fact of all—God dwelling in His people and bringing them into unity as a completed Temple.

Historically, Jesus was pictured as the God of Creation, the King Eternal, the Servant High Priest, and the Son of Man. He was, allegorically, the blood and flesh that covered Adam and Eve, the ark of Noah's salvation, the only son in Abraham's total surrender of Isaac, Joseph the rejected ruler, and the rock smitten in the desert wilderness, bringing forth the mighty river of life from the love of God. He is seen as the Beginning and the End.

Because God used the historical to record His will, the New Testament contained the historical impregnated with spiritual truths. The resulting works confronted the carnal mind, drawing a defining line—one was either born of the Spirit and received truth, or carnal and angry.

Summary

The Bible is the most incredible book known to man! Its pages contain every provision to satisfy every need of mankind. To the natural man, the historical dimension of the Bible is the gateway that leads him to recognize the holiness of God and the sinfulness of man. He can see the need for salvation and is drawn to repent and be reconciled to the Father. God uses the letter of the Word to bring us to the place where the life of the Word impregnates our soul.

Once we are born again and receive the indwelling Spirit of God, the Bible is our food. God whispers His secrets in the ear of His Bride and we feast upon a banquet of unimaginable splendor! Because Jesus prevailed to open the Book and sent the Holy Ghost to teach it to us, the spirit man is made privy to the heart of God in a way the natural man has no access to. Sometimes we may not feel as though we understand anything we read, but we can trust that the Holy Spirit is working within—in the secret places, often invisible to our conscious under-standing—according to our needs and His will in meeting them. Our faith and perseverance will be rewarded when the words do come to life in our conscious understanding.

The Bible contains mysteries, parables, allegories, and histories that we can only understand as the Holy Ghost reveals them to us. God made it this way to protect His Word from Satan and from the natural man.

Study Questions

119. Why is it important that we understand the Bible from both the historical and spiritual aspects?
120. Why is it easier to understand the historical (physical) facts of the Bible?
121. Why did God seal the spiritual truths written in His Word?
122. What are the four primary forms of expression in the Bible?
123. When Jesus said, "tear this Temple down and in three days I will raise it up" was He speaking physically or Spiritually? Why is this important for us to understand today?
124. Why is the Old Testament pertinent today?
125. Why is it important that we understand the seven Jewish feasts?
126. What is God's creative masterpiece?
127. What is the difference between a mystery and a parable? Why does God use them?
128. Define allegory. What is the first allegory in the Bible?
129. How does God bear witness to, or prove, His allegories?
130. What are some "types and shadows" of Jesus in the Old Testament buried in the history of Israel?

SEVEN

The Bible Was Written Both Historically and Spiritually, Part 2

Spiritual History: Allegorical Unfolding

Another important dynamic of the Spirit's infusion of truth into the historical context is confrontation. As man rejected truth, trusting in his carnal reasoning, God confronted his slide into apostasy with a dramatic increase in warnings. Once man persisted in having his own way, God then spoke in forms of divine conundrum and the natural man was lost as to the meaning and enraged by what appeared preposterous to him.

The New Testament opens with a looking back to things recorded under the influence of the Holy Spirit's perspective. Matthew is not alone in this feast on the inward parts of the Lamb, but the fact that God chose to begin the writings of the New Covenant with such an open confrontation of religion is in itself very instructive.

It is true that Matthew as well as the other writers did not begin at once to provide these important documents to the world, but after the death and resurrection of Jesus, they recognized the need as the Spirit prompted them.

We do well to note here that at the time Matthew began to write the Gospel, he knew that the high priest and the elders had paid the soldiers stationed at the tomb of Jesus to lie about Jesus' resurrection. These were the soldiers who experienced the earthquake, the angel of the Lord coming like lightning to the tomb of Jesus, and the fear they knew in the presence of that mighty angel. What sorrow Matthew and the other disciples must have suffered to find out that the spiritual leaders felt compelled to bribe those soldiers to lie. The soldiers said that the disciples came and stole the body of Jesus while they slept. What possible sum of money facilitated such a fabrication in the face of the resurrection and the fearfulness they encountered under the judgmental eye of the angel of God? I cannot imagine! That bribe revealed the certainty of the total apostasy of the religious house of that hour. The disciples learned the same thing that Jesus did on the mountain of temptation— the same spirit that rejected the prophets and could not believe God, even in the face of irrefutable evidence, now ruled the priests who influenced their nation.

It is certain that these leaders obtained and read the writings of the men who believed in Jesus as the Messiah. When men reject God's merciful invitation (Jesus invited His kinsmen to join Him), God's anger turns to confrontation. The leaders who read the Gospels became enraged by what was written, which was a consequence of their rejection of the truth. It led to their destruction.

The Christian Church is on the brink of just such a disaster. These things were written for our admonition, on whom the ends of the world have come (1 Cor. 10:11). If we forget that this blindness in Israel happened, in part, for our benefit, we might view their mistakes with arrogance and make our own guilt before God worse. The strange sound that truth made in the ears of these errant leaders is indeed a warning to God's children today. The leaders of Israel will come to see that Jesus is the Messiah when the absolute truth that He embodies is welcomed by the Christian Church. God will not and cannot reveal Himself in the fragmented, divided, fighting doctrines of men and devils.

Confrontation, the New Testament, and the Spiritual History View

The Forty-Two Generations from Abraham to Jesus
Matthew starts with a loaded genealogy, the message clearly confronts the religious leaders while it tells of God's redeeming grace reaching out beyond the nation of His delight to the entire world. Matthew's view of Jesus is that of the King. This is the Gospel of the Kingdom and Jesus is King of everything!

> *The book of the generation of Jesus Christ, the son of David, the son of Abraham.* Matthew 1:1 (KJS)

Matthew starts with David, in whose lineage Jesus was born according to the flesh. Once the royal lineage was defined, he moved on to Abraham. It is "this Kingdom" that the King of glory reigns over, and Abraham is the father of the Kingdom.

Then Matthew brings in the four women. The Jewish people were proud of the four matriarchs who gave birth to their nation. These women of barren wombs and lonely hearts touched the very fabric of Israel with their stories of triumph. Sarah, Rebecca, Leah, and Rachel all contributed to the glory of God by their virtue and fidelity to the birthing of this people. These four women were celebrated by the people of Israel, and for a good reason—they birthed a nation. Contrary to historical preference, however, they are not the four mentioned by Matthew! In fact, the four women mentioned by Matthew were all Gentiles, regarded by the Jewish leadership as unacceptable, and all were faithful to God. The first woman mentioned is Tamar.

> *And Judas begat Phares and Zara of Thamar; and Phares begat Esrom; and Esrom begat Aram;* Matthew 1:3 (KJS)

Tamar was a Canaanite, married to Er, eldest son of Judah. Unable to conceive before her husband Er died, she was married to but was rejected by his brother. He also died while married to her. Sent back to her family by her father-in-law, Judah, to wait for his last son (still a child) to grow up, she eventually realized that Judah was not going to call for her. Posing as a prostitute on the roadside, she waited for Judah and ended up having twins by him. It was through this woman that God blessed Judah's lineage! She does not seem like the kind of woman God would want to mention in the family tree—she was an outsider, possibly cursed (after all, two sons die while married to her), and, finally, posed as a prostitute. There she is, though, in the lineage of Jesus, Son of God! Tamar was willing to sacrifice herself for the lineage of her husband. She was faithful, courageous, and persistent.

Next, Matthew mentions Rahab. Salmon begat Boaz of Rahab. During this time, Israel had come into the promised land and God had saved this city prostitute who protected His servants. Rahab risked her own life to rescue the Hebrew spies. She encouraged the people of God with her confidence that God had indeed given the city to them. Still, Rahab was a woman from Jericho, a Gentile from a cursed city. How clearly Matthew described the depths that God would bring man from through Christ Jesus, redeeming us from the curse of the law.

> 7 Know ye therefore that they which are of faith, the same are the children of Abraham. 8 And the Scripture, foreseeing that God would justify the heathen through faith, preached before the gospel unto Abraham, [saying], In thee shall all nations be blessed. 9 So then they which be of faith are blessed with faithful Abraham. 10 For as many as are of the works of the law are under the curse: for it is written, Cursed [is] every one that continueth not in all things which are written in the book of the law to do them. 11 But that no man is justified by the law in the sight of God, [it is] evident: for, The just shall live by faith. 12 And the law is not of faith: but, The man that doeth them shall live in them. 13 Christ hath redeemed us from the curse of the law, being made a curse for us: for it is written, Cursed [is] every one that hangeth on a tree: 14 That the blessing of Abraham might come on the Gentiles through Jesus Christ; that we might receive the promise of the Spirit through faith. Galatians 3:7-14 (KJS)

> And Salmon begat Boaz of Rahab; and Boaz begat Obed of Ruth; and Obed begat Jesse; Matthew 1:5 (KJS)

Ruth came next, the Moabite whose tender care of her widowed Jewish mother-in-law, Naomi, brought her not only into Israel but into the lineage of the King. God understood the attitude that Ruth faced was still prevalent in the days of Jesus. Matthew knew well the story of the near-kinsman who had the right of redemption. He refused it because he didn't want to mar his inheritance by marrying Ruth. The carnal man is not a good judge when it comes to eternal things. The Moabites were descendants of Lot and his daughter. Ruth placed value on being part of the people of God. Putting her own sorrow aside, she chose to minister to Naomi and ended up being ministered to.

The fourth woman was Bathsheba. As Matthew wrote, "David begat Solomon, of her who had been the wife of Uriah."

These are wonderful names in this lineage of Jesus. They embody the very message of salvation preached by Jesus. These women were women of faith. They were women of courage and they were also Gentiles, mentioned as a reminder that God always brought in Gentiles, and women at that. Their reputations did not make them seem valuable to anyone but God the Savior. The Great Potter, Reconciler, and Redeemer made His boast in this genealogy of His Son. Those women are not mentioned as women of shame. Quite the contrary, they were placed here by God as examples of good and blessings in the lineage.

These names picked at the pride of the self-righteous. They were like beacons shining out through the genealogy of Jesus, condemning the knowledge of good and evil and embracing the unwanted. As Matthew tells the story of reconciliation, the carnal mind would surely miss the Spirit's view and feel like he was trying to sully the name of Abraham or David or Solomon...or all the people of God. The Spirit of God proclaiming amnesty sounded belittling to the natural man.

This lesson was not given only to confront the leaders who rejected Jesus two thousand years ago. Christian leaders today can just as easily be caught by a misguided concept of morality and distance themselves from the very people Jesus came to save. We have people we are proud of in the Church and we also have people we wouldn't want to be associated with...Salvation by grace means salvation by unmerited favor from God. The good news of Jesus Christ is the power of God unto salvation.

Matthew's summary of the genealogy is the next point of confrontation to the carnal mind, with its one-dimensional view.

> *So all the generations from Abraham unto David are fourteen gener-*
> *ations; and from David unto the carrying away to Babylon fourteen*
> *generations; and from the carrying away to Babylon unto the Christ*
> *fourteen generations.* Matthew 1:17 (ASV)

In Luke's genealogy, one notices a great disparity between the number of generations Matthew used and the accepted historical account. Reasoning finds conflict where the Spirit reveals. Jesus is the Door to salvation; we know that because He said so.

> *7 Then said Jesus unto them again, Verily, verily, I say unto you, I am the door of the sheep. 8 All that ever came before me are thieves and robbers: but the sheep did not hear them. 9 I am the door: by me if any man enter in, he shall be saved, and shall go in and out, and find pasture.* John 10:7-9 (KJS)

Jesus is the Door. In Ezekiel's vision of the temple, the dimensions of the door to the holy of holies were seven cubits by six cubits.

> *3 Then went he inward, and measured the post of the door, two cubits; and the door, six cubits; and the breadth of the door, seven cubits.* Ezekiel 41:3 (KJS)

Seven is the number representative of perfection in the Bible. Six is the number of man (man was created on the sixth day). Thus, the door into the temple was to be a perfect man, and so it was! God used numbers just as He used names in the Bible to tell of things He would later reveal. The birth of Jesus was certainly the "entering in" through the Door for the people of God!

When numbers are multiplied in the Bible, they mean something with the same connotation but describing a revelation that affects the people of God. When multiplied, the dimensions of the door equal forty-two.

Under the leadership of Moses, the children of Israel visited forty-two encampments from the time they left Egypt until they "entered in" to the land of promise. The earthly ministry of Jesus lasted three and a half years, or forty-two months. The Jewish priesthood would not understand that Matthew, under the unction of the Holy Ghost, was proclaiming Jesus the Door by the numbers of the genealogy. The wilderness wandering for the people of God had ended now that "Joshua" was here (Jesus is the Greek pronunciation for the Hebrew name Joshua)! Joshua, not Moses, took the children of Israel over the Jordan River and into the land that fulfilled the promise God made to Abraham. The Kingdom had come!

There even seems to be a bit of humor in the genealogy. To the uninitiated eye, there appears to be a mistake in Matthew's math. He happened to be a tax collector before he came to follow Jesus...

The Church today ignores the deeper things that only the Spirit of God can reveal. The carnal mind puzzles over the things it cannot explain and ignores the obvious need for the Holy Spirit's explanation. The intellect of man is no match for the mysteries of God. The simplicity of the statement by Jesus, "I am the Door," is backed up by prophecy, veiled in mystery, and included in the temple's architecture.

His Name Shall Be Called Emmanuel

Having told of the virgin birth without mentioning either the angelic visit to Mary or any priestly validation, Matthew jumped right to Isaiah's prophecy. Matthew could have mentioned Zacharias, John the Baptist's father, the priest who encountered the same angel while in the temple burning incense. He was told of his son's ministry to forerun that of the Messiah, but Matthew did not include that information. Instead, he quoted the prophecy about the Messiah's name and came to a confusing conclusion.

> 21 And she shall bring forth a son, and thou shalt call his name JESUS: for he shall save his people from their sins. 22 Now all this was done, that it might be fulfilled which was spoken of the Lord by the prophet, saying, 23 Behold, a virgin shall be with child, and shall bring forth a son, and they shall call his name Emmanuel, which being interpreted is, God with us. Matthew 1:21-23 (KJS)

How is that again? His name shall be called Jesus, for He shall save His people from their sin. This fulfills the prophecy that a virgin shall be with child and call his name Emmanuel, which being interpreted is, God with us? J-E-S-U-S is not how to spell Emmanuel or God with us, so how could Matthew say that? After two thousand years of Christianity, we just accept this as the truth. However, to the priesthood, who believed that Jesus was an impostor, this seemed like a human contrivance to facilitate a myth. If a writer could make up the story as he went along, *anyone* could fit the criteria. This challenge of authenticity has only one remedy, faith in the words of Jesus. Matthew understood that God is a Savior. No one else can offer salvation by grace! Is the Church today paying attention to this startling fact? Prophecy can have a spiritual interpretation that is beyond the human intellect's ability to substantiate it, making it foolishness to the natural man.

Oriental Astrologers Come Seeking Jesus

If Matthew wanted to validate the authenticity of Jesus' ministry by telling the story of the Eastern mystics seeing a star, it never would have succeeded in Israel. God had forbidden His people to go to soothsayers, astrologers, and the like for spiritual counsel. The sign those men spoke of, however, came from God. The Bible tells us that God gives signs for the unbelievers (John 4:48, 1 Cor. 14:22). These astrologers were despised by the religious leadership, which had become very self-important. At least the astrologers believed in God's sign! The outsiders and uninitiated, with no religious kingdom to protect, came by faith seeking the King. It might appear that God was trying to make it difficult for His Christ by sending three wise men, but He was not.

We know that this was not the first word from God on the subject. First, He told Zacharias the priest while he burned incense in the temple of God. This priest, punished with dumbness by the angel of the Lord for doubting, was told openly that his son would prepare the way for the Messiah. Who could have been more trustworthy than one of God's own ministers? The message Zacharias received was accompanied by not one, but three mighty signs. His barren wife was going to have a child in her old age. Not just a child, a boy. In addition, Zacharias came from the temple encounter unable to talk and remained that way until John the Baptist was born. God did start talking to His priests in His temple, but they wouldn't hear and believe. The mystics came near the end of a long line of witnesses and were much less credible to the priesthood. We can see, then, that as the hard, doubting heart pushes God's message aside, the messengers become more and more difficult to believe.

The message God shares with us here is that He gives signs and His own people can become too skeptical to believe them. The wise men did not find Jesus because they saw the star. They found Him because they went to the governor, who called the Jewish scribes and elders together. The astrologers inquired of them concerning where the King would be born, so the scribes and elders went to the Scriptures. That's the same way everyone finds Jesus—someone who knows the Word of God should be able to tell a seeker how to find Him.

This was another challenge to the leadership of Israel, who knew that God had warned them not to listen to sorcerers. However, these men were not trying to lead, they were themselves seeking to bow at the feet of Israel's King. To the natural mind, one could not be an astrologer and be accepted as a truthful witness. Notice that God used this question of where the Messiah would be born to openly confront His errant leadership.

The astrologers brought a witness from the Scriptures proving that what the shepherds said about the angelic visitation and the proclamation over Bethlehem was true. News of this magnitude travels fast! If you do not believe the shepherds, the next witness who comes your way may be even less credible. When hearts are hard, God confronts that hardness with challenges. Herod believed the wise men enough to send his army to kill the innocent babies of Bethlehem. The astrologers, the shepherds, and even the Scriptures pointed to the same place and time, yet the religious leaders could not see what had taken place.

Isn't this a picture of where most of the Christian community is now? The ministers who say that they trust in God to provide, but who sell bonds to finance building projects, would be confronted by men who instead believe and act on their beliefs. These men from the Orient traveled a great distance to bow to the new King and bring Him gifts, while the leaders who were awaiting this King would not acknowledge He existed.

Joseph the Dreamer

When the wise men left, they were warned not to return to Herod so they went home by a different route. After their departure, the angel of the Lord warned Joseph in a dream to take the child Jesus and flee into Egypt. Matthew, led by the Holy Ghost, keeps referring to Joseph and his dreams. This does not confront the Church of the twenty-first century but, oh, how it stirred the leaders of that day, who saw the obvious parallels drawn between this man and Joseph, the dreamer of Genesis. These things were an insult to them because it seemed as though Matthew was stretching every comparison to force conclusions. Doubt is the second worst enemy of a doubter. Satan is the worst.

By His simple use of a name and a behavior, God draws a parallel picture of men who can be led by the slightest impulse from Him. Who, today, would move under such hardship, armed only with a dream in the night and faith in the God who gave it? God wants to show His people what a disaster it truly is to drift away from Him and to trust in human reasoning. "Broken cisterns" are no substitute for hearing the voice of God.

We see evidence of a war being waged in the first two chapters of Matthew. For those who believe that the Bible is merely a historical document, the apparent inconsistencies present grounds for dismissing the authority of the Scriptures. To those who see with eyes of the Spirit, the gospel message of forgiveness for all people is reiterated and reinforced. This is the battle line for the minds of earth's multitudes. Standing for truth is not a popular place to stand, but reformation is necessary in order for revival to come. It is no secret that revival is needed now like rain before the harvest.

> 1 When Israel [was] a child, then I loved him, and called my son out of Egypt. 2 [As] they called them, so they went from them: they sacrificed unto Baalim, and burned incense to graven images. Hosea 11:1-2 (KJS)

When he described the return from Egypt, Matthew quoted from a passage of Scripture that pointed to the past and the people of Israel burning incense to graven images. Any scholar would have contested Matthew's interpretation. However, the wonderful truth is that the New Testament pictures Jesus as a many-membered Body. The Church is His Body!

Egypt is a symbolic picture of Christianity after its leadership has stopped hearing the voice of Jesus. Rejection of Jesus by Herod (who sought to destroy Him) is what sent Jesus into Egypt. His own people could no longer recognize Him. Rejection of Joseph by his brothers is what sent Joseph into Egypt and how Israel ended up there. Joseph commanded his brothers to take his bones out of Egypt when God came to get them out. He knew that God would not leave His people in this religious place, where men used God's people to built great monuments to gods of clay. The promise is as true today! God is going to send deliverance to His people who are slaves to minister "kings" who use them to build monuments to their greatness.

The priests of Matthew's day were enraged by his divinely guided use of Scripture, just as men are today. In any case, it takes the Spirit of God to teach these things of revelation knowledge.

17 That the God of our Lord Jesus Christ, the Father of glory, may give unto you the spirit of wisdom and revelation in the knowledge of him: 18 The eyes of your understanding being enlightened; that ye may know what is the hope of his calling, and what the riches of the glory of his inheritance in the saints, 19 And what [is] the exceeding greatness of his power to us-ward who believe, according to the working of his mighty power, 20 Which he wrought in Christ, when he raised him from the dead, and set [him] at his own right hand in the heavenly [places], 21 Far above all principality, and power, and might, and dominion, and every name that is named, not only in this world, but also in that which is to come: 22 And hath put all [things] under his feet, and gave him [to be] the head over all [things] to the church, 23 Which is his body, the fulness of him that filleth all in all. Ephesians 1:17-23 (KJS)

25 Husbands, love your wives, even as Christ also loved the church, and gave himself for it; 26 That he might sanctify and cleanse it with the washing of water by the word, 27 That he might present it to himself a glorious church, not having spot, or wrinkle, or any such thing; but that it should be holy and without blemish. 28 So ought men to love their wives as their own bodies. He that loveth his wife loveth himself. 29 For no man ever yet hated his own flesh; but nourisheth and cherisheth it, even as the Lord the church: 30 For we are members of his body, of his flesh, and of his bones. 31 For this cause shall a man leave his father and mother, and shall be joined unto his wife, and they two shall be one flesh. 32 This is a great mystery: but I speak concerning Christ and the church. Ephesians 5:25-32 (KJS)

Matthew understood that Jesus had come to dwell in the hearts of His disciples. As they came into unity, the Church would manifest Christ to the world. We are His Body! The nation of Israel is a physical kingdom that pictures God's promise of a new nation, a holy nation. The Church is also a new nation and a holy nation. In the Old Testament, God used the twelve tribes of Israel to describe the Church of the New Testament, which is why Matthew included that reference from the past.

Going all the way back to Exodus, we read that God sent Moses to confront Pharaoh. God told him to say, "Let my son go." Jesus came from those Hebrews, and their God was planning a salvation that would encircle the globe.

After Jesus died on the cross, it became necessary for both Hebrews and Gentiles to be born again of the Spirit. God took out a people for His name from every nation on earth. He promises to bring the people of Abraham's physical lineage back to Himself in the last days. He will do it by showing them that Jesus is their Messiah. They will see Jesus in the perfected Church.

We want to look one more time at this rainbow in Matthew's Gospel and witness the beauty of the refracted light. The light behind the glory is prophetic, composed of long-forgotten words of the prophets, illuminating the historical, proving God true even in the midst of total apostasy. What Saul of Tarsus could not see, Paul the apostle did see—the same flesh, a different man. There is hope, even for those hostile to the revelation of Jesus Christ, through the power of the Holy Ghost!

Herod Kills the Babies in Bethlehem

16 Then Herod, when he saw that he was mocked of the wise men, was exceeding wroth, and sent forth, and slew all the children that were in Bethlehem, and in all the coasts thereof, from two years old and under, according to the time which he had diligently enquired of the wise men. 17 Then was fulfilled that which was spoken by Jeremy the prophet, saying, 18 In Rama was there a voice heard, lamentation, and weeping, and great mourning, Rachel weeping [for] her children, and would not be comforted, because they are not. Matthew 2:16-18 (KJS)

There is the historical, brutal and unflinching—the jealous rage of the governor, killing the innocents to protect his earthly throne. This is more than just an insecure ruler fighting to stay in power—this is what the flesh thinks of God as King. Herod was nothing more than a governor appointed by Rome, yet, Matthew called Herod the "king of Israel." He wants us to understand that this conflict was king against King. Matthew wrote of these events this way to ensure that his readers would not miss the wider view. There are two kingdoms in conflict here, make no mistake about that.

Matthew said that the children slain in Bethlehem were a fulfillment to a prophecy given by the prophet Jeremiah, saying that Rachel would weep for her children in Ramah. How could Matthew say that? Ramah and Bethlehem are two distinctly different places! How would Bible scholars today respond to a minister treating that prophecy as Matthew did? It appears that he ignored the place mentioned, the time frame of Rachel's life, and the fact that Jeremiah reassured Rachel that her children would return from the land of the enemy. How could Bethlehem's slain children possibly return from the land of the enemy?

Let's look at what God spoke through the prophet.

> 15 Thus saith the LORD; A voice was heard in Ramah, lamentation, [and] bitter weeping; Rahel weeping for her children refused to be comforted for her children, because they [were] not. 16 Thus saith the LORD; Refrain thy voice from weeping, and thine eyes from tears: for thy work shall be rewarded, saith the LORD; and they shall come again from the land of the enemy. Jeremiah 31:15-16 (KJS)

God had allowed blindness in part to happen to His beloved people, Israel, in order to bring the nations of the world into the Kingdom. Their rejection of Jesus, as we have already discussed, was all a part of God's plan.

This special priesthood was chosen to provide the blood of the perfect sacrifice. They were kept from understanding God's plan to make it clear that God brought it all to pass, not man. To keep Satan from getting glory over God's people and using this work against them, God told of His will in Old Testament prophecies and allegories. As we are told in the book of Job (28:7), "There is a path which no fowl knoweth, and which the vulture's eye hath not seen." The path of the revelation of Jesus is such a path. Satan's eye cannot see this path. Neither can our carnal minds!

Man's intellect says that there are inconsistencies, errors, and evidence of misinterpretations in the Bible. In so doing, he only proves that there is a path unseen by the natural eye. Much of what man says about God and His Word is criticism generated by ignorance. Man, who thought the world flat with the sky filled with round objects, has boasted himself the smartest intelligence in the universe!

In this prophecy of Jeremiah's, God told of the day that Rachel would weep because her children "were not." Next, He told Rachel, "Weep not for thy work will be rewarded." Finally, he said, "They will come out of the land of the enemy." The babies killed in Bethlehem fit into this picture of Ramah because of the allegories contained in the Old Testament story of Jacob and Rachel.

Herod's army represents the reception the Jews would give to Jesus, their Messiah. Clearly, their wrong judgments placed them in the land of the enemy. There is no way these descendants of Abraham would have crucified their own King unless they were under the dominion of the enemy, Satan.

Rachel is an allegorical representation of the New Testament Church and the covenant of grace. Jacob served Laban for seven years to gain her as his wife. On the night of their wedding, Laban gave Leah to him instead. The next morning, when Jacob discovered what Laban had done, he confronted him. Laban said that according to their law, the elder had to marry first. Leah, then, represents the law. She was not Jacob's desire, but she was useful. God opened her womb and she was fruitful while Rachel was barren.

When Rachel realized that she was barren, she gave her handmaid to Jacob to have children in her place. Leah gave Jacob her maid as well, so he had one wife and two bondservants bearing children. The law was productive until grace brought forth. Grace came by a miracle birth! Once Rachel had a child, the wombs of the three women who represented the law were closed and never brought forth children again.

When God was finished with the covenant of servitude to an external law, He was finished with it for all time. Once the blood of Jesus was shed, the sacrifices of the Old Testament were finished forever. All Biblical references to future events that require blood to be shed for the sacrifice, including the last three Jewish Feasts, are symbolic. The shedding of the blood of Jesus is what all Old Testament sacrifices were symbolic of. Once His blood was brought before the Father in heaven, no other blood would ever be acceptable.

In Exodus 12, God foretold of the very day Jesus would die. The Passover lamb was killed on the fourteenth day of the first month and Jesus was crucified on that very day. The Passover lamb was slain by the Jewish people to celebrate the blood covering, which protected them from the death angel. The same nation had to shed the blood of Jesus, the everlasting protection from the angel of death. That precious blood made the atonement for all of mankind. The salvation of God came through Israel. No wonder Satan hates them so much! Within this prophecy of Jeremiah's, God promised Israel that they would come out of the land of their enemy.

With God opening Rachel's womb, we see a picture of the New Testament Church operating under grace, bringing in Jewish men and women to the Kingdom of Christ. The first of the many thousands of souls that God brought into salvation were all Hebrews (Acts 2). The same people who denounced Him at His crucifixion, while under the influence of Satan, now believed. The womb of grace opened!

The veil in the temple, which separated the holy place from the most holy place, was torn in two from top to bottom. This meant that man was no longer separated from the presence of God. From that moment on, every man could confess his sins and, under the blood protection of Jesus as High Priest, enter into the presence of God.

Let's look at the story of Rachel, comparing the things recorded there with what has indeed happened in light of Jeremiah's prophecy.

Rachel's first son was Joseph. He is a perfect picture of Jesus. Remember, Rachel was always a part of Abraham's lineage. The New Testament Church of grace began when Mary, a Jewish virgin, was chosen by God to be the womb that held His Son. Mary did not merit God's favor, she was "given" God's favor. She accepted by faith the words of the angel. After that, she called herself blessed (Luke 1:48)!

Mary is another allegory showing that God's new people are all part of the New Kingdom through faith in Him. A new people, both Jew and Gentile...a new Kingdom, with every inhabitant there only because of faith in God. What a Kingdom this will be when God is finished with His work in man! No man had any part in the birth of Jesus. Likewise, no man can bring about spiritual birth by any human efforts. This Kingdom is a miracle from start to finish.

Comparing the lives of Jesus and Joseph, we see many striking similarities: Both were born by a miracle of God. Both were the favorites of their fathers. Both were hated by their brethren because of their favored status. Both were sold for silver. Both were sold by a man named Judah, or Judas, as the Greek spelling would be. Joseph's coat was dipped in blood and Jesus' coat was dipped in His own blood. After being rejected by their own people, both were accepted by Gentiles. Both became rulers.

Joseph was the wisdom behind Egypt's storing of food, saving multitudes from starvation during a grievous famine. Those saved included his own brothers and father. Jesus is the Bread of heaven that will feed a multitude, including his Jewish brothers, who will come to Him in the last days for bread.

Clearly, Rachel's son, Joseph, was a picture of the early Church manifesting Jesus to the world. Rachel had a second son named Benjamin. She died in childbirth near Bethlehem. The Church will give birth in these last days to a son that will grow into the full stature of the man Christ Jesus.

As God's people come to maturity in these last days, they will manifest the glory of God through Jesus Christ. Notice that the tribe of Benjamin played an important role in the New Testament Church. The apostle Paul, who wrote much of the New Testament, was of the tribe of Benjamin.

What did the early Church weep over? She wept because the Jewish leaders and many of her Jewish brothers would not come out of the land of the enemy and accept Jesus as their Messiah.

In Ephesians 4, it says that God "gave some apostles, some prophets, evangelists, pastors, and teachers for the perfecting of the saints, for the work of the ministry, for the edifying of the Body of Christ *until* we all come into the unity of the faith, and the knowledge of the Son of God, unto a perfect man." Notice, these ministries will operate only *until* we all come into the measure of the stature of the *fullness* of Christ. The Church has a glorious work to do! She is going to get it done, not because of who she is or what she knows, but because of her faith in Jesus, the great indwelling God.

The word "until" means that there will be a change at a certain point. Until we reach that point, the fivefold ministry will edify the assembly. Once the creative work of God transforms the Church by her faith in Him, the Church will be edified from the inside by that which every joint supplies. As a woman brings forth a baby from her own body, the baby takes on its own identity. It is the same with the Church. This mature Church is described allegorically as Benjamin, because he is a full brother to Jesus as Benjamin was to Joseph. The whole creation is waiting for the manifestation of the sons of God. These "sons" are led by the Spirit of God, just as Jesus confessed that He was. The Son does nothing of Himself but only what He sees the Father do. The mature Church will operate the same way.

> *Then answered Jesus and said unto them, Verily, verily, I say unto you, The Son can do nothing of himself, but what he seeth the Father do: for what things soever he doeth, these also doeth the Son likewise.*
> John 5:19 (KJS)

God is working His perfecting grace in us to bring glory to Himself. The Bible tells us that God will bring many sons unto glory, for both He that sanctifies and they that are sanctified are all one.

9 But we see Jesus, who was made a little lower than the angels for the suffering of death, crowned with glory and honour; that he by the grace of God should taste death for every man. 10 For it became him, for whom [are] all things, and by whom [are] all things, in bringing many sons unto glory, to make the captain of their salvation perfect through sufferings. 11 For both he that sanctifieth and they who are sanctified [are] all of one: for which cause he is not ashamed to call them brethren, 12 Saying, I will declare thy name unto my brethren, in the midst of the church will I sing praise unto thee. Hebrews 2:9-12 (KJS)

Just as Joseph was rejected by his brothers, so Jesus was rejected by the Jews. When a famine came on all the earth, the sons of Jacob went down into Egypt for bread. They saw Joseph there but did not recognize him. He did not make himself known to his brothers at that time, but said that "until he saw Benjamin," they could not come back to see him.

The Christian Church is trying to win the Hebrew nation to Jesus, but until the Church comes to the place of perfect unity (all speaking the same thing in truth) and to the full stature of the man Christ Jesus (Benjamin was the only full brother to Joseph), He is not going to make himself known to them. No earthly effort will avail anything. Again, why would God want to bring His Jewish children into Christianity now? It is divided by doctrines, full of envy and strife. Since no one knows what is truth among all the teachings, lies are taught as truth. The bottom line remains: a house or kingdom divided against itself cannot stand.

When Benjamin did come with his brothers to Egypt, Joseph still did not make himself known to them. As they departed, he had his steward put his cup into Benjamin's sack. That cup is symbolic of total surrender. Jesus spoke of it in His agony in Gethsemane. Jesus prayed, "Father let this cup pass from me, nevertheless, not my will but thine be done." God is waiting for the same total surrender in His Church before the rest of His promises come to pass.

Multitudes of Christians throughout the world today are willing to drink from the cup of total obedience, but they must first be taught the absolute truth about God's will and Word and work so that their surrender can be according to His will and Word and work. Total surrender to any other doctrine will not be the drinking of that cup of obedience. Faith in God's Word, not in human efforts, will produce the perfect Church. Self-effort will never bring perfection to the Body of Christ.

Through Jeremiah's prophecy, God spoke comfort to the men and women who, down through the ages, have grieved for the people of Israel. The blindness and unbelief brought against them by Satan will not last forever.

Paul, an example from the tribe of Benjamin, fervently desired that his countrymen would come to the same revelation of Jesus that he had. In his letters, Paul acknowledged that his ministry was to the Gentiles, but he said that he wished he could be accursed for the sake of his kinsmen if it meant they would come in. Rachel was weeping then and could not be comforted. Paul grieved because his beloved Israel had met the Messiah and rejected Him. Thank God for His promise: "Weep not for your work will be rewarded." In the end, no matter how Satan rages, "Your children will come again to their own border."

Thank God for the mysteries, allegories, parables, and history of the precious Word of God!

Summary

It is difficult for us to comprehend how extraordinarily confrontational Matthew's Gospel was to the Jewish religious leaders of antiquity. We often take for granted the truths it contains, thinking we see things so much more clearly than they did. However, once the veil is lifted and we glimpse the many layers of spiritual revelation residing in even just the first few chapters, we begin to grasp how very difficult it is to accept revelation knowledge if our hearts are hardened and our sight is dimmed. Our understanding of the Word is so very limited unless we have the indwelling Holy Spirit to teach us what the Lamb prevailed to open for us.

Let us be honest before the Lord, humbly confessing our spiritual poverty and our need for His mercy. As His searchlight penetrates those dark recesses of our hearts, revealing our iniquity and pride, let us allow Him to cleanse us of our carnal ways. The Lord's desire is for His Church to be overflowing with spiritual Christians, filled with the Spirit, led by the Spirit, and mature. What He sees now is largely a Church full of carnal Christians, bogged down by strongholds, bondages, unforgiveness, envy, strife, divisions, and immaturity (1 Cor. 3:1-4, Heb. 5:11-6:3).

There is much we can learn from the mistakes of the Jewish leaders if we are willing to admit how similar today's circumstances are to those of Jesus' day. We must never forget the longsuffering heart of God, the love that is willing to forgive us and cast our sins into the sea of forgetfulness if we will but turn from our wayward doctrines and embrace His truth.

In Psalm 113, it says that God must humble Himself to behold what takes place upon the earth, that He is willing to scoop us out of the muck and mire we get stuck in and cleanse us of all unrighteousness. How great a love is that! The grace of our Lord Jesus pursues us, He longs for us to be one with Him. There is so much we miss out on when we allow sin of any kind to separate us from that abundance of life that God has for His sons. What greater calling is there in all the universe than to be a joint heir with Christ, seated in the heavenlies with our Savior? What lie could possibly be worth holding onto if it means we will miss out on the fullness of life God has always desired for His children? The remedy is simple: invite that searchlight of His Spirit to expose the things in our hearts that hold us back, repent, and surrender them to the hand of the Potter, obey His voice, and praise His name for His infinite love and forgiveness. It's time to go back to the absolutes!

Study Questions

131. When will the Jewish nation come to see Jesus as the Messiah?
132. What is significant about the genealogy of Matthew?
133. What is the Spirit revealing to us in the numbers of the genealogy of Matthew and Ezekiel's vision of the Temple?
134. The first two chapters of Matthew are an excellent example of historical facts revealed spiritually. How can we be protected from just an intellectual understanding of God's Word?
135. What did it mean when the veil in the Temple was torn in two, from top to bottom, the day Jesus was crucified?
136. What are some of the parallels between Joseph whose story we read in Genesis and Jesus?
137. What will produce the perfect Church?
138. What is God's desire for His Church?

Answer Key

What are Absolutes?

1. *Why is it so bad that the Church has forsaken the fountain of living waters and hewn out broken cisterns that can hold no water?* The fountain of living waters is God present with his people, alive and speaking. Not men talking about God but Him actually talking. In the Old Testament account of the Exodus of Israel from Egypt, Moses represented God's chosen leadership and God spoke to him constantly. God missed nothing that went on in the camp and he made decisions for Moses to implement. Cisterns are man's answer to the need of water. They don't require a walk with God that the fountain does and they are stationary.

2. *What is the purpose of the Holy Spirit and why do we need Him so much in our churches?* The Holy Spirit is the teacher sent from God who will lead us into all truth. When the Holy Ghost is doing the teaching, we can be assured that we are receiving only pure truth. Only the God who wrote the Bible can interpret the Bible for the Church in truth.

3. *Why is man's leadership so destructive to the Church?* Man's leadership rejects God's appointed head of the Church, Jesus Christ! Replaces God's revelation with doctrines, teaches lies for truth and when truth is brought rejects it. This is clearly shown in the four Gospels and the Book of Acts.

4. *What should man's leadership be replaced with—and how do we do that?* Saul of Tarsus is a good example for us. A Leader who loved God, and was serious about doing his will. Taught by the religious leaders of his day the current theologies he began destroying God's Church. Confronted by Jesus on the road to Damascus he began to fast and pray for Truth. God sent him a man who knew the truth, and was lead by the Spirit of God. God saw his humility, forgave him his sins and filled him with His Spirit, all this for us to see and do.

5. *Define the true Church of Christ.* The true Church of Christ is a living organism created by God with Christ Jesus as her head. She walks in absolute truth because Jesus is absolute truth. She is built on the revelation of God that comes from God—not man—and the gates of hell cannot prevail against her. Jesus gave Himself for her, that he might sanctify and cleanse her with the washing of water by the Word to present her to Himself without spot or wrinkle, blameless in His sight, on earth.

6. *Why is truth so important to the Church?* Without the anchor of truth any wind of doctrine will blow her. (Eph. 4:14)

7. *What is an absolute?* An absolute is a perfect truth that cannot change under any circumstance.

8. *What will bring the Church back to a firm foundation?* A Reformation. The voice of Jesus crying out and a people who hear that voice and humble themselves and pray.

ABSOLUTE 1

9. *What is God's promise of victory?* God's promise of victory for the Church is victory over all her enemies, including sin.

10. *What is Christ's command about perfection in the Sermon on the Mount?* "Be ye therefore perfect as your Father in heaven is perfect" (Matthew 5:48).

11. *Did Jesus expect His followers to keep that command by their own power of commitment? If not why did He speak it?* No. The perfect man can only come from the perfect man, Christ Jesus. Faith in perfect grace starts the process and the empowering of the Holy Ghost within every believer provides power that the flesh does not possess. Who the potter is makes the difference.

12. *Explain why "mature" and "perfect" which are translations of the same Greek word require context to define different concepts.* The Greek word from which these two words are translated means "coming to fullness" or "completeness". "Perfect" calls for the highest standard. The word "mature" while it implies fullness of age does not hold the same standard. The Perfected man is God's desire for His creation, (remember He created Adam perfect) and His creative work brings Him glory, why would He not demand the highest standard?

13. *What does it mean to be born again?* In John Chapter 3, Jesus tells us that we must be born again to see the Kingdom of God. Knowing God exists, or being a member of a church does not constitute being born of the Spirit. Believing that Jesus Himself hears our confession of, and repentance from sin, and that He alone can and will forgive us, brings new birth. By inviting Him to live inside of us we acknowledge His rightful ownership of us. It is important to understand that He accepts us as we are, and that we cannot make ourselves worthy, not even by keeping the commandments. Accepting His Amnesty by faith, faith in his blood as *shed* for our sins and faith in His unmerited favor of us.

14. *Explain the difference between the old man and the new man.* The old man is our "flesh" man, our mind, nature and appetites. The new man is the Spiritual man born in our hearts when Jesus comes to live inside of us. The new man is perfect from birth, but he must grow and mature just as our flesh man does.

15. *What can't the new man do according to God's word?* The new man cannot sin.

16. *What provision has God made to help us grow stronger spiritually? How is that growth accomplished?* He created the Church. Ministers are spiritual parents ordained by God to give spiritual babies spiritual food. The Bible is both the milk and meat needed for spiritual growth. The meat is revelation based and requires a knowledge of the Bible. It is also all truth. Milk is readily digested by the carnal mind, it makes sense therefore a small amount of faith can receive it. Milk is made from the Blood and meat contains it. We overcome by the Blood of the Lamb.

17. *What is the difference between the first Adam and the last Adam?* The first Adam bowed his knee to the flesh and rejected God's will. The Last Adam, Jesus, bowed his knee to God and rejected the will of the flesh. The first Adam brought a curse on himself and his descendants and the last Adam freed us from that curse. The first Adam brought death on humanity, the last Adam brought life. The first Adam was made a living soul, the last Adam a quickening spirit.

18. *What is the difference between being "blameless" and being "perfect"?* Blameless is innocence within a legal context. Perfection is being all that God wanted from His creative masterpiece man. Jesus was more than Blameless, He did only what God showed Him to do. He stopped the storms, cast out demons, opened the eyes of the blind and protected the guilty with just His faith in the Father.

19. *How are we reconciled to God?* We are reconciled in His body of flesh through His death.

20. *What if we do sin after we become Christians?* Sin is not expected to be a part of a Christian's life. If we do sin, we have an advocate with the Father, Jesus Christ the righteous. He is the propitiation (substitution payment) for our sins. We have His blood covering over us (imputed righteousness) and He promises to cleanse us of all unrighteousness (in the flesh).

21. *What is the purpose of the fivefold ministry?* The perfecting of the holy ones, the work of the ministry, the edifying of the body of Christ, until all Christians come into the unity of the Faith, unto the knowledge of the Son of God, unto the full stature of the man Christ Jesus, unto a perfect man. So that we are no longer children tossed around by every wind of doctrine, by the slight of men and cunning craftiness whereby they lie in wait to deceive.

22. *What are the two miracles born of God's fivefold ministry?* Unity, believing and teaching the same thing and the will of God realized on the earth, the perfect man.

23. *How do we overcome the world?* Our faith in Jesus and in His work within us. We cannot overcome by works, but by a new birth. He that is born of God overcomes the world by faith.

24. *Is it true that a Christian will sin as long as he is living on the earth? Is a Christian in the flesh just because he is alive?* The answer to both these questions is of course No. The Bible teaches that once the Spirit of God comes into a living person they are no longer in the flesh. Paul's letter to the

Roman Church states very clearly in chapter 8 that we are not in the flesh but in the spirit, if the Spirit of God dwells within us. We are a new creation and we are IN Christ Jesus, once we are born again.

ABSOLUTE 2

25. *Why didn't God want Adam and Eve to eat of the tree of the knowledge of good and evil?* He knew that they would no longer see themselves as He saw them but would immediately begin to judge themselves with human reasoning and be separated from Him. Because Adam believed being naked was a sin, it became a sin to him. Sin in man brought death.

26. *What was the certain outcome of their disobedience?* Once Eve accepted the premise contained in Satan's challenge (the premise that knowledge of good and evil was the missing ingredient for becoming like God, that it was good for her and God lied, she would **not** die) religions were the certain outcome. Adam was not deceived but he traded his Father-son, faith-based, relationship with God for a relationship rooted on the value that his own actions could create—all religions are based on this very thing.

27. *What was missing from the fruit of the tree of the knowledge of good and evil?* It did not contain God's criteria of what was good or what was evil. It provided no guidelines for judgment, Adam and Eve obtained judgment without any Godly criteria to judge by. The human mind became the judge.

28. *What did man lose when he began judging himself as evil? What was the result of that loss?* Man, judging himself as evil, lost his faith in God's love for him. Because of that loss of faith, we now believe that we must do something religious to please God to stay saved.

29. *What does the tree of life represent? The tree of the knowledge of good and evil?* The tree of life represents obedience to the word of God through faith. The tree of knowledge of good and evil represents the way of works not based upon the will of God. Man the potter, man the judge.

30. *Why was Cain's sacrifice unacceptable to God?* God taught Adam and Eve that He accepts only the blood of a living sacrifice. Cain brought God "his best" as a sacrifice even though God had requested a living sacrifice and the shedding of its blood. Today many Christians unwittingly do the same thing. Salvation is by faith in God's grace, only in that. It is not by works (doing good things, or even keeping God's commandments). If you are not washed in the Blood of Jesus, your name is not written in the Book of Life, even if you keep all the commandments. If you are a Christian you will want to keep the commandments of God, but not for your salvation. Remember Saul of Tarsus kept all the commandments yet fought the Son of God. Once saved by Grace he counted all those things as dung. It is much more difficult to hold to salvation by faith than it is to do "your best" to please God.

31. *How do we attain the righteousness of God? How does that differ from works?* We are saved by grace, through faith. Grace is unmerited favor, a gift from God Himself—it is unearned. "Works" come from the belief that God would not give us such a gift, that we have to earn the very salvation He died to give us.

32. *Was God saying that He didn't want man to know the difference between good and evil? How could we be good and not do evil?* The tree of the knowledge of good and evil did not describe what was good or what was evil, it only said there is good and there is evil. It opened Adam and Eve to a new way of thinking. Under this influence anything could become "good" even sacrificing your own children to a false god. Anything could become evil, such as Jesus setting the woman caught in adultery free from her accusers. This is not the same thing as understanding what is good because the Bible says it is. Remember however that God's own priesthood, mixing human judgment and the commands of God, condemned the guiltless and crucified God in the flesh, judging Him an evil man. An example of man judging what is good and what is evil. There are thousands of things men say are good in religions around the world but they lead to murder and hatred. This is not from the tree of life. This is not from God.

33. *What are the two keys to doing right?* We must understand that God is the Potter and we are only the clay. We must hear His voice and obey His commands.

34. *Why are trials so important to our walk with God?* As God designs our life, He proves us through times of tribulation. When the fire of God comes to try the word of God within us, we must live that word. Hearing the Word of God isn't enough, we must put it into application and times of trial confront us to do just that.

35. *What does it mean to be reconciled to God? To be justified?* To be reconciled to God through Christ Jesus is to be covered with His blood that was shed for us. Christ is the atonement for our sins. God justifies us by declaring us free from guilt and acceptable unto Him through the righteousness of Jesus, which we accept by faith.

36. *What does Christ mean when He describes himself as the Potter?* We are God's creation and He will finish us according to His will and purpose for man.

37. *Explain the difference between the way God's commandments were intended to be used and what man did with them. Why does it matter?* God gave Israel commandments in order to provide a framework for judgment. Up until then, men used random criteria to judge good and evil. The Ten Commandments give man perimeters. Man took the commandments and based his faith on whether or not he could keep them. This was not God's intended use of the commandments. The Old Testament legal system formed a protective covering around man based on the blood covering and faith in God's unmerited favor. When we base our faith on whether or not we keep the commandments we end up hiding from God just like Adam and Eve.

38. *Explain why the fruit of the tree of knowledge of good and evil is so destructive to the Church.* The knowledge of good and evil is destructive to faith because it accuses us and insists that God is angry without a remedy. This mindset is destructive to the Church because it rejects the perimeters established by God and establishes its own. It is destructive to the Body of Christ because it denies that the power of God is able to finish the workmanship of man. Instead, man crowns himself potter over his own life.

ABSOLUTE 3

39. *Why is the Church earthbound and lost?* The Church is for the most part being led by the Natural man, with the power to reason and a disastrous view of good and evil asserting itself as guide in spiritual matters. The Church lacks a true understanding of what God wants.

40. *Why did God give the Spirit of Truth to the Church?* God gave His Spirit of Truth to keep the Church in every matter of importance, so that she can make right decisions and know the Truth.

41. *What are the two spirits that Paul reveals to us in 1 Corinthians 2:12-15?* In 1 Corinthians 2:12-15 he talks about the spirit of the world and the spirit which is of God.

42. *How can we tell the difference between the two spirits?* 1 John 4:1 tells us to try the spirits: "Beloved, believe not every spirit, but try the spirits whither they are of God: because many false prophets are gone out into the world. Every spirit that confesses not that Jesus Christ is come in the flesh is not of God..." Notice the test is not, "did" Jesus come in the flesh, (atheists say Jesus was a good man) "is" come in the flesh is about now. Today! Is Jesus in the flesh today? The answer of course is Yes. He said He'd come to dwell in us. That same power that was in His flesh is now in our flesh. False spirits tell you Jesus was on the earth and that He will return one day, but they do not confess that He is in his people, in their flesh, living His life through them now. Confronted with this truth many will say they know it—but they don't know it experientially. They don't believe Jesus is on earth in a many member Body, and in heaven at the same time.

43. *Where does this lack of understanding in the Church come from?* The understanding we lack in the Church comes from refusing to allow the Holy Ghost to be the only one to teach the absolutes of Truth.

44. *Why did Nicodemus have so much trouble understanding what Jesus talked to him about in John 3?* Nicodemus could not understand the things Jesus said because he was relating spiritual truths to physical things. He was looking in the wrong realm for his answers.

45. *Why should Nicodemus have recognized Jesus as the Messiah?* The coming of the Messiah was foretold in the Hebrew Scriptures. Nicodemus was a rabbi, a teacher, and he should have been able to spiritually discern the truth about Jesus based on what he knew of the Old Testament prophecies.

46. *What did Nicodemus believe qualified him to be in the Kingdom of God? What is the answer Jesus gave him?* Nicodemus believed he was in the Kingdom of God because he was a descendant of Abraham. The truth is that he needed to be born again into the spiritual kingdom. The physical kingdom of Israel while precious to God, was only a shadow of the magnificent fulfillment of His will—a Kingdom where men full of His Spirit walk with him daily.

47. *How are we protected from our reasoning?* The Church has an open door to God through prayer and the Holy Ghost. We can clear any confusion between doctrines and reasoning by going to Jesus like his disciples did. The Word of God in the hands of the Holy Ghost is sharper than any two edged sword able to cut between soul (thought from the flesh) and Spirit (answers from God) (Heb. 4:12).

48. *What happened to Saul of Tarsus on the road to Damascus?* He was confronted by Jesus Himself, who he did not believe was the Messiah. A man of integrity, he humbled himself and repented. Traveling at noon day was a picture of the brightest light the natural man knew. Saul knew the Scriptures as well as any natural man could. He was blinded by the light of Christ. The transcendent glory of Christ Jesus revealed, out shinning the noonday sun!

49. *Why is it important to the Church to understand how Satan wages war?* Satan knows that he can manipulate man's desire to serve God by using false information to challenge him. The Church needs to understand this so she can turn to Jesus to clarify confusion, to allow Him to be the Head in all things. Man was created without the ability to discern truth from lies, so the Church needs the Holy Spirit for absolute Truth.

50. *Why did God leave man vulnerable to lies?* He left us vulnerable to lies because only He knows all truth. He wants us to see how much we need Him, and to believe when we come to Him He will help us. He told us that He would send the Church the Spirit of Truth, and He did. The day He birthed the Church in Jerusalem, The Spirit came! God is the great provider. Man did not need to know truth from lies because God doesn't lie. Satan is the father of lies.

51. *What prevents the world from receiving the Holy Ghost?* The Holy Ghost is a gift to all born-again believers, but Jesus said the world cannot receive the Spirit of Truth because it cannot see Him.

52. *How was Paul the Christian different from Saul of Tarsus?* He was a new creation. Paul as a Christian was led by the Spirit of Christ, which exhibited love and a nature totally different than that of Saul of Tarsus. Saul the Jew intellectually interpreted God's wishes and will, thought he was pleasing God, when in fact he was fighting Him.

53. *What did God use Ananias to represent and why is that significant to us?* God asked Ananias to represent heaven's mercy extended to an offender—Love, peace, and healing. It gives us a picture of God's mercy towards us as we wrestle between the things of the flesh and the things of the Spirit.

54. *What does the natural man need to receive the things of God and how does he get it?* The natural man can never receive the things of God. However, when a man is born again of the Spirit, he gains spiritual knowledge and discernment between the spiritual and physical realms.

ABSOLUTE 4

55. *What is the dynamic of the voice of Jesus that makes it stand out from all other voices?* The distinguishing dynamic of the voice of Jesus Christ is Truth. Whatever He spoke, to whomever He spoke, it was always absolute Truth. The words of Jesus were Spirit and life and they were true to the revelation all Scriptures hold from beginning to end.

56. *What does water represent in the Bible? What does blood represent? How is this significant in Moses' first miracle?* Water represents outward cleansing. Blood represents total redemption before God. Moses' first miracle in Egypt was turning the water to blood. Moses' ministry represented the Law and under the light of the Law allowed man to see mercy's river of Blood. The Law of God condemned sin, demanded justice, and there for the repentant, provided the blood of sacrificial cleansing. Under God's legal system there was to be a river of blood.

57. *What was the purpose of the Law?* The law of God established criteria for man to judge by, thereby defeating the power of the knowledge of good and evil with its random criteria. The Law is to bring man to a place of repentance, where he sees that he can't keep it by his own power, and directs him back to God for forgiveness and cleansing.

58. *What is wrong with man's view of God as judgmental? What is the truth?* After declaring God the Creator of all things the Bible tells us that Satan accused God of having evil intentions toward man. The father of lies wants to accuse God of being angry with man. The truth is that the commands of God are meant to protect man. No one wants to be murdered, or to have his or her mate commit adultery. As we look at what God intended we see the animal substitution for man, the blood of animals covering the sins of God's people. The payment for sin was provided with the Law! All God ever asked for was repentance. Jesus became the last payment for sin, the last blood shed. God the Creator dying for the creature.

59. *What do God's children have to be rescued from and why?* Two things. Man must be rescued from the guilt of his sins. And he must also be rescued from false religion with its lie based theology. When the judgment we use is not truth-based, we doubt the voice of God when it speaks truth because it doesn't agree with what we believe to be truth. Sound confusing? Satan hoped so. God gives us a picture of this through the rejection of Moses by his peers, and Jesus by the Priesthood who should have known He was their Messiah.

60. *Why couldn't Moses take the children of Israel into the Promise Land?* Moses represents the Law, and the Promise land represents the victory over our enemies that only God could promise. The Law cannot take us into the promise land, only Grace can. Joshua (Jesus) was able to take the Children of Israel in. The Law and its limitations are all part of the plan of God.

61. *What is the parallel between Moses' first miracle and Jesus' first miracle?* Moses' first miracle was turning water into blood. Jesus' first miracle was turning the water into wine(symbolic of blood). Both covenants of God are based on the Blood.

62. *What does the story of Elijah teach us?* Elijah showed us God's intervention when lie-based religion takes his people into confusion. He also showed us how to distinguish true ministers of God from false ministers. First he restored the altar that was broken down. The Altar represents surrender to God's will. Next he washed the sacrifice, which is the believer, with water, and the water a minister of God uses is the Word of God (Ephesians 5:25-27). He asked that they fill four barrels with water and bring them three times. Four, in the Bible means "Revelation" and three is the number God used for Himself. So Elijah ministered the Truth until the Believer had been immersed in the Word of God and saw God. Truth does that! Then the Holy Spirit Baptism consumed the sacrifice. All religions denounce the deeds of the flesh. Only God's fire can consume the flesh with its self-will and appetites. John the Baptist and Jesus show this same exact story. John baptized with water, (the disciples of Jesus had been washed in this water) then Jesus baptized them with the Holy Ghost and Fire. See the difference?

63. *What is the function of the prophets of God?* The prophets of God are the eyes of the nation and the voice of God. Under the calling of God, they see the direction God intends to lead His people. They are also the voice of God that leads to restoration. The voice of the prophet is linked to the presence of God and thereby ministers to the exact need of the hour. They bring judgment when judgment is needed in order to reinstate truth. They bring mercy to rejoice against judgment when repentance comes, reflecting the merciful nature of God.

64. *What is God teaching us through the Transfiguration of Jesus on the mountain where he appeared with Moses and Elijah and heard God say, "This is my Son, hear ye Him"?* God was teaching us that Jesus is above the highest expectation of the Law, even with its river of Blood. He is above the highest vision of the Prophetic voice, even with its consuming fire. A Christian is not measured by the voice of the Law or the vision of Prophets. He is measured by Christ. The Church is to become a perfect man, the full stature of the man Christ Jesus. The Law can bring us out, but it can never take us into the full stature of Christ. The fire of Elijah's confrontation and restoration was but a promise of the indwelling fire of the Holy Ghost. Our God is a consuming fire!

65. *What did Jesus say about His voice?* Jesus said that His sheep (those who follow him) will hear His voice and they would not follow a stranger.

66. *What is our only means of hearing God's voice in His written Word?* The human intellect cannot hear the voice of God by reading the Bible, but our spirit man can. The indwelling Spirit is our only means of hearing God's voice in the written Word.

67. *Besides our knowing His voice, what additional assurance does Christ give us that ensures an intimate relationship between us and Him?* When Jesus said that His sheep would know His voice, He also said that He knows the sheep. He assures us that we will be okay because we hear His voice, that He will not forsake us if we wander off. He rescue us.

68. *What is the simple truth about prayer?* There is no formula for success. God just wants us to come and talk to Him. He will hear us and answer.

69. *How is communion as a ritual offensive to God?* Communion means to communicate, to fellowship. John said that the Word of God became flesh and we beheld Him as the only begotten of God. We fellowship with God through His Word and He speaks to us from His Word. Why substitute a wafer when we have His real flesh, The Word of God?

70. *What is the spiritual significance of the Last Supper?* As the disciples ate the Passover with Him, He revealed Himself as the Passover Lamb. This Lamb is symbolic of My body, take and eat. I must be killed, My blood applied to the door post of your hearts and the angel of death will passover you! When He said "This is my Body," He wasn't just talking about the bread that He was holding. He was talking about the entire feast.

71. *What is revealed to us about communion through the word God gave Moses in exodus 12 about how to eat the Passover Lamb?* In Exodus 12 we are commanded to roast the flesh, (Jesus the Word) with fire (the Holy Ghost, the spirit of Truth) and not to eat it raw (using the carnal mind to understand the meaning). The Bible must be interpreted and taught by the Holy Spirit. We are told to eat the inward parts (things not seen on the surface). The Holy Spirit opens the Word and we find the hidden truths—the hidden manna of the Bible.

72. *How and why does Satan try to keep us out of the Bible and what is God's provision that protects us from Satan's lies?* Lies have caused confusion about what the Bible teaches and because even Bible schools don't agree on basic doctrines, man is left believing that the Bible must be too complicated to understand. If professors who teach the Bible don't know who is right, who would? Satan's sowing of lies has had a devastating effect on Bible reading in the home. Satan wants to keep believers out of their Bibles because the Word of God has a life giving effect. The spirit man receives nourishment from the Scriptures even when the intellect doesn't comprehend what is being said. The Word of God is like a seed that is planted. Jesus said that is what He did, and the disciples remembered what He said even after He was resurrected. Satan also knows that God has given the Holy Ghost to every believer to lead and guide them into all truth. This is not intended for man to stay home alone, ignoring the assembling of Saints and the fivefold

ministry. Over and over in the Bible, the people of God have followed after false teachers and God has sent a single man to confront the lies. Majority does not mean safety or truth.

73. *Why is it important for us to know the difference between when God's word is creative and when it is instructive?* When God is creating, He is giving us a promise that only He can and will fulfill. When He is instructing, we need to learn and obey. If we confuse the two, we try to become the creator and potter and do the things that only the power of God can do. This ends in failure and discouragement and destroys faith in our relationship with the Father—because we want to please Him and believe we cannot. Faith pleases God and only faith can appropriate the promises that constitute the will of God for our lives.

74. *What is the difference between the historical and spiritual dimensions of the Bible?* The historical dimension of the Bible invites us to seek God for reconciliation. It shows us of God's love and constant intervention for man. The historical does not reveal the mind of God however, beyond His desire for fallen man to repent of his sins and come back to the Father. There is a door of hope for the natural man to see and believe if he chooses to. The spiritual dimension of the Bible holds the revelation of God's secrets and is the anchor of Truth.

75. *What is the heritage of the Church?* The Bible, God's Spirit, a message, and the power which is by God (revealed for the uniting of His people with a common understanding of all scriptures) and the power to live out the things which the Spirit reveals, that God alone would be exalted.

76. *What was the result of Israel's mixing truth with religion and what did God do about it?* The result was confusion and God sent a prophet—Elijah—a man of God sent to restore the absolutes of truth by signs and wonders.

77. *How does the story of Elijah from 1 Kings 18 compare with God's ministry today?* True ministers of God, using the written word of God, wash the saints of God until the Holy Ghost and fire consumes the sacrifice leaving that which cannot be burned.

78. *What was the significance of John the Baptist baptizing Jesus?* John (expressing the spirit of Elijah), being the son of a Priest of the tribe of Levi, washed the last sacrifice—Jesus, the Lamb of God, in order to fulfill the law that demanded a perfect sacrifice for sin.

79. *Water (washing of the Word) is only part of the plan of salvation. What is the rest of it?* The water cleanses, creating a clean heart and surrendered will, the Holy Ghost and fire transforms. When the fire of God is finished, a believer is changed in a way that only God can change him. The new man lives through the fire, and the old flesh man, is consumed. The fire turns the sand to glass and we become transparent, the world then sees Jesus in us.

80. *Why did God demolish the common language of man in the descendants of Noah and how is this significant today?* God demolished the common language of man so they would stop trying to build a tower to get to heaven

by their own works. They were unable to work together because they no longer understood one another. The Church today has a confusion of languages. Denominations today who do not agree, say they can still work together, even though they do not understand one another. God will not let the flesh man mount up and be the head of religion any more today than He did back then. Confusion of languages within the Church is proof that man has made himself head. Today men say we can work together even if we don't understand each other. Can we?

81. *What is God's plan for ending the confusion of tongues?* When the Church was born on the day of Pentecost, God broke the power of confusion of languages by His Holy Ghost: "One body, one Spirit, one Lord, one faith, one baptism, one God" (Ephesians 4:3): We have a common language through the Holy Ghost.

ABSOLUTE 5

82. *Why did Christ send us the Holy Ghost?* Jesus sent the Holy Ghost to dwell in the heart of every believer so that He can lead and guide us into all truth.

83. *What did God do in His word to assure that truth would be revealed?* To assure that truth would be preserved, God concealed spiritual truths within historical events.

84. *What is the spiritual significance of leaven? What is the difference between the Holy Ghost's leaven and man's leaven?* Leaven signifies life. The leaven of the Holy Ghost helps us understand things spiritually through God's Spirit of Revelation. No matter what the flesh sees, the Holy Ghost reveals the truth. Man's leaven, on the other hand, is man's interpretation of the Bible. Man's intellect cannot discern or understand spiritual things. The "life" man's leaven gives to scriptures is the root of division. Denominations come from this leaven. Beware of it.

85. *Name the seven Jewish feasts. Which was the first to allow leaven? Why?* The seven feasts are: Unleavened bread, Passover, First Fruits, Pentecost, Trumpets, Atonement, Tabernacles. The feast of Pentecost was the first at which God allowed leaven. Leaven could be in that feast because Jesus had been crucified and the Bible unsealed. On that feast day, the Holy Ghost was poured out upon the 120 disciples of Jesus in the upper room. The teacher sent from God had arrived. The Spirit of Revelation and Truth!

86. *Define the church as the Body, Bride, and Building of Christ.* The Church defined as the "Body" of Christ is a declaration of the Word of God made manifest in the flesh in every generation. The Church defined as the "Bride" of Christ is a declaration of the work of God perfected in the spirit in every generation. The Church defined as the "Building" of Christ is a declaration of the will of God uniting in vision and purpose the saints in every generation.

87. *Why does the Church need to come back to knowing all truth?* Jesus is the Word of God. The Word become flesh, John said. To twist that precious word into lies, misrepresents Jesus. Satan knows that men who want to serve Jesus and are looking for His return, when taught lies of twisted truth, will reject Truth when it's preached to them—to their destruction. What happened to the Jewish people is a warning to the Church. Believing a lie means you think the truth (Jesus) is a lie and reject Him. To be saved you must believe in Jesus. Say it this way: "to be saved you must believe in truth." Jesus said, "I am the Truth."

88. *How does God plan to reveal Jesus to the world?* The Church which is His Body will be made one with the Word (Jesus) and that Word is pure truth. When the Church lives the Word of God, as the Spirit leads her to, the world will see Christ in us.

89. *What is our assurance of victory over flesh?* Ephesians 5:30 teaches that, "We are members of His body, of His flesh, and of His bones." We are members of His flesh. His flesh was brought to total surrender to God by the Spirit of God which dwelt within Him. That same Spirit dwells in us with the same power for the same outcome. The Body of Christ as we observed in the Gospels, was led by the Spirit, defeated the flesh by the same Spirit, and obeyed the same Spirit unto death.

90. *Why did Jesus need the Apostles? What significance does that have for us today?* When Jesus was born of Mary to walk among His people on earth, their needs were more than one man could possibly meet. He sent out the twelve Apostles in His name. At any moment, His work could go on in more than a dozen places. Today, the Church is to provide physical hands and feet while God provides the Spirit's power and wisdom.

91. *What is God's promise concerning His Church?* The promise God gives concerning the Church is perfection—a Church without spot or wrinkle. Washed in the Blood of Jesus and covered in his Flesh. Just as Adam and Eve.

92. *What is the fivefold ministry and what is its purpose?* The fivefold ministry is comprised of apostles, prophets, evangelists, pastors, and teachers. They are anointed by God for the perfecting of the holy ones (all believers are the "holy ones," or "saints" as some translate the word) for the work of the ministry, for the edifying of the Body of Christ.

93. *What is God's plan for His Church?* To grow into the full stature of the man Christ Jesus, into a perfect man. So that the world can see Jesus. To establish His Kingdom on the revelation of Jesus and show His power over flesh. To live the expressed image of God in front of the world, and glorify Him in His creation.

94. *Will we know when the Church has reached perfection?* Yes. The Church will be perfected when she is in unity globally, no longer tossed to and fro by every wind of doctrine. When the ministries all speak the same thing, have the same judgment, and see eye to eye on what is truth in the Bible. Too

many Christians have resigned themselves to the fact that confusion will always exist in the Body of Christ, and it will not. We have been taught to pray that God's will be done on earth as it is in Heaven. When we pray believing, we will have what we ask.

95. *How are we made perfect?* When we accept Christ as our Savior, He impregnates our spirit with His own Spirit, and a new man forms inside of us. We are His Workmanship, Created in Christ Jesus, so He works on us and in us until His will is accomplished. There is an inside man (the new man) and there is an outside man (flesh). The new man is born of God and cannot sin. We pray for this and we believe His word on it. Faith in Him is the victory!

96. *What tool does God give us that enables us to rest in His promises?* Faith. When we have faith that God will do all that He has promised we can rest.

97. *What is the only work God requires of us?* 1 John 3:23 teaches us that our work is to believe in Jesus Christ and to Love one another.

98. *How does Christ's true Church differ from the Church lead by man?* The Bible tells us that the true Church will be built up into a unity of incorruptible faith and belief. The differences between the true Church and world Church are manifested in the leadership (Christ or man), what each group is taught (truth or lies), and where each group is being led, (New Jerusalem, which means Peace) or Babylon (which means confusion of tongue, or babble). These two groups are brought out in the book of Revelation.

99. *Why did God bring Jews from all over the world to Jerusalem when He started His Church?* When God started the Church, Jews scattered by Babylon came up to Jerusalem from all over the world to celebrate the Feast of Pentecost. After the Holy Ghost fell, those Jews heard the disciples preaching the Gospel of Jesus in their own languages. God wanted them and us to understand that if we make man the head of God's people He will confuse the speech until we don't understand each other. When the Holy Ghost came, the church was under God's ordained Head, and the confusion of languages was erased. The same will happen today. We've made man the head and confusion is evident. We Christians don't understand each other. The Holy Ghost as teacher will correct this.

100. *Why must we submit to the Holy Ghost?* We must submit to the Holy Ghost so that He can protect us from our inability to discern the truth. The Holy Ghost is the only authority that has all truth.

ABSOLUTE 6

101. *How are we saved?* We are saved from our sins and their punishment by grace through faith.

102. *Once we've been converted to Christ, who is then to be trusted with the completion?* Once we are born again of the spirit we become the workmanship of God. We must obey the word and follow him in faith. The Bible tells

us that obedience is better than sacrifice but we must remember that praying instead of becoming discouraged about the things we want changed in us, puts our faith in His working and keeps our eyes on Him. Jesus becomes our confidence that we will be what He wants us to be.

103. *What is the one thing that we need in all that we do, that we might please God?* Faith. Without faith it's impossible to please God (Heb. 11:6).

104. *What were the three beginnings in Genesis and which one succeeded? Why?* The three beginnings in Genesis are Adam, a perfect man; Noah, a perfect man; and Abraham, an idol worshipper when God called him. Abraham was the only one who succeeded. Adam failed God and his failure brought death to mankind. Noah's descendants took the covenant God gave Noah and decided to make a name for themselves by building a tower to God. God showed us through these stories that even perfect men could not carry the hopes of the human race on their shoulders. Abraham succeeded because he believed God and obeyed Him, no matter what the cost. This man's life showed both faith without works and faith by works. He believed God and it was counted unto him for righteousness.

105. *What is the significance of the Book of Exodus for us?* The Book of Exodus is the story of God's success. God sent a ministry, under the leadership of the Holy Ghost, (cloud by day, pillar of fire by night) to lead His people out of Egypt. The combination of God's ministry and God's presence took the children of Israel out of religious bondage and into the Promised Land of God. The fivefold ministry is ordained by God to do the same thing for us today.

106. *What are Satan's two plans for mankind?* 1) When possible, keep people in bondage to sin; 2) If they escape the bondage of sin by coming to Jesus, defeat them through religious corruption and lies.

107. *Describe the three-part work of salvation.* 1) Jesus paid the debt for our sins on the cross at Calvary; 2) Jesus shed His blood for our cleansing and healing; 3) God covered us with the flesh of the sacrifice.

108. *Why is it so important that we understand that we are covered with His flesh?* Being covered with His flesh describes a finished work. It says that God sees Jesus as my righteousness. I am **in Christ, my life is hid with Christ in God.** I am dead, it is a finished work. Only faith can see it, but it was finished on Calvary. I cannot strive to accomplish it, I must believe to receive it. Believing it's finished because God said it is.

109. *What are the key points regarding salvation that God reveals to us in the story about Cornelius in the Book of Acts?* The Bible tells us that Cornelius was a man who prayed to God, fasted, and gave alms to the poor—a "righteous" man. Yet the Bible tells us that at this point in his life, he was not even born again. Cornelius was subsequently saved, but not because of what he did right. When Peter told him about Jesus, Cornelius believed that what Jesus did and said was for him personally. Cornelius was saved by grace—by faith. Through this story, Jesus teaches us that we are not saved by good works, but only by believing on Him.

110. *Why is the true meaning of the word "grace" so unsettling to man?* The true meaning of grace reveals that it is freely given—unmerited—no strings attached—a gift of Divine love and mercy. Our natural man cannot comprehend such a gift, so we continue to try and earn salvation. The cost of salvation has already been paid—by Jesus on the cross.

111. *What is the only way believers overcome sin?* Faith in the work of God, grace and mercy comprise the only way for a believer to overcome sin. This is the victory that overcomes the world, even our faith.

112. *What is our inheritance through Christ?* In His will and Testament, Jesus left us His faith, His mind, and His Spirit, as well as His victory over flesh and Satan and sin.

113. *What is the most important thing we can believe as followers of Christ? Why?* Believing that we are products of the workmanship of Christ. If we trust that we are His workmanship and His creative work that turns us into what He desires, we will stop trying to make ourselves into what He wants us to be. Once we understand that Jesus is the Builder ordained by God to do this work our spirit man will enter into rest and cease from his own labors.

114. *Why is it important that we understand the pictures God gave us in the Tabernacle?* It's a pattern of God's will finished. It's the blue print by which we must build if we desire to build in the work of God. It is the picture of Christ and His Bride triumphant over all enemies. The Church will come to unity and perfection just as simply and certainly as the Tabernacle of Moses was built because the builder and maker is God. It is a promise of an appointed time and event and no matter how much Satan rages or broadcasts lies, God's Word will shine brighter and brighter.

115. *What was the law unable to do? Why?* The law could not bring man to perfection because its success depended on man's obedience. Flesh did not have the power or faith to walk in total obedience to God's commands.

116. *How did Jesus fulfill all prophecy about Himself?* When God was manifested in the flesh, He turned from the weakness of the flesh and relied on the power of the Spirit. Jesus denied the flesh and elevated the will of God. Through surrender to the revealed Word, Jesus pursued victory in order to restore the unaltered Word and the secured revelation to man. He secured all sixty-six books of the revelation of Himself.

117. *How do we stop serving sin?* Under Grace, the scriptures teach us that it is a simple matter of yielding yourself. To whom ever you yield yourself servant to obey his servant you are to whom you obey. It is as easy for a believer to yield to righteousness as it is to sin. The convicting presence of Jesus within our soul and the power of the indwelling Holy Ghost are the formula for victory. We must allow God to create within us a clean heart and to change the way we think. We are instructed to allow the mind of Christ to be in us—and this mind surrendered to God's commands all the way to death: We can to, because greater is He that is within us then he that is in the world.

118. *What is the most important dynamic of the Holy Ghost?* The most important dynamic of the Holy Ghost is Love. When men are truly filled with the Holy Ghost, love is evident.

ABSOLUTE 7, Part 1

119. *Why is it important that we understand the Bible from both the historical and spiritual aspects?* The historical aspect is important because it shows the consistency of God's love toward man. The spiritual aspect is important because it introduces an intimacy through which God is manifested to us as real and desiring relationship with His children, not far off and unapproachable.

120. *Why is it easier to understand the historical (physical) facts of the Bible?* We understand the physical dynamics of the Bible with our natural mind. We feel safest in the physical realm. The problem with the spiritual aspect is that we cannot comprehend it without being born again of the Spirit. The Kingdom of God is invisible to the carnal mind.

121. *Why did God seal the spiritual truths written in His Word?* The spiritual level of the Bible is God's way of writing His secrets to His Bride and being sure that only She sees and understands them. God sealed the Bible to insure the integrity of signs involving future events. He wanted to deny access to the carnal mind. In that way, He enters the hearts of His people on invitation, and teaches them the truths of His word internally. God's desire was to guarantee His way of salvation would not become merchandise sold to the highest bidder—but that it would remain free to all who desire to receive. He sealed the Bible because His kingdom is at war with Satan. Satan twists God's words and deceives the carnal mind. Additionally, He raised up the Jewish priesthood to kill the living sacrifices for sin, the last sacrifice they were ordained to slay was Jesus the Messiah. Would this priesthood knowingly sacrifice their own Messiah for the world's (and their own) salvation? Not very likely.

122. *What are the four primary forms of expression in the Bible?* The Bible contains four primary forms of expression: allegory, parable, mystery, and history.

123. *When Jesus said, "tear this Temple down and in three days I will raise it up" was He speaking physically or Spiritually? Why is this important for us to understand today?* Jesus was speaking spiritually. The Jewish priesthood tore his body down (on the Cross) and in three days He raised it back up. This is important for us today because the Bible is still taught in the physical realm. In light of this spiritual declaration and fulfillment how could men teach that the "Anti-Christ" will enter a physical temple in Jerusalem? And they do teach that. Jesus said, "My Body is the New Temple." Satan knows that, so why would he want to enter a stone building that means nothing to God? The assembly of saints is the Temple. We are a Temple not made with hands eternal in the heavens.

124. *Why is the Old Testament pertinent today?* The Old Testament is full of stories that are allegorical pictures to us of the spiritual things that took place in the New Testament and are still taking place today. The Old Testament stories remain constants of definition. The Old Testament explains the details unseen by the carnal eye. New Testament truths illuminated by Old Testament parameters complete the revelation of Jesus Christ.

125. *Why is it important that we understand the seven Jewish feasts?* The seven feasts describe seven historical phenomenon, events that would change the world and finish the very will of God in His people. They are a description of the will of God and the chronological order of significant events. The first four feasts were allegories defining the events in the four Gospels. The last three feasts reveal things that will come to God's people in the last days.

126. *What is God's creative masterpiece?* God's creative masterpiece is 1.) man living the full potential God intended for him, 2.) man living as a son of God would live, 3.) the Church under the ministries of God coming to maturity and attaining the full stature of the man Christ Jesus, 4.) the assembly growing up into Him as the Head of the Body. When the masterpiece is finished the world will see the manifestation of the Sons of God.

127. *What is the difference between a mystery and a parable? Why does God use them?* A mystery is something hidden or secret, not obvious to the intellect. A parable is God exercising dominion over His Word. He alone holds the interpretation and we must go to Him for understanding. Parables can be stories of historical events where God has controlled the events and names of people to conceal a spiritual revelation. Jesus used every day events to convey deeper truths because once they were opened the information would be voluminous. Jesus spoke in parables and mysteries to first prepare His ministries, He could establish a flow of information to a select group to whom He later explained what He had said. This was not meant to exclude anyone, but the ministries of God are parental and they needed to be older than their spiritual children. Once the Church was birthed, thousands of these people were taught the truth by the Apostles.

128. *Define allegory. What is the first allegory in the Bible?* An allegory is a type or shadow, a symbolic representation of what is really being talked or written about, presented as a story or picture. The first allegory in the Bible was Adam and Eve, caught in sin and covered with the flesh of a substitutionary sinless animal whose blood was shed for their sin. This depicting the death of Jesus paying for our sins with His own blood and covering us with His flesh so God would forever after look upon us and see Him. Our lives are hid with Christ in God.

129. *How does God bear witness to, or prove, His allegories?* When God put an allegory into the historical context of the Bible, He reiterated the principle in the prophetical context. As a third witness Jesus lived the principle in the Gospels. There is no allegory that stands alone without witness in the same way.

130. *What are some "types and shadows" of Jesus in the Old Testament buried in the history of Israel?* From Abraham's binding of Isaac on the sacrificial altar, to the Passover Lamb and the shedding of blood for the remission of sins, Christ Jesus and His roles as High Priest and Sacrifice are described. The Tabernacle of Moses describes Jesus, the tabernacle of God. The Rock that followed Israel during their wilderness wanderings was Jesus—the rock in a weary land, the very river of life. Rachel's son Joseph was also a picture of Jesus even to the name of his betrayer who would sell him for silver. Joseph's brother Judah or Judas in Greek, sold him for silver.

ABSOLUTE 7, Part 2

131. *When will the Jewish nation come to see Jesus as the Messiah?* After Jesus died on the cross, it became necessary for both Hebrews and Gentiles to be born again of the Spirit. God will bring the people of Israel, Abraham's physical lineage, back to Himself by showing them that Jesus is their Messiah. They will see Jesus in the perfected Church—a church perfect in unity (all speaking the same things in truth) and in the full stature of the man Christ Jesus. Christ in you the hope of glory.

132. *What is significant about the genealogy of Matthew?* The genealogy of Matthew places four women in the lineage of Jesus—four Gentile women of questionable repute. These women were Tamar (dressed as a prostitute and seduced her father-in-law to continue her dead husbands lineage), Rahab (a prostitute in Jericho who rescued the Hebrew spies and encouraged the people of God), Ruth (a moabite from the lineage of Lot and his daughter), and Bathsheba (who bore David's child while married to another man). They are mentioned in the lineage because they were women of faith who embody the very message of salvation preached by Jesus. They were mentioned as a reminder that God always brought in Gentiles—and women. These names confront self-righteousness and embrace the unwanted.

133. *What is the Spirit revealing to us in the numbers of the genealogy of Matthew and Ezekiel's vision of the Temple?* The total generations mentioned by Matthew was forty two, the same number of encampments that Israel used from Egypt to crossing into the Promised Land. In Ezekiel's vision of the Temple the dimensions of the door into the Holy Place was 6 cubits by 7cubits. Seven is significant of perfection, six is symbolic of man. God told us through the Prophet that the way into the presence of God would be through a perfect man—Jesus, the perfect man. Seven times six equals forty two—the generations total and number of months in Jesus' earthly ministry. Matthew was proclaiming Jesus to be the Door.

134. *The first two chapters of Matthew are an excellent example of historical facts revealed spiritually. How can we be protected from just an intellectual under-standing of God's Word?* For a believer the first step is humbling before God to request all truth. Reformation comes to the Church at great cost. The Holy Ghost was sent to lead and guide the Church into all truth.

Unfortunately once we believe something to be true it is difficult to see a need to change. God has been faithful to hold back His rain from the Church when it has gone astray. Today men can make sermons and act as though the power of God is in a meeting when He is not. Lives transformed by the power of God's presence is proof that He is in our midst. The greater part of the Christian community has settled for momentum without power. Young people are disenfranchised and the Church is acting more worldly to attract them. If we deny that we need God back in our churches, those who bring the delivering message of Reformation will be ignored or called too spiritual, or fought. God will restore truth to the Church, but it may be a small remnant who will hear what the Spirit says unto the Church. We have to admit something is wrong amid all the conflicting doctrines and seek God's remedy seriously.

135. *What did it mean when the veil in the Temple was torn in two, from top to bottom, the day Jesus was crucified?* The tearing of the veil signified that man was no longer separated from the presence of God. From that moment on, every man could confess his sins and, under the blood protection of Jesus as High Priest, boldly enter into the presence of God.

136. *What are some of the parallels between Joseph whose story we read in Genesis, and Jesus?* Both were born by a miracle intervention of God; both were favorites of their fathers; both were hated by their brothers because of their closeness to their fathers; both were sold for silver, both were sold by a man named Judah (Judas was the Greek pronunciation); both coats were dipped in blood; both were rejected by their own people and accepted by the gentiles; both became rulers; both have Gentile brides; both feed the multitudes; both went down into Egypt.

137. *What will produce the perfect Church?* Our faith in God's work and in His Word, and total surrender to His will, will produce the perfect Church. Stopping our self-efforts to accept His working in us. Realizing that for His will to be done in us requires a miracle. That's why we were instructed by Jesus to pray for His will to be done on earth.

138. *What is God's desire for His Church?* Perfection—a Church without spot or wrinkle. A Church overflowing with spiritual Christians, filled with the Spirit of God, led by the Spirit of God, and mature—no longer blown by winds of doctrine—no longer divided.

Glossary

Please note: The following entries provide extended definitions of many of the key words used in this book. Words denoted with an "H" are taken from the original Hebrew of the Old Testament; words denoted with a "G" are taken from the original Greek of the New Testament. The numbers at the beginning of the entry are the Strong's key numbers.

A

Absolute

Webster's Dictionary: 1. being entirely without flaw and meeting supreme standards of excellence; 2. pure; 3. free from restrictions; 4. definite. It also means existing in or based on fact. Synonyms of "absolute" are factual, genuine, and perfect.

Abomination

H: 8251 shiqquwts {shik-koots'} or shiqquts {shik-koots'}; from 08262; TWOT - 2459b; n m AV - abomination 20, detestable things 5, detestable 1, abominable filth 1, abominable idols 1; 28
1) detestable thing or idol, abominable thing, abomination, idol, detested thing
H: 8441 tow`ebah {to-ay-baw'} or to`ebah {to-ay-baw'}
act part of 08581; TWOT - 2530a; n f; AV - abomination 113, abominable thing 2, abominable 2; 117
1) a disgusting thing, abomination, abominable; 1a) in ritual sense (of unclean food, idols, mixed marriages); 1b) in ethical sense (of wickedness etc)
H: 3577 kazab {kaw-zawb'}; from 03576; TWOT - 970a; n m AV - lie 23, lying 2, leasing 2, deceitful 1, false 1, liar 1, lies + 01697 1; 31
1) a lie, untruth, falsehood, deceptive thing
G: 946 bdelugma {bdel'-oog-mah}; from 948; TDNT - 1:598,103; n n; AV - abomination 6; 6
1) a foul thing, a detestable thing; 1a) of idols and things pertaining to idolatry
Nave's (1814): falsehood: General Scriptures concerning
Ex 20:16 23:1 Le 6:2-7 19:11,12,16 Job 13:4 21:34 27:4 31:5,6,33 36:4 Ps 5:6,9 10:7 12:2,3 28:3 31:18 34:13 36:3 50:19,20 52:2-5 55:21,23 58:3 59:12 62:4 63:11 101:5,7 109:2 116:11 119:29,69,163 120:2-4 144:8,11 Pr 2:12-15 3:3 6:12,13,17-19 10:9,10,18,31 11:9 12:17,19,20,22 13:5 14:5,8,25 17:4,7 19:5,9,22,28 20:17 21:6 26:18,19,24-26,28 27:14 Ec 5:6 Isa 28:15 32:7 57:11 59:3,4,12,13 63:8 Jer 7:8,28 9:3,5,6,8 12:6 50:36 Eze 22:9 Ho 4:1,2 Ob 1:7 Mic 6:12 Na 3:1 Zep 3:13 Mt 25:44-46 Joh 8:44,45 Eph 4:25,29 Col 3:9 1Ti 1:9,10 4:2 1Pe 3:10,16 Re 21:8,27 22:15
(see Absolute 7 for a discussion of "abomination")

Adam (man)

H: 0120 'adam {aw-dawm'}; from 0119; TWOT - 25a; n m AV - man 408, men 121, Adam 13, person(s) 8, common sort + 07230 1, hypocrite 1; 552
1) man, mankind; 1a) man, human being; 1b) man, mankind (much more frequently intended sense in OT); 1c) Adam, first man; 1d) city in Jordan valley
G: 76 Adam {ad-am'}; of Hebrew origin 0121; TDNT - 1:141,21; n pr m AV - Adam 9; 9
Adam = "the red earth"
1) Adam, the first man, the parent of the whole human race
Nave's (3214): created Ge 1:26,27 2:7 5:1,2 De 4:32 Job 4:17 10:2,3,8,9 31:15 33:4 35:10 Ps 8:5 100:3 119:73 138:8 139:14 Ec 7:29 Isa 17:7 42:5 43:7 45:12 64:8 Jer 27:5 Zec 12:1 Mal 2:10 Mr 10:6 Heb 2:7; created in the image of God Ge 1:26,27 9:6 Ec 7:29 1Co 11:7 15:48,49 Jas 3:9; design of the creation of Ps 8:6-8 Pr 16:4 Isa 43:7; dominion of Ge 1:26,28 2:19,20 9:2,3 Jer 27:6 28:14 Da 2:38 Heb 2:7,8; equality of Job 31:13-15 Ps 33:13-15 Pr 22:2 Mt 20:25-28 23:8,11 Mr 10:42-44 Ac 10:28 17:26 Ga 3:28; insignificance of Job 4:18,19 15:14 22:2-5 25:4-6 35:2-8 38:4,12,13 Ps 8:3,4 144:3,4; little lower than the angels Job 4:18-21 Ps 8:5 Heb 2:7,8; mortal Job 4:17 Ec 2:14,15 3:20 1Co 15:21,22 Heb 9:27; spirit Job 4:19 32:8 Ps 31:5 Pr 20:27 Ec 1:8 3:21 12:7 Isa 26:9 Zec 12:1 Mt 4:4 10:28 26:41 Mr 14:38 Lu 22:40 23:46 24:39 Joh 3:3-8 4:24 Ac 7:59 Ro 1:9 2:29 7:14-25 1Co 2:11 6:20 7:34 14:14 2Co 4:6,7,16 5:1-9 Eph 3:16 4:4 1Th 5:23 Heb 4:12 Jas 2:26; (1411) depravity of man Ge 8:21 6:5-7,11-13 8:21 De 32:10 2Ch 6:36 Job 4:17-19 9:2,3,20,29,30 11:12 14:4 15:14-16 25:4-6 Ps 5:9 14:1-3 51:5 53:1-3 58:1-5 94:11 130:3 143:2 Pr 10:20 20:6,9 21:8 Ec 7:20,29 8:11 9:3 Isa 1:5,6 42:6,7 43:8 48:8 51:1 53:6 64:6 Jer 2:22,29 6:7 13:23 16:12 17:9 Eze 16:6 36:25,26 37:1-3 Ho 6:7 14:9 Mic 7:2-4 Mt 7:17 12:34,35 15:19 Mr 7:21-23 Lu 1:79 Joh 1:10,11 3:19 8:23 14:17 Ac 8:23 Ro 2:1 3:9-19,23 5:6,12-14 6:6,17,19,20 7:5,11,13-15,18-21,23, 25 8:5-8,13 11:32 1Co 2:14 3:3 5:9,10 2Co 3:4,5 5:14 Ga 3:10,11,22 5:17,19-21 Eph 2:1-3,11,12 4:17-19,22 5:8,14 Col 1:13,21 2:13 3:5,7 2Ti 2:26 Tit 3:3 Jas 3:2 4:5 1Pe 1:18 2:9,25 1Jo 1:8,10 2:16 3:10 5:19 Re 3:17

Adoption

G: 5206 huiothesia {hwee-oth-es-ee'-ah}; from a presumed compound of 5207 and a derivative of 5087;
TDNT - 8:397,1206; n f; AV - adoption 3, adoption of children 1, adoption of sons 1; 5
1) adoption, adoption as sons; 1a) that relationship which God was pleased to establish between himself and the Israelites in preference to all other nations; 1b) the nature and condition of the true disciples in Christ, who by receiving the Spirit of God into their souls become sons of God
Nave's (138): General Scriptures concerning Ge 15:3; Of children, instances of - Of Joseph's sons Ge 8:5,14,16,22
Of Moses Ex 2:5-10 Ac 7:21 Heb 11:24; Of Esther Es 2:7; Spiritual Ex 4:22,23 Nu 6:27 De 14:1 26:18 27:9 28:10 32:5,6 2Sa 7:14 1Ch 22:10 28:6 2Ch 7:14 Pr 14:26 Isa 8:18 43:6,7 63:8,16 Jer 3:19 31:9,20 Ho 1:9 11:1 Mt 5:9,45 13:43 Lu 6:35 Joh 1:12,13 11:52 Ac 15:17 Ro 8:14-19,21,29 9:8,26 2Co 6:17 Ga 3:26,29 4:5-7 Eph 1:5 2:19 3:6,15 Php 2:15 Heb 1:5 2:10,13 12:6,7,9 1Jo 3:1,2,10 4:4 Re 21:7; typified, in Israel Ex 4:22

Allegory

Webster's Dictionary: 1) the expression by means of symbolic figures and actions of truths or generalizations about human existence; 2) a symbolic representation
(see Absolute 7 for an in-depth explanation of this term)

Anointing

H: 04888 mishchah {meesh-khaw'} or moshchah {mosh-khaw'}; from 04886; TWOT - 1255a,1255b; n f

AV - anointing 24, anointed 1, ointment 1; 26
1) consecrated portion, anointing oil, portion, ointment, anointing portion; 1a) ointment
(used to consecrate by anointing); 1b) anointing portion
G: 5545 chrisma {khris'-mah}; from 5548; TDNT - 9:493,1322; n n AV - anointing 2,
unction 1; 3
1) anything smeared on, unguent, ointment, usually prepared by the Hebrews from oil and
aromatic herbs. Anointing was the inaugural ceremony for priests
Nave's (334): God Preserves those who receive Ps 18:50 20:6 89:20-23; Saints receive Isa
61:3 1Jo 2:20; In consecration of high priests Ex 29:7,29 40:13 Le 6:20 8:12 16:32 Nu 35:25
Ps 133:2; Of priests Ex 28:41 30:30 40:15 Le 4:3 8:30 Nu 3:3; Of spiritual gifts 2Co 1:21 1Jo
2:20,27; Typified Ex 40:13-15 Le 8:12 1Sa 16:13 1Ki 19:16; Symbolic of Jesus Mt 26:7-12 Joh
12:3-7
Unger's: (Spiritual significance) The anointing with oil in the OT is symbolic of
endowment with the Spirit of God for the duties of the office to which a person is consecrated; in NT terms an anointing is an endowment, or unction, of the Holy Spirit given to a
believer for a specific purpose to the glorification of God and the edification of the Body of
Christ.

Atonement
H: 3722 kaphar {kaw-far'}; a primitive root; TWOT - 1023,1024,1025,1026; v; AV -
atonement 71, purge 7, reconciliation 4, reconcile 3, forgive 3, purge away 2, pacify 2,
atonement...made 2, merciful 2, cleansed 1, disannulled 1, appease 1, put off 1, pardon 1,
pitch 1; 102
1) to cover, purge, make an atonement, make reconciliation, cover over with pitch; 1a)
(Qal) to coat or cover with pitch; 1b) (Piel); 1b1) to cover over, pacify, propitiate; 1b2) to
cover over, atone for sin, make atonement for; 1b3) to cover over, atone for sin and persons
by legal rites; 1c) (Pual); 1c1) to be covered over; 1c2) to make atonement for; 1d)
(Hithpael) to be covered
G: 2643 katallage {kat-al-lag-ay'}; from 2644; TDNT - 1:258,40; n f; AV - reconciliation 2,
atonement 1, reconciling 1; 4
1) exchange; 1a) of the business of money changers, exchanging equivalent values; 2)
adjustment of a difference, reconciliation, restoration to favor; 2a) in the NT of the
restoration of the favor of God to sinners
that repent and put their trust in the expiatory death of Christ
Nave's (510): atonement — For tabernacle and furniture Le 16:15-20,33; -In consummation of the Levites Nu 8:21; For those defiled by the dead Nu 6:11; Made for houses Le
14:53; By meat offerings Le 5:11-13; -By jewels Nu 31:50; -By money Ex 30:12-16 Le 5:15,16
2Ki 12:16; -By incense Nu 16:46-50; day of, Time of Ex 30:10 Le 23:27 25:9 Nu 29:7; How
observed Ex 30:10 Le 16:2-34 23:27-32 Nu 29:7-11 Ac 27:9 Heb 5:3 9:7,19,22; made by
animal sacrifices Ex 29:36 30:12-16 Le 1:4 4:20,22-35 5:6-10 6:7 9:7 10:17 12:6-8 14:12-32
16:6,10,11,15-19,24-34 17:11 19:22 Nu 15:22-28 28:22,30 29:5,10,11 Heb 9:22; made by
Jesus, Divinely ordained Lu 2:30,31 Ga 4:4,5 Eph 1:3-12,17-22 2:4-10 Col 1:19,20 1Pe 1:20
Re 13:8; A mystery 1Co 2:7; With context 1Pe 1:8-12; Made but once Heb 7:27 9:24-28
10:10,12,14 1Pe 3:18; Redemption by Mt 20:28 Ac 20:28 Ga 3:13 1Ti 2:6 Heb 9:12 Re 5:9;
Typified Ge 4:4 Heb 11:4 Ge 22:2 Heb 11:17,19 Ex 12:5,11,14 1Co 5:7 Ex 24:8 Heb 9:20 Le
16:30,34 Heb 9:7,12,28 Le 17:11 Heb 9:22; General Ps 40:6,7 Isa 53:4-12 Da 9:24-27 Zec
13:1 Mt 26:28 Lu 22:20 24:46,47 Joh 1:29,36 6:51 11:49-51 Ac 17:2,3 20:28 Ro 3:24-26 4:25
5:1,2,6-11,15-21 1Co 1:17,18,23,24 15:3 2Co 5:18,19 Ga 1:3,4 4:4,5 Eph 1:7 2:13-18 5:2,25
Col 1:14,19-22 1Th 5:9,10 1Ti 2:5,6 Tit 2:14 Heb 1:3 2:9,17 9:12-15,25,26 10:1-20 12:24
13:12,20,21 1Pe 1:18-20 2:24 3:18 1Jo 1:7 2:2 3:5 4:10 5:6 Re 1:5 5:9 7:14 12:11
(see Absolute 7 for a look at the spiritual meaning of the Feast of Atonement)

B

Babylon

H: 0894 Babel {baw-bel'}; from 01101; TWOT - 197; n pr loc; AV - Babylon 257,
Babylonian + 01121 3, Babel 2; 262 Babel or Babylon = "confusion (by mixing)"
1) Babel or Babylon, the ancient site and/or capital of Babylonia (modern Hillah) situated
on the Euphrates
G: 897 Babulon {bab-oo-lone'}; of Hebrew origin 0894; TDNT - 1:514,89; n pr loc AV -
Babylon 12; 12; Babylon = "confusion"
1) a very large and famous city, the residence of the Babylonian kings, situated on both
banks of the Euphrates. Cyrus had formerly captured it, but Darius Hystaspis threw down
its gates and walls, and Xerxes destroyed the temple of Belis. At length the city was reduced
to almost solitude, the population having been drawn off by the neighbouring Seleucia,
built on the Tigris by Seleucus Nicanor; 2) of the territory of Babylonia
Nave's (585): Tower of Babel Ge 11:1-9; Prophecies concerning Ps 87:4 137:8,9 Isa 13:1,
14:4-26, 21:1-10 46:1,2 47:1, 48:14,20 Jer 21:4-10 25:12-14 27:1-11 28:14 32:28 34:2,3
42:11,12 43:1, 46:13-26 49:28-30 50:1, 51:1, Eze 21:19 26:1, 29:17-20 30:10 32:11 Da 2:21-38
4:10-26 5:25-29 7:1, Hab 1:5-11 Zec 2:7-9; figurative Re 14:8 16:19 17:1, 18:1; Jews carried
to 2Ki 25:1,1Ch 9:1 2Ch 33:11 36:17-21 Jer 32:2 39:1, 52:1; Conquest of Egypt by 2Ki 24:7;
Prophecies of conquests by 2Ki 20:16-19 Jer 20:4-7 21:1, 22:1,25:1-11 27:1, 28:1, 29:1,
32:28,29 34:1, 36:29 38:17,18 43:8-13 46:13-26 Eze 12:1, 17 19:1, 21:1, 24:1, 26:1, 29:18-20
30:1, 32:1; Prophetic denunciations against Ps 137:8,9 Isa 13:1 14:21 43:14-17 47:1 Jer 50:1
51:1
Unger's: In the NT Babylon symbolizes confusion, or apostate Christendom, that is, ecclesi-
astical Babylon, the great harlot (Rev. 17:5-18). Its power will be destroyed by the greater
power of the Kingdom of Christ.

Baptism

H: 07364 rachats {raw-khats'}; a primitive root; TWOT - 2150; v AV - wash 53, bathe 18,
wash away 1; 72
to wash, wash off, wash away, bathe; 1a) (Qal); 1a1) to wash, wash off, wash away; 1a2) to
wash, bathe (oneself); 1b) (Pual) to be washed; 1c) (Hithpael) to wash oneself
H: 03526 kabac {kaw-bas'}; a primitive root; TWOT - 946; v AV - wash 47, fuller 4; 51
1) to wash (by treading), be washed, perform the work of a fuller; 1a) (Qal) washer, fuller,
treader (participle); 1b) (Piel) to wash (garments, person); 1c) (Pual) to be washed; 1d)
(Hothpael) to be washed out
G: 907 baptizo {bap-tid'-zo}; from a derivative of 911; TDNT - 1:529,92; verb; AV - baptize
(76), wash 2, baptist 1, baptized + 2258 1; 80
1) to dip repeatedly, to immerse, to submerge (of vessels sunk);2) to cleanse by dipping or
submerging, to wash, to make clean with water, to wash one's self, bathe; 3) to overwhelm
Nave's (614) John's Mt 3:5-8,11,13-16 21:25 Mr 1:4,5,8-10 11:30 Lu 3:7,8,12,21 7:29,30 20:4
Joh 1:25,26,28,31,33 3:23 10:40 Ac 1:5,22 10:37 11:16 19:3,4; Of the Holy Spirit Isa 44:3 Joe
2:28,29 Zec 12:10 Mt 3:11,16 Mr 1:8 Lu 3:16,22 24:49 Joh 1:32,33 3:5 Ac 1:5 2:1-4,38,41
8:15-17 10:38,44,45,47 11:15,16 19:2,6 1Co 12:13 Tit 3:5,6 1Pe 3:20,21
    In its most fundamental sense, the word baptism (Greek "baptizo," Strong's #907) means
washing. As earthen vessels, God has made a provision for us to be washed and cleansed of
the impurities of the flesh by the water of the Word and the fire of the Holy Spirit. Just as
we use water and fire to cleanse and purify physical objects (think of bathing, washing
dishes, or refining metal) so does God use spiritual water and spiritual fire to cleanse and
purify His own. If we look closely at the Scriptures, we see that this cleansing is an internal
process meant to *sanctify* us from self unto the Lord.

Baptism into Christ is a spiritual process, not visible to the human eye, or completed in a day. The purpose of this cleansing is to bring a believer into complete identification with Christ in His sufferings, death, and resurrection. There is no outward ceremony that can produce such an identification, but only an inward change, going from being dead in sin to being dead to sin. Physical rituals can symbolize our identification with Christ and our forsaking of the world, but in themselves are not the very essence of what baptism means for us as believers. God tells us that He does not look upon the outward appearance of man, but instead He looks upon the heart.

In the Old Testament, baptism is typified many times. The following are several examples: Noah and his family on the ark; the nation of Israel passing under the cloud; the brazen laver in the tabernacle of Moses; Israel's crossing of the Jordan River; Elijah's sacrifice in 1 Kings 18; the three Hebrew boys in the fiery furnace; and the refiner's fire described in Malachi. In each shadow, we gain an understanding of the cleansing power of the Word of God and the fire of the Holy Spirit.

Baptism addresses the believer's second experience in his approach to God. The first is *justification* through faith in the cleansing power of the atoning blood of Jesus and its personal efficacy for the sinner. Jesus embodies the two cleansing agents of blood and water that were used in the ceremonial laws of the Old Testament. When the soldiers pierced Jesus' side after His death on the cross, blood and water flowed forth. He both fulfilled and abolished the blood sacrifices and ceremonial washings of the Old Testament by His perfect and final sacrifice on Calvary. He brought forth the New Covenant, of which His blood covering and cleansing word are a vital part. That which flowed from His side is our reconciliation and our redemption! With His ascension to the throne at the right hand of God, Christ received His glory and He received His power to baptize us with the Holy Spirit and with fire, thus becoming our all in all. Thereby, we can understand the words of 1 John 5:5-12. Outside of Christ, there is no justification and no sanctification. He is the blood and the water and the One who baptizes us with the fire of the Holy Spirit!

The sanctification of baptism has two primary aspects: the washing of the water of the Word and the cleansing by fire, which comes with the filling of the indwelling Spirit of God. It helps to use the illustration that God has given us of the animal sacrifice. We know that Jesus is the Passover Lamb, and that to fulfill all righteousness He had to be baptized of John's baptism of repentance for remission of sins just as the physical Passover lamb had to be washed. This washing identified the sinless Christ with our sins, and caused John to recognize Him as the Lamb who takes away the sins of the world. Jesus is the final and ultimate sacrifice for sin, the Blood applied to the doorposts of our hearts.

In Romans 12:1, believers are described as living sacrifices to God. Because His redeeming love paid the debt for our sins through His giving of Himself completely, it is our reasonable service to freely offer ourselves to Him completely. We must follow Christ's example and walk the way of the cross so that the righteousness that Jesus fulfilled may be fulfilled in us, His Body the Church. He comes to dwell within us in order that He might live out His perfect, sinless life in His Church. It is only as our flesh is dealt with through sanctification that He can be lifted up in His Church so that men are drawn to Him.

We must understand the pictures the Old Testament gives us of how sacrifices were handled because they give us the ability to understand how God deals with us as living sacrifices. If we remain ignorant of what the Old Testament tells us about sacrificial laws, we remain ignorant of His dealings with us as well.

Just as the ox in 1 Kings was doused with water and burned with fire from heaven, we are to be washed with water and burned with Holy Spirit fire as well. This is God's ideal way of dealing with our flesh: He cleanses us with His Word in order to create within us a desire to obey and to be conformed to the image of the Son. Once we truly desire to become like Jesus because we are saturated in the Word, we are a sacrifice ready to be consumed in the fire. Our washing with water turns us into flammable material, but the water is only part of the plan. Fire does what water alone cannot do, it very effectively turns our dead flesh into ash, producing a sweet aroma in the nostrils of God! What remains is a clean vessel, a vessel purged of every impurity that would hinder the Spirit from filling it completely, a vessel usable as a spontaneous reflex of the mind of God. This vessel is the new man purified from the old man, it is gold purified from dross in the refiner's fire.

Hopefully, we are beginning to see that we have in ourselves no power to produce sanctification, but that we must depend upon God for it. Thankfully, we have in Him a faithful provider! We know that Jesus is the Word, and the Word comes to live inside of us both to give us a will and a means to do His good works. God has given the Body of Christ, the Church, the gift of fivefold ministry to lead it to perfection, the full stature of the man Christ Jesus. He provides His ministry to do exactly what Elijah did on Mount Carmel—to wash the sacrifice with the water of the Word and call down the heavenly fire to consume it. Before His ascension to the heavenlies, Jesus told the soon-to-be-apostles (His ordained ministers) that they were to baptize (wash) believers in just this way.

As the sacrifice, our part is to believe. We must receive the Word and obey it in surrender, which is what Romans 6:16 tells us. This is what makes us flammable, what brings our will into line with God's will. This aspect of cleansing is typified by the brazen laver, in which the priests washed themselves before entering the holy place of the tabernacle. The laver was made of looking glasses, which shows us that looking into the Word gives us a true reflection of who we are and what needs to be cleansed in us.

The priests washed their hands and feet, their service and their walk. They applied the water of the laver for cleansing, and so must we, as a nation of kings and priests, apply the Word to our lives personally in order to be cleansed.

Blood

H: 01818 dam {dawm}; from 01826 (compare 0119); TWOT - 436; n m AV - blood 342, bloody 15, person + 05315, bloodguiltiness 1, bloodthirsty + 0582 1, vr blood 1; 361
1) blood; 1a) of wine (fig.)
H: 01826 damam {daw-man'}; a prim root [compare 01724, 01820]; TWOT - 439; v AV - silence 6, still 6, silent 4, cut off 3, cut down 2, rest 2, cease 2, forbear 1, peace 1, quieted 1, tarry 1, wait 1; 30
1) to be silent, be still, wait, be dumb, grow dumb; 1a) (Qal); 1a1) to be silent; 1a2) to be still, die; 1a3) to be struck dumb; 1b) (Niphal) to be silenced, be made silent, destroyed; 1c) (Poal) to make quiet; 1d) (Hiphil) to make silent (cause to die)
G: 129 haima {hah'-ee-mah}; of uncertain derivation; TDNT - 1:172,26; n m AV - blood 99; 99
1) blood; 1a) of man or animals; 1b) refers to the seat of life; 1c) of those things that resemble blood; 2) blood shed, to be shed by violence, slay, murder
Nave's (857): Is the life Ge 9:4 Le 17:11,14 19:16 De 12:23 Mt 27:4,24; Sacrificial, Without shedding of, no remission Heb 9:22; Sprinkled on door posts Ex 12:7-23 Heb 11:28; Of sacrifices, typical of the atoning blood of Christ Heb 9:6-28; Of Christ Mt 26:28 Mr 14:24 Lu 22:20 Joh 6:53-56 19:34 Ac 20:28 Ro 3:24,25 5:9 1Co 10:16 11:25 Eph 1:7 2:13,16 Col 1:14,20 Heb 9:12-14 10:19,20,29 12:24 13:12,20 1Pe 1:2,18,19 1Jo 1:7 5:6,8 Re 1:5,6 5:9 7:14 12:11

Body

H: 06106 `etsem {eh'tsem}; from 06105; TWOT - 1673c; n f AV - bone 104, selfsame 11, same 5, body 2, very 2, life 1, strength 1; 126
1) bone, essence, substance; 1a) bone; 1a1) body, limbs, members, external body; 1b) bone (of animal)
1c) substance, self

G: 4983 soma {so'-mah}; from 4982; TDNT - 7:1024,1140; n n AV - body 144, bodily 1, slave 1; 146
1) the body both of men or animals; 1a) a dead body or corpse; 1b) the living body; 1b1) of animals; 2) the bodies of plants and of stars (heavenly bodies); 3) is used of a (large or small) number of men closely united into one society, or family as it were; a social, ethical, mystical body; 3a) so in the NT of the church; 4) that which casts a shadow as distinguished from the shadow itself
Nave's (867): Called house 2Co 5:1; house of clay Job 4:19; the temple of God 1Co 3:16 6:3,15,19; Corruptible Job 17:14 1Co 15:53,54; Resurrection of 1Co 15:19-54
Unger's: The apostle Paul used the exquisite figure of the human body to portray the spiritual unity of the believers in this age. This mystical body is formed by the cleansing, regenerating work of the Spirit, an operation that not only unites Christians to one another but to Christ (Rom. 6:3-4; Gal. 3:27).

Bread

H: 03899 lechem {lekh'-em}; from 03898; TWOT - 1105a; n m AV - bread 237, food 21, meat 18, shewbread + 06440 5, loaves 5, shewbread + 04635 3, shewbread 2, victuals 2, eat 1, feast 1, fruit 1, provision 1; 297
1) bread, food, grain; 1a) bread; 1a1) bread; 1a2) bread-corn; 1b) food (in general)
G: 740 artos {ar'-tos}; from 142; TDNT - 1:477,80; n m AV - bread 72, loaf 23, shewbread + 4286 + 3588 4; 99
1) food composed of flour mixed with water and baked; 1a) the Israelites made it in the form of an oblong or round cake, as thick as one's thumb, and as large as a plate or platter hence it was not to be cut but broken; 1b) loaves were consecrated to the Lord; 1c) of the bread used at the love-feasts and at the Lord's Table; 2) food of any kind
Nave's (909): Called the staff of life Eze 4:16 5:16 14:13; kinds of bread of affliction 1Ki 22:27 Ps 127:2 Ho 9:4 Isa 30:20; Leavened (made with yeast) Le 7:13 23:17 Ho 7:4 Am 4:5 Mt 13:33; Unleavened (made without yeast) Ge 19:3 Ex 29:2 Jud 6:19 1Sa 28:24; Manna Nu 11:8; how prepared mixed with oil Ex 29:2,23; Honey Ex 16:31; Kneaded Ge 18:6 Ex 8:3 12:34 1Sa 28:24 2Sa 13:8 Jer 7:18 Ho 7:4; figurative
Isa 55:2 1Co 10:17 2Co 9:10; **Christ John 6:32-35;**
symbolic of the body of Christ Mt 26:26 Ac 20:7 1Co 11:23,24
Unger's: "Bread of Life" prefigures Christ as the supplier of true spiritual nourishment. He is the bread of heaven, and God's Word, like bread, is the spiritual staff of life (Matt. 4:4).

Bride

H: 03618 kallah {kal-law'}; from 03634; TWOT - 986a; n f AV - daughter in law 17, bride 9, spouse 8; 34
1) bride, daughter-in-law; 1a) daughter-in-law; 1b) bride, young wife
H: 03634 kalal {kaw-lal'}; a primitive root; TWOT - 985,986; v AV - perfected 1, made perfect 1; 2
1) to complete, perfect, make complete, make perfect; 1a) (Qal) to perfect
Nave's (916): figurative Ps 45:10-17 Eze 16:8-14 Re 19:7,8 21:2,9 22:17
Unger's: The Church is alluded to (Rev. 21:9) as "the bride, the wife of the Lamb." The implication here is that just as a man leaves his father and mother to cleave to and become one flesh with his wife, so Christ desires to cleave to and become one with the Church.

C

Candlestick

H: 5214 niyr {neer}; a root probably identical with that of 05216, through the idea of the gleam of a fresh furrow; TWOT - 1360; v AV - break up 2; 2

1) (Qal) to break up, freshly plough or till

H: 5216 niyr {neer} or nir {neer} also neyr {nare} or ner {nare}; or (fem.) nerah {nay-raw'} from a primitive root [see 05214; 05135] properly, meaning to glisten; TWOT - 1333b; n m AV - lamp 35, candle 9, light 4; 48
1) lamp

H: 4500 manowr {maw-nore'}; from 05214; TWOT - 1361a; n m AV - beam 4; 4
1) beam; 1a) beam (carrying the heddles in a loom)

H: 4501 m@nowrah {men-o-raw'} or m@norah {men-o-raw'}; from 04500 (in the original sense of 5216); TWOT - 1333c; n f AV - candlestick 40; 40
1) lamp stand

G: 3087 luchnia {lookh-nee'-ah}; from 3088; TDNT - 4:324,542; n f AV - candlestick 12; 12
1) a (candlestick) lamp stand, candelabrum

Nave's (985): of the tabernacle — Made after divine pattern Ex 25:31-40 37:17-24 Nu 8:4; Place of Ex 26:35 40:24,25 Heb 9:2; Furniture of Ex 25:38 37:23 Nu 4:9,10; Burned every night Ex 27:20,21; Trimmed every morning Ex 30:7; Carried by Kohathites Nu 4:4,15; Called the lamp of God 1Sa 3:3; of the temple — Ten branches of 1Ki 7:49,50; Of gold 1Ch 28:15 2Ch 4:20; Taken with other spoils to Babylon Jer 52:19; symbolical Zec 4:2,11 Re 1:12,13,20 2:5 11:4

"The Tabernacle of Moses": Represents Jesus, the Light of God; names: Lampstand, candlestick, pure candlestick, the candlestick of God. Golden Candlestick — 1. No specific dimensions; 2. 3 stages of the almond plant - unopened bud/knop, flower, fruit; 3. Lamp of oil rests on the fruit; 4. Made of beaten gold, one beaten work; 5. 6 branches ; one main shaft of 4 fruit 4 flowers 4 buds and 3 shoots on each side. 7 lamps of oil from 6 branches, each comprised of 3 fruit+3 flowers + 3 buds = 9 ornaments—having their sources in three originating buds. All added up they equal 66 ornaments — A confirmation to God's selection of 66 books of the Bible that testify of the plan of redemption.

Carnal

G: 4559 sarkikos {sar-kee-kos'}; from 4561; TDNT - 7:98,1000; adj AV - carnal 9, fleshly 2; 11
1) fleshly, carnal; 1a) having the nature of flesh, i.e. under the control of the animal appetites; 1a1) governed by mere human nature not by the Spirit of God; 1a2) having its seat in the animal nature or aroused by the animal nature; 1a3) human: with the included idea of depravity; 1b) pertaining to the flesh; 1b1) to the body: related to birth, lineage, etc

Church

G: 1537 ek {ek} or ex {ex}; a primary preposition denoting origin (the point whence action or motion proceeds), from, out (of place, time, or cause; literal or figurative; prep AV - of 367, from 181, out of 162, by 55, on 34, with 25, misc 97; 921
1) out of, from, by, away from

G: 1577 ekklesia {ek-klay-see'-ah}; from a compound of 1537 and a derivative of 2564; TDNT - 3:501,394; n f AV - church 115, assembly 3; 118
1) a gathering of citizens called out from their homes into some public place, an assembly; 1a) an assembly of the people convened at the public place of the council for the purpose of deliberating; 1b) the assembly of the Israelites; 1c) any gathering or throng of men assembled by chance, tumultuously; 1d) in a Christian sense; 1d1) an assembly of Christians gathered for worship in a religious meeting; 1d2) a company of Christian, or of those who, hoping for eternal salvation through Jesus Christ, observe their own religious rites, hold their own religious meetings, and manage their own affairs, according to regulations prescribed for the body for order's sake; 1d3) those who anywhere, in a city, village, constitute such a company and are united into one body; 1d4) the whole body of

Christians scattered throughout the earth; 1d5) the assembly of faithful Christians already dead and received into heaven

Nave's (1132): courts Ps 65:4 84:2,10 92:13 96:8 100:4 116:19 Isa 1:12 62:9 Zec 3:7; house of God Ge 28:17,22 Jos 9:23 Jud 18:31 20:18,26 21:2 1Ch 9:11 24:5 2Ch 5:14 22:12 24:13 33:7 36:19 Ezr 5:8,15 7:20,23 Ne 6:10 11:11 13:11 Ps 42:4 52:8 55:14 84:10 Ec 5:1 Isa 2:3 Ho 9:8 Joe 1:16 Mic 4:2 Zec 7:2 Mt 12:4 1Ti 3:15 Heb 10:21 1Pe 4:17; sanctuary Ex 25:8 Le 19:30 21:12 Nu 3:28 4:12 7:9 8:19 10:21 18:1,5 19:20 1Ch 9:29 22:19 24:5 28:10 2Ch 20:8 26:18 29:21 30:8,19 Ne 10:39 Ps 20:2 28:2 63:2 68:24 73:17 74:3,7 77:13 78:69 150:1 Isa 16:12 63:18 La 2:7,20 4:1 Eze 5:11 42:20 44:5,27 45:3 48:8,21 Da 8:11,13,14 9:17,26 11:31 Heb 8:2 9:1,2; house of prayer Isa 56:7 Mt 21:13; tabernacle Ex 26:1 Le 26:11 Jos 22:19 Ps 15:1 61:4 76:2 Heb 8:2,5 9:2,11 Re 13:6 21:3; temple 1Sa 1:9 3:3 2Ki 11:10,13 Ezr 4:1 Ps 5:7 11:4 27:4 29:9 48:9 68:29 Isa 6:1 Mal 3:1 Mt 4:5 23:16 Lu 18:10 24:53; Zion Ps 9:11 48:11 74:2 132:13 137:1 Isa 35:10 Jer 31:6 50:5 Joe 2:1,15; My Father's house Joh 2:16 14:2; holy Ex 30:26-29 40:9 Le 8:10,11 16:13 19:30 21:12 Nu 7:1 1Ki 9:3 1Ch 29:3 2Ch 3:8 Isa 64:11 Eze 23:39 1Co 3:17; church NT Mt 16:18 18:17 Ac 2:47 1Co 11:18 14:19,23,28,33,34 15:9 Ga 1:13; assembly of the saints Ps 89:7 Ps 111:1; body of Christ Eph 1:22,23 Col 1:24; branch Isa 60:21; bride Re 21:9;

Church of: God Ac 20:28 1 Ti 3:15; firstborn Heb 12:23; city of God Heb 12:22; congregation of saints Ps 149:1; congregation of the poor Ps 74:19; dove So 2:14 5:2; family Eph 3:15; flock Eze 34:15 1Pe 5:2; fold Joh 10:16; God's heritage Joe 3:2 1Pe 5:3; heavenly Jerusalem Ga 4:26 Heb 12:22; kingdom Mt 6:33 12:28 19:24 21:31Mt 3:2 4:17 10:7 5:3,10,19,20 Ps 103:19 145:12 Mt 16:28 Lu 1:33 Joh 18:36 Ps 45:6 145:11,13 Mt 6:10 Lu 23:42; place of God's throne Eze 43:7; vineyard Jer 12:10 Mt 21:41; Salt and light of the world

Mt 5:13; Militant So 6:10 Php 2:25 2Ti 2:3 4:7 Phm 1:2; God provides ministers for Jer 3:15 Eph 4:11,12; Is clothed in righteousness Re 10:8

Circumcision

H: 05243 namal {naw-mal'} a primitive root; TWOT - 1161; v AV - cut off 2, cut down 2, circumcised 1; 5

1) (Qal) to circumcise, become clipped, be circumcised, be cut off

G: 4061 peritome {per-it-om-ay'}; from 4059; TDNT - 6:72,831; n f AV - circumcision 35, circumcised 1; 36

1) circumcised; 1a) the act or rite of circumcision, "they of the circumcision" is a term used of the Jews; 1a1) of Christians gathered from among the Jews; 1a2) the state of circumcision; 1b) metaph.; 1b1) of Christians separated from the unclean multitude and truly consecrated to God; 1b2) of the extinction of passions and the removal of spiritual impurity

G: 4059 peritemno {per-ee-tem'-no}; from 4012 and the base of 5114; TDNT - 6:72,831; v AV - circumcise 18; 18

1) to cut around; 2) to circumcise; 2a) cut off one's prepuce (used of that well known rite by which not only the male children of the Israelites, on the eighth day after birth, but subsequently also "proselytes of righteousness" were consecrated to Jehovah and introduced into the number of his people); 2b) to get one's self circumcised, present one's self to be circumcised, receive circumcision; 2c) since by the rite of circumcision a man was separated from the unclean world and dedicated to God, the word is transferred to denote the extinguishing of lusts and the removal of sins

Nave's (1140): Institution of Ge 17:10-14 Le 12:3 Joh 7:22 Ac 7:8 Ro 4:11; A seal of righteousness Ro 2:25-29 4:11; Performed on all males on the eighth day Ge 17:12,13 Le 12:3 Php 3:5; Neglect of, punished Ge 17:14 Ex 4:24; Covenant promises of Ge 17:4-14 Ac 7:8 Ro 3:1 4:11 9:7-13 Ga 5:3; figurative Ex 6:12 De 10:16 30:6 Jer 4:4 6:10 9:26 Ro 2:28,29 15:8 Php 3:3 Col 2:11 3:11

According to "The New Unger's Bible Dictionary," Christians are said to be circumcised in Christ (Col. 2:11). This circumcision is asserted to be "circumcision made without hands," that is, a spiritual reality and not a physical rite, the antitype and not the type. Physical circumcision was a putting off of a part of the flesh as a symbol of covenant relationship of God's people with a holy God. Christian circumcision is removal of not a part, but the entire "body of flesh." "The body of the flesh" is the physical body controlled by the old fallen nature that all possess, saved as well as unsaved. The "removal of" is positional truth, that is, truth that arises as a result of the believer's being placed in Christ by the Spirit's cleansing work. Because the sin nature was judged by Christ in His death, so the believer by virtue of his organic union and identification with his Lord shares that "removal" that Christ accomplished, just as he shares Christ's fullness and is declared to be "complete" in Him (Col. 2:10). The believer's circumcision is not only a spiritual reality consisting in the putting off of the body of the flesh; it is more precisely Christ's circumcision, effected by Him and imputed to the believer: "In Him you were also circumcised...by the circumcision of Christ" (Col. 2:11). Our Lord's circumcision mentioned in this passage has no reference to His physical circumcision when He was eight days old, but is a meaningful term the apostle applies to Christ's death to the sin nature. It is the truth enunciated in Rom. 6:10, "For the death that He died, He died to sin, once for all," and 8:3, "For what the law could not do, weak as it was through the flesh, God did: sending His own son in the likeness of sinful flesh and as an offering for sin, He condemned sin in the flesh." It is thus apparent that the cleansing work of the Holy Spirit (Rom. 6:3-4; 1 Cor. 12:13; Col. 2:12) effects spiritual circumcision.

Cloud

H: 06051 `anan {aw-nawn'}; from 06049; TWOT - 1655a; n m AV - cloud 81, cloudy 6; 87
1) cloud, cloudy, cloud-mass; 1a) cloud-mass (of theophanic cloud); 1b) cloud
G: 3509 nephos {nef'-os}; apparently a root word; TDNT - 4:902,628; n n; AV - cloud 1; 1
1) a cloud, a large dense multitude, a throng; 1a) used to denote a great shapeless collection of vapor obscuring; the heavens as opposed to a particular and definite masses of vapor with some form or shape 1b) a cloud in the sky
Nave's (1167): figurative Jer 4:13 Ho 6:4 13:3; symbolical Re 14:14; pillar of Ex 13:21,22 14:19,24 16:10 19:9,16 24:16-18 33:9,10 34:5 40:36-38 Le 16:2 Nu 9:15-23 10:11,12,33-36 11:25 12:5,10 14:10 16:19,42 De 1:33 31:15 1Ki 8:10,11 2Ch 7:1-3 Ne 9:12,19 Ps 78:14 105:39 Isa 4:5 6:1,4 Eze 10:18,19 11:22,23 Mt 17:5 Lu 2:8,9 9:34,35

Communion

G: 2842 koinonia {koy-nohn-ee'-ah}; from 2844; TDNT - 3:797,447; n f AV - fellowship 12, communion 4, Communication 1, distribution 1, contribution 1, to communicate 1; 20
1) fellowship, association, community, communion, joint participation, intercourse; 1a) the share which one has in anything, participation; 1b) intercourse, fellowship, intimacy; 1b1) the right hand as a sign and pledge of fellowship (in fulfilling the apostolic office); 1c) a gift jointly contributed, a collection, a contribution, as exhibiting an embodiment and proof of fellowship
G: 2844 koinonos {koy-no-nos'}; from 2839; TDNT - 3:797,447; n m AV - partaker 5, partner 3, fellowship 1, companion 1; 10
1) a partner, associate, comrade, companion; 2) a partner, sharer, in anything; 2a) of the altar in Jerusalem on which the sacrifices are offered; 2a1) sharing in the worship of the Jews; 2b) partakers of (or with) demons; 2b1) brought into fellowship with them, because they are the authors of heathen worship
Nave's (1193): with God Ps 16:7 Joh 14:16-18,23 1Co 16:1 ... 2Co 6:16 13:14 Ga 4:6 Php 2:1,2 1Jo 1:3 Re 3:20

Of saints 1Sa 23:16 Ps 55:14 119:63 133:1-3 Am 3:3 Mal 3:16 Lu 22:32 24:17,32 Joh 17:20,21
Ac 2:42 Ro 12:15 1Co 10:16,17 12:12,13 2Co 6:14-18 Eph 4:1-3 5:11 Col 3:16 1Th 4:18
5:11,14 Heb 3:13 10:24,25 Jas 5:16 1Jo 1:3,7

> *Behold, I stand at the door, and knock: if any man hear my voice, and open the*
> *door, I will come in to him, and will sup with him, and he with me.* Revelation 3:20
> (KJS)

"Communion" is defined in Webster's Dictionary as: An act or instance of sharing; intimate fellowship or rapport, communication, intercourse.

The Greek word "koinonia" (Strong's #2842) is defined as fellowship with or participation in anything; a communion, fellowship, society. The Greek root word is "koinonos," (Strong's #2844) which broadly means to lie in common or open to all. In the New Testament, the words "communion" and "fellowship" represent this Greek term. Praise God! The essential meaning of the word "communion" is that God has made a way for all of mankind to have fellowship with Him, to partake of the Body of Christ by becoming an actual part of it through salvation! He is the Vine, and communion means that we can be so intimately associated with Him as to be a living appendage of the Vine, an engrafted branch! To commune with Him is to fellowship with Him so closely that we actually become one with Him! That is good news!

Jesus defined Himself as the Bread of Life in the passage found in John 6:25-63. After reading those Scriptures, it is easier to see that Jesus did not command His disciples to begin ritually eating bread and drinking wine in remembrance of Him. Instead, He commanded them to partake of Him spiritually and follow Him in His obedience unto death. As they gathered to eat their last meal together, the Passover, He revealed Himself to the disciples as the Passover Lamb.

Jesus imparted a spiritual and fundamental truth to the disciples in the picture of the Passover. If we try to interpret such spiritual things by way of our carnal mind, we come up with things like communion rituals and transubstantiation. The Holy Ghost was sent to interpret the Bread of Life to us, and the Spirit's interpretation is the only one that matters.

In the same way, Paul's references to communion and the Lord's supper were symbolic of this New Testament fellowship made available to all by the suffering, death and resurrection of Jesus. Paul was not inferring a physical ritual.

If a man speaks the truth in his heart, he will admit that a cracker and a cup of wine or grape juice can alone do nothing to make him feel a connection to Jesus. Performing a ritual is a religious exercise, and can cause one to feel righteous if they believe that righteousness comes from such a performance. However, religious feelings are not to be confused with intimate fellowship and living and active communication with the living and active God. God seeks those who worship Him in spirit and in truth, not in outward forms springing from the human will.

A ritual means nothing to God and has no power to hear you in your darkest hour. The only power big enough to truly deliver and change us is the very hand of the Lord Himself. If we confess our sins He is faithful and just to forgive us of our sins and cleanse of all unrighteousness (1 John 1:9); no ritual need be present as a go-between.

There is much confusion in Christianity today concerning what the Bible says about communion. In order to provide a definition of the word "communion" according to God's heart on the matter, we must carefully look at what the Word indeed tells us communion is.

> *And having taken bread, having given thanks, he brake and gave to them, saying,*
> *`This is my body, that for you is being given, this do ye—to remembrance of me.'*
> *In like manner, also, the cup after the supping, saying, `This cup [is] the new*
> *covenant in my blood, that for you is being poured forth.* Luke 22:19-20 (YLT)

To misread what God is telling us about His Son in this passage is to misunderstand what He is saying. First, we know that Jesus referred to Himself as the Bread of Life in John 6. Jesus is the Word, and the Word is to be our spiritual nourishment, our Bread. We also know that wine is a picture of the Spirit of God upon the Word, and that the cup symbolizes obedience unto death (as we can see from Jesus' prayers in the Garden of Gethsemane). The Spirit is the divine life force. Here, Jesus explains that He is the embodiment of the New Testament, the way, the truth, and the life. Jesus is our spiritual food and our spiritual drink, and without eating and drinking Him, our spirit man is not fed and does not grow.

Jesus called His disciples, on the night of the Passover, to follow Him and to take Him internally as sustenance and life. He explained that the way to follow Him was to drink the same cup of obedience that He was willing to drink for our redemption. Jesus is the firstfruits of the Spirit, the firstborn among many brethren, the Son whose image God has predestinated us to be conformed to. God desires each child born again into His kingdom to reach the full stature of Jesus Christ, and the way He has ordained for that to be accomplished is that we would take up our own cross daily and live a life of surrender to His will just as Jesus did.

In His High Priestly prayer, Jesus petitioned God to make us one with Him just as Jesus and God are one. That is certainly true communion—becoming intimately identified with Christ by partaking of His life and His sufferings.

By the power of God, Jesus was able to completely deny His flesh and live a life of sinless perfection. He overcame Satan and the world and eternally reigns as Lord of all things because He loved not His life unto death. He calls us to walk in His footsteps, to commune with Him, to lay down our lives for His sake as He did for ours. "This do in remembrance of me...."

In 1 Corinthians 10 and 11, God opens up to us the way that He defines idolatry. According to God, an idol is anything that we bow down to other than Him. If we lean on our understanding instead of Him, it is idolatry. If we give into temptations of the flesh we serve them, and bow down to them as gods. Paul told us that we must choose which altar we want to sacrifice ourselves upon, the altar of God or the altar of the fleshly self-life. By the same token, we can choose to partake of the Lord's spiritual food or partake of that which idols provide.

Paul draws the sharp contrast between true communion with the Most High God and communion with a dumb idol. Communion with the Lord is living and active, and meets our needs on every level. This is unlike any fellowship the world can concoct, for it is a connection between our body, soul, and spirit, and the Spirit of God. According to Psalm 139, God knows us completely, more intimately than we can comprehend. He longs to pour Himself into us in order that He might fill us with His very being. In doing so, God can reach into the very depths of who we are, shine His light on all that He sees and overcome everything inside that works against Him.

It is through this intimate fellowship with God, through trusting Him enough to allow Him access to every place within, that He can make us and mold us into a vessel He can use to bring glory to Himself. If we shy away from Him because of fear, we do not truly know His heart. If we keep Him at arm's length, we do not trust that He only wants the best for us. Both are traps of the enemy.

When Adam walked and talked with God in the cool of the evening He was having communion with the Lord. Adam was a perfect son of God, and he was able to spend time with God just as a son spends time with his father. God is the perfect father, and loves His children completely. He wants nothing more than to give us the very best of what He has, and He has everything! In Luke 11:11, God tells us that if we ask Him for bread He will not give us a stone. What a loving and perfect Father He is!

The oneness between Jesus and the Father is communion. The constant communication that took place between Jesus and His Father was brought about by complete submission to and dependence upon God. That is communion in its very highest form, and the very sort of communion God longs to have with us. We can have that by submitting our will completely to Him, as Jesus did.

Condemnation

H: 07561 rasha` {raw-shah'}; a primitive root; TWOT - 2222; v AV - condemn 15, wickedly 10, wicked 4, departed 2, trouble 1, vexed 1, wickedness 1; 34
1) to be wicked, act wickedly; 1a) (Qal); 1a1) to be wicked, act wickedly; 1a2) to be guilty, be condemned
1b) (Hiphil); 1b1) to condemn as guilty (in civil relations); 1b2) to condemn as guilty (in ethical or religious relations); 1b3) to act wickedly (in ethics and religion)
G: 2631 katakrima {kat-ak'-ree-mah}; from 2632; TDNT - 3:951,469; n n AV - condemnation 3; 3
1) damnatory sentence, condemnation
Unger's: As far as the justified believer is concerned, he faces no condemnation or judgment (Rom. 8:1). The guilt of his sin has been removed (Rom. 3:7), and he stands positionally "in Christ" and hence accepted "in the Beloved" (Eph. 1:6).

Conversion

H: 07725 shuwb {shoob}; a primitive root; TWOT - 2340; v AV - return 391, ...again 248, turn 123, ...back 65, ...away 56, restore 39, bring 34, render 19, answer 18, recompense 8, recover 6, deliver 5, put 5, withdraw 5, requite 4, misc 40; 1066
1) to return, turn back; 1a) (Qal); 1a1) to turn back, return; 1a1a) to turn back; 1a1b) to return, come or go back; 1a1c) to return unto, go back, come back; 1a1d) of dying; 1a1e) of human relations (fig); 1a1f) of spiritual relations (fig); 1a1f1) to turn back (from God), apostatize; 1a1f2) to turn away (of God); 1a1f3) to turn back (to God), repent; 1a1f4) turn back (from evil); 1a1g) of inanimate things; 1a1h) in repetition; 1b) (Polel); 1b1) to bring back; 1b2) to restore, refresh, repair (fig); 1b3) to lead away (enticingly); 1b4) to show turning, apostatize; 1c) (Pual) restored (participle); 1d) (Hiphil) to cause to return, bring back; 1d1) to bring back, allow to return, put back, draw back, give back, restore, relinquish, give in payment; 1d2) to bring back, refresh, restore; 1d3) to bring back, report to, answer; 1d4) to bring back, make requital, pay (as recompense) ; 1d5) to turn back or backward, repel, defeat, repulse, hinder, reject, refuse; 1d6) to turn away (face), turn toward; 1d7) to turn against; 1d8) to bring back to mind; 1d9) to show a turning away; 1d10) to reverse, revoke; 1e) (Hophal) to be returned, be restored, be brought back; 1f) (Pulal) brought back
G: 1994 epistrepho {ep-ee-stref'-o}; from 1909 and 4762; TDNT - 7:722,1093; v AV - turn 16, be converted 6, return 6, turn about 4, turn again 3, misc 4; 39
1) transitively; 1a) to turn to; 1a1) to the worship of the true God; 1b) to cause to return, to bring back; 1b1) to the love and obedience of God; 1b2) to the love for the children; 1b3) to love wisdom and righteousness; 2) intransitively; 2a) to turn to one's self; 2b) to turn one's self about, turn back; 2c) to return, turn back, come back

Covenant

H:1285 b@riyth {ber-eeth'}; from 01262 (in the sense of cutting [like 1254]); TWOT - 282a; n f AV - covenant 264, league 17, confederacy 1, confederate 1, confederate + 01167 1; 284
1) covenant, alliance, pledge; 1a) between men; 1a1) treaty, alliance, league (man to man); 1a2) constitution, ordinance (monarch to subjects); 1a3) agreement, pledge (man to man); 1a4) alliance (of friendship); 1a5) alliance (of marriage); 1b) between God and man; 1b1)

alliance (of friendship); 1b2) covenant (divine ordinance with signs or pledges); 2) (phrases); 2a) covenant making; 2b) covenant keeping; 2c) covenant violation

G:1242 diatheke {dee-ath-ay'-kay}; from 1303; TDNT - 2:106,157; n f AV - covenant 20, testament 13; 33

1) a disposition, arrangement, of any sort, which one wishes to; be valid, the last disposition which one makes of his earthly possessions after his death, a testament or will; 2) a compact, a covenant, a testament; 2a) God's covenant with Noah, etc.

Nave's (1279): -Sacred Jos 9:18-21 Ga 3:15; -Binding Jos 9:18-20 Jer 34:8-21 Eze 17:14-18 Ga 3:15; -Binding, not only on those who make them, but on those who are represented De 29:14,15; -Blood of Ex 24:8; -Book of Ex 24:7; -The Mosaic law called a covenant Ex 34:28; -of men with men Breach of, punished 2Sa 21:1-6 Jer 34:8-22 Eze 17:13-19; -of God with men Confirmed with an oath Ge 22:16 26:3 50:24 Ps 89:35 105:9 Lu 1:73 Heb 6:13,17,18; Binding Le 26:1 ... Jer 11:2,3 Ga 3:15; Everlasting Ge 8:20-22 9:1-17 Ps 105:8,10 Isa 54:10 61:8; God faithful to Le 26:44,45 De 4:31 7:8,9 Jud 2:1 1Ki 8:23 Ps 105:8-11 106:45 111:5 Mic 7:20; Repudiated by God on account of Jews' idolatry Jer 44:26,27 Heb 8:9; Broken by the Jews Jer 22:9 Eze 16:59 Heb 8:9;

Punishments for breaking of Le 26:25-46; instances of Of the sabbath Ex 31:16; Of the Ten Commandments Ex 34:28 De 5:2,3 9:9; With Adam Ge 2:16,17; Noah Ge 8:16 9:8-17; Abraham Ge 12:1-3 15:1 ... 17:1-22 Ex 6:4-8 Ps 105:8-11 Ro 9:7-13 Ga 3:1; -the second covenant Jer 31:31-34 Heb 8:4-13 12:18-24 13:20;

Covering

H: 03680 kacah {kaw-saw'}; a primitive root; TWOT - 1008; v AV - cover 135, hide 6, conceal 4, covering 2, overwhelmed 2, clad 1, closed 1, clothed 1; 152

1) to cover, conceal, hide; 1a) (Qal) conceal, covered (participle); 1b) (Niphal) to be covered; 1c) (Piel)

1c1) to cover, clothe; 1c2) to cover, conceal; 1c3) to cover (for protection); 1c4) to cover over, spread over; 1c5) to cover, overwhelm; 1d) (Pual); 1d1) to be covered; 1d2) to be clothed; 1e) (Hithpael) to cover oneself, clothe oneself

H: 03847 labash {law-bash'} or labesh {law-bashe'}; a primitive root; TWOT - 1075; v AV - clothe 51, put on 22, put 18, array 6, wear 4, armed 3, came 3, apparel 1, apparelled 1, clothed them 1, came upon 1, variant 1; 112

1) to dress, wear, clothe, put on clothing, be clothed; 1a) (Qal); 1a1) to put on clothes, be clothed, wear

1a2) to put on, be clothed with (fig.); 1b) (Pual) to be fully clothed; 1c) (Hiphil) to clothe, array with, dress

G: 4028 perikalupto {per-ee-kal-oop'-to}; from 4012 and 2572;; v AV - cover 1, blindfold 1, overlay 1; 3

to cover all around, to cover up, cover over

G: 4018 peribolaion {per-ib-ol'-ah-yon}; from a presumed derivative of 4016; n n AV - covering 1, vesture 1; 2

1) a covering thrown around, a wrapper; 1a) a mantle; 1b) a veil

Create

H: 01254 bara' {baw-raw'}; a primitive root; TWOT - 278; v AV - create 42, creator 3, choose 2, make 2, cut down 2, dispatch 1, done 1, make fat 1; 54

to create, shape, form; 1a) (Qal) to shape, fashion, create (always with God as subject); 1a1) of heaven and earth; 1a2) of individual man; 1a3) of new conditions and circumstances; 1a4) of transformations; 1b) (Niphal) to be created; 1b1) of heaven and earth; 1b2) of birth; 1b3) of something new; 1b4) of miracles; 1c) (Piel); 1c1) to cut down; 1c2) to cut out; 2) to be fat; 2a) (Hiphil) to make yourselves fat

G: 2936 ktizo {ktid'-zo}; probably akin to 2932 (through the idea of proprietor-ship of the manufacturer); TDNT - 3:1000,481; v AV - create 12, Creator 1, make 1; 14
1) to make habitable, to people, a place, region, island; 1a) to found a city, colony, state; 2) to create; 2a) of God creating the worlds; 2b) to form, shape, i.e. to completely change or transform

Cross
G: 4716 stauros {stow-ros'}; from the base of 2476; TDNT - 7:572,1071; n m AV - cross 28; 28
1) an upright stake, esp. a pointed one; 2) a cross; 2a) a well known instrument of most cruel and ignominious punishment, borrowed by the Greeks and Romans from the Phoenicians; to it were affixed among the Romans, down to the time of Constantine the Great, the guiltiest criminals, particularly the basest slaves, robbers, the authors and abetters of insurrections, and occasionally in the provinces, at the arbitrary pleasure of the governors, upright and peaceable men also, and even Roman citizens themselves; 2b) the crucifixion which Christ underwent
Nave's (1282): figurative Mt 10:38 16:34 Mr 8:34 10:21 Lu 9:23 14:27 1 Co 1:17, 18 Ga 5:11 6:14 Php 3:18

D-E

Doctrine
H: 03948 leqach {leh'-kakh}; from 03947; TWOT - 1124a; n m AV - doctrine 4, learning 4, fair speech 1; 9
1) learning, teaching, insight; 1a) instruction (obj); 1b) teaching (thing taught); 1b1) teaching-power
1b2) persuasiveness
G: 1322 didache {did-akh-ay'}; from 1321; TDNT - 2:163,161; n f AV - doctrine 29, has been taught 1; 30
1) teaching; 1a) that which is taught; 1b) doctrine, teaching, concerning something; 2) the act of teaching, instruction; 2a) in religious assemblies of the Christians, to speak in the way of teaching, in distinction from other modes of speaking in public
Nave's (1469): General scriptures concerning Joh 7:16,17; Guidelines set forth from the leaders in Jerusalem Ac 15:6-29; false Mt 5:19 15:9,13 Ro 16:17,18 1Co 3:1-4,11,21 11:18,19 2Co 2:17 11:3,4 Ga 1:6-8 Eph 4:14 Col 2:4,8,18-23 1Ti 1:3,4,6,7,19 4:1-3,7 6:3-5,20,21 2Ti 2:14,16-18 3:6-9,13 4:3 Tit 1:10,11,14 3:10,11 Heb 13:9 2Pe 2:1-22 1Jo 4:3 2Jo 1:7-9 Jude 1:4-11

Earth
H: 0776 'erets {eh'-rets}; from an unused root probably meaning to be firm; TWOT - 167; n f AV - land 1543, earth 712, country 140, ground 98, world 4, way 3, common 1, field 1, nations 1, wilderness + 04057 1; 2504
1) land, earth; 1a) earth; 1a1) whole earth (as opposed to a part); 1a2) earth (as opposed to heaven); 1a3) earth (inhabitants); 1b) land; 1b1) country, territory; 1b2) district, region; 1b3) tribal territory; 1b4) piece of ground; 1b5) land of Canaan, Israel; 1b6) inhabitants of land; 1b7) Sheol, land without return, (under) world
1b8) city (-state); 1c) ground, surface of the earth; 1c1) ground; 1c2) soil; 1d) (in phrases); 1d1) people of the land; 1d2) space or distance of country (in measurements of distance); 1d3) level or plain country; 1d4) land of the living; 1d5) end(s) of the earth; 1e) (almost wholly late in usage); 1e1) lands, countries; 1e1a) often in contrast to Canaan
G: 1093 ge {ghay}; contracted from a root word; TDNT - 1:677,116; n f AV - earth 188, land 42, ground 18, country 2, world 1, earthly + 1537 + 3588 1; 252

1) arable land; 2) the ground, the earth as a standing place; 3) the main land as opposed to the sea or water; 4) the earth as a whole; 4a) the earth as opposed to the heavens; 4b) the inhabited earth, the abode of men and animals; 5) a country, land enclosed within fixed boundaries, a tract of land, territory, region
Nave's (1527): Primitive condition of Ge 1:6,7 Job 26:7 Ps 104:5-9; Design of Isa 45:18; Cursed of God Ge 3:17,18 Ro 8:19-22; God's footstool Isa 66:1 La 2:1; Given to man Ps 115:16; Early divisions of Ge 10:1 11:1 De 32:8; Perpetuity of Ge 49:26 De 33:15 Ps 78:69 104:5 Ec 1:4 Hab 3:6; A new earth Isa 65:17 66:22 Re 21:1; created by God Ge 1:1 2Ki 19:15 2Ch 2:12 Ne 9:6 Ps 90:2 102:25 115:15 146:6 Pr 8:22-26 Isa 37:16 45:18 Jer 10:12 27:5 32:17 51:15 Joh 17:24 2Pe 3:5 Re 10:6 14:7; by Christ Joh 1:3,10 Heb 1:10 destruction of Ps 102:25-27 Isa 24:19,20 51:6 Mt 5:18 24:3,14,29-31,35-39 Mr 13:24-37 Lu 21:26-36 Heb 1:10-12 2Pe 3:10-13 Re 20:11 21:1

Eden
H: 05731 `Eden {ay'-den}; the same as 05730; TWOT - 1568; AV - Eden 17; 17 Eden= "pleasure"; n pr m loc
1) the first habitat of man after the creation; site unknown; n pr m; 2) a Gershonite Levite, son of Joah in the days of king Hezekiah of Judah
Nave's (1548): 1. The garden of Eden Ge 2:8-17 3:23,24 4:16 Isa 51:3 Eze 28:13 31:9,16,18 36:35 Joe 2:3; 2. A marketplace of costly merchandise 2Ki 19:12 Isa 37:12 Eze 27:23 Am 1:5

Edify
G: 3618 oikodomeo {oy-kod-om-eh'-o} also oikodomos {oy-kod-om'-os} Ac 4:11; from the same as 3619; TDNT - 5:136,674; v AV - build 24, edify 7, builder 5, build up 1, be in building 1, embolden 1; 39
1) to build a house, erect a building; 1a) to build (up from the foundation); 1b) to restore by building, to rebuild, repair; 2) metaph.; 2a) to found, establish; 2b) to promote growth in Christian wisdom, affection, grace, virtue, holiness, blessedness; 2c) to grow in wisdom and piety

Eternal
H: 06924 qedem {keh'-dem} or qedmah {kayd'-maw}; from 06923; TWOT - 1988a; AV - east 32, old 17, eastward 11, ancient 6, east side 5, before 3, east part 2, ancient time 2, aforetime 1, eternal 1, misc 7; 87 n m
1) east, antiquity, front, that which is before, aforetime; 1a) front, from the front or east, in front, mount of the East; 1b) ancient time, aforetime, ancient, from of old, earliest time; 1c) anciently, of old (adverb); 1d) beginning; 1e) east adv; 2) eastward, to or toward the East
G: 166 aionios {ahee-o'-nee-os}; from 165; TDNT - 1:208,31; adj AV - eternal 42, everlasting 25, the world began + 5550 2, since the world began + 5550 1, for ever 1; 71
1) without beginning and end, that which always has been and always will be; 2) without beginning; 3) without end, never to cease, everlasting
Nave's (1740): Eternity — God inhabits Isa 57:15 Mic 5:2; God rules Jer 10:10; unclassified scriptures relating to Ps 30:12 41:13 72:17 90:2 110:4 119:142 Mt 6:13 18:8 2Co 9:9 Jude 1:6
Nave's (3086) life everlasting — Called Spirit of God Job 27:3; Tree of Ge 2:9 3:22,24 Pr 3:18 13:12 Re 2:7; What can a man give in exchange for Mt 16:26 Mr 8:37; The one who loses it will save it Mt 10:39 16:25,26 Lu 9:24 Joh 12:25; Life of Christ, a ransom Mt 20:28 Mr 10:45 1Ti 2:6; from God Ge 2:7 De 8:3 30:20 32:39,40 1Sa 2:6 Job 27:3 34:14,15 Ps 22:29 30:3 68:20 104:30 Ec 12:7 Isa 38:16-20 Ac 17:25-28 Ro 4:17 1Ti 6:13 Jas 4:15; spiritual Joh 3:3-16 5:24-26,40 6:27,33,35,40,47 10:10 11:25,26 14:6 17:2,3 20:31 Ro 6:4,5,8,11,13,22,23 8:10 1Jo 1:1,2

F

Faith

H: 0530 'emuwnah {em-oo-naw'} or (shortened) 'emunah {em-oo-naw'}; from 0529; TWOT - 116e; n f AV - faithfulness 18, truth 13, faithfully 5, office 5, faithful 3, faith 1, stability 1, steady 1, truly 1, verily 1; 49
1) firmness, fidelity, steadfastness, steadiness
G: 4102 pistis {pis'-tis}; from 3982; TDNT - 6:174,849; n f AV - faith 239, assurance 1, believe + 1537 1, belief 1, them that believe 1, fidelity 1; 244
1) conviction of the truth of anything, belief; in the NT of a conviction or belief respecting man's relationship to God and divine things, generally with the included idea of trust and holy fervor born of faith and joined with it; 1a) relating to God; 1a1) the conviction that God exists and is the creator and ruler of all things, the provider and bestower of eternal salvation through Christ; 1b) relating to Christ; 1b1) a strong and welcome conviction or belief that Jesus is the Messiah, through whom we obtain eternal salvation in the kingdom of God; 1c) the religious beliefs of Christians; 1d) belief with the predominate idea of trust (or confidence) whether in God or in Christ, springing from faith in the same; 2) fidelity, faithfulness; 2a) the character of one who can be relied on
Nave's (1808): General scriptures concerning 2Sa 22:31 Ps 2:12 5:11 7:1 9:9,10 18:30 32:10 33:18,19 34:1-8,22 36:7 40:4 64:10 78:5-7 84:5,12 112:5,7,8 118:8,9 125:1 147:11 Pr 3:5 14:26 22:19 28:25 29:25 30:5 Isa 10:20 14:32 26:3 30:15 57:13 Jer 17:7,8 39:18 Na 1:7 Mt 9:22 21:21,22 Mr 9:23,24 11:23,24 Lu 7:50 8:48-50 17:5 18:8 Joh 11:25-27 Ac 3:16 13:48 26:18 Ro 1:16,17 4:1-25 5:1 9:31-33 10:6-10 11:20,23 15:13 1Co 1:21 2:5 12:8,9 2Co 1:24 Ga 3:1-29 5:22 Eph 2:8 6:16 Col 1:23 2:12 1Th 2:13 5:8 2Th 2:13 1Ti 1:5,19 2:15 4:10 6:11,12,17 2Ti 4:7,8 Heb 4:1-11 6:1,7,12,18 10:35,38,39 11:1-39 13:5,6 Jas 1:6 2:1-26 1Pe 1:5,7,9,21 3:5 1Jo 3:21 5:4 Re 22:7; faith in Christ (1808) enjoined Ex 14:13 Nu 21:34 De 1:21-31 3:2,22 7:17-21 20:1 31:6-8,23 Jos 1:5-9 10:25 Jud 6:14-16 2Ki 19:6,7 2Ch 15:7 16:9 20:15,17,20 32:7,8 Ne 4:14 Job 35:14 Ps 4:5 27:14 31:19,24 37:3,5,7,39,40 55:22 62:8 115:9,11 130:7 Pr 3:5,6,24-26 16:3 Isa 26:4,20 35:3,4 37:6 41:10,13,14 43:1,2,5,10 44:2,8 50:10 Jer 42:11 49:11 Joe 2:21 3:16 Hab 2:3,4 Zep 3:16,17 Zec 8:9 9:12 Mt 6:25-34 17:18-20 Mr 1:15 11:22-24 Lu 12:22-32 17:6; examples of faith in Christ Isa 28:16 Mt 7:24,25 8:2,13 9:22,29 11:6,28-30 14:27 15:28 17:7 Mr 5:36 9:23 16:16 Lu 6:46-49 7:9,50 8:50 17:6 18:42 Joh 1:12 3:14-16,18,36 5:24 6:20,29,35,45,47 7:38 9:35 11:25,26,40 12:36,44,46 13:7,20 14:1,11,12 16:27,33 18:37 20:27,29,31 Ac 3:16 10:43 15:9,11 16:31 20:21 26:18 Ro 3:22-28 9:33 10:4,9 Ga 2:16 3:1-29 5:6 Eph 1:12-14 3:12,17 4:13 Php 3:9 Col 2:7 1Ti 1:16 2Ti 1:13 2:1 3:15 Heb 4:16 6:19 10:22 12:2 13:7 1Pe 1:8 2:6,7 2Pe 1:1 1Jo 3:23 5:4,5,10,13,14 Jude 1:21 Re 1:17 3:18,20; trial of 1Ch 29:17 Ps 26:2 81:7 Mt 13:19-22 24:21-25 Lu 8:13,14 2Th 1:3-5 Heb 6:13-15 Jas 1:3,12 1Pe 1:7; sum total of religious belief and life Ro 1:8 Jude 1:3
NT Definition: "Faith is the substance of things hoped for, the evidence of things not seen." (Heb. 11:1)

Fasting

H: 6684 tsuwm {tsoom}; a primitive root; TWOT - 1890; v AV - fast 20, at all 1; 21
1) (Qal) to abstain from food, fast
G: 3521 nesteia {nace-ti'-ah}; from 3522; TDNT - 4:924,632; n f AV - fasting 7, feast 1; 8
1) a fasting, fast; 1a) a voluntary, as a religious exercise; 1a1) of private fasting; 1a2) the public fast as prescribed by the Mosaic Law and kept yearly on the great day of atonement, the tenth of the month of Tisri (the month Tisri comprises a part of our September and October); 1b) a fasting caused by want or poverty
Nave's (1822) Observed on occasions of public calamities 2Sa 1:12; Afflictions Ps 35:13 Da 6:18; Private afflictions 2Sa 12:16; Approaching danger Es 4:16; Ordination of ministers Ac 13:3 14:23; Accompanied by prayer Da 9:3; Confession of sin 1Sa 7:6 Ne 9:1,2; Humiliation

De 9:18 Ne 9:1; During forty days Moses De 9:9,18; Jesus Mt 4:1,2 Mr 1:12,13 Lu 4:1,2; Habitual by John's disciples Mt 9:14; by Anna Lu 2:37; by Pharisees Mt 9:14 Mr 2:18 Lu 18:12; by Cornelius Ac 10:30; by Paul 2Co 6:5 11:27; In times of bereavement of the people of Jabesh-gilead, for Saul and his sons 1Sa 31:13 1Ch 10:12; of David, at the time of Saul's death 2Sa 1:12; of Abner's death 2Sa 3:35; Prolonged for three weeks, by Daniel Da 10:2,3; for forty days, by Moses Ex 24:18 34:28 De 9:9,18; Elijah 1Ki 19:8; Jesus Mt 4:2; Unclassified scriptures Ezr 8:21-23 Ps 35:13 69:10 Isa 58:3-7 Jer 14:12 Da 10:3 Joe 1:14 2:12,13 Zec 7:5 8:19 Mt 6:16-18 9:14,15 17:21 Ac 27:9,33,34 1Co 7:5

Isaiah 58:1-14—1 Cry aloud, spare not, lift up thy voice like a trumpet, and shew my people their transgression, and the house of Jacob their sins. 2 Yet they seek me daily, and delight to know my ways, as a nation that did righteousness, and forsook not the ordinance of their God: they ask of me the ordinances of justice; they take delight in approaching to God. 3 Wherefore have we fasted, [say they], and thou seest not? [wherefore] have we afflicted our soul, and thou takest no knowledge? Behold, in the day of your fast ye find pleasure, and exact all your labors. 4 Behold, ye fast for strife and debate, and to smite with the fist of wickedness: ye shall not fast as [ye do this] day, to make your voice to be heard on high. 5 Is it such a fast that I have chosen? a day for a man to afflict his soul? [is it] to bow down his head as a bulrush, and to spread sackcloth and ashes [under him]? wilt thou call this a fast , and an acceptable day to the LORD? 6 [Is] not this the fast that I have chosen? to loose the bands of wickedness, to undo the heavy burdens, and to let the oppressed go free, and that ye break every yoke? 7 [Is it] not to deal thy bread to the hungry, and that thou bring the poor that are cast out to thy house? when thou seest the naked, that thou cover him; and that thou hide not thyself from thine own flesh? 8 Then shall thy light break forth as the morning, and thine health shall spring forth speedily: and thy righteousness shall go before thee; the glory of the LORD shall be thy reward. 9 Then shalt thou call, and the LORD shall answer; thou shalt cry, and he shall say, Here I [am]. If thou take away from the midst of thee the yoke, the putting forth of the finger, and speaking vanity; 10 And [if] thou draw out thy soul to the hungry, and satisfy the afflicted soul; then shall thy light rise in obscurity, and thy darkness [be] as the noonday: 11 And the LORD shall guide thee continually, and satisfy thy soul in drought, and make fat thy bones: and thou shalt be like a watered garden, and like a spring of water, whose waters fail not. 12 And [they that shall be] of thee shall build the old waste places: thou shalt raise up the foundations of many generations; and thou shalt be called, The repairer of the breach, The restorer of paths to dwell in. 13 If thou turn away thy foot from the sabbath, [from] doing thy pleasure on my holy day; and call the sabbath a delight, the holy of the LORD, honorable; and shalt honor him, not doing thine own ways, nor finding thine own pleasure, nor speaking [thine own] words: 14 Then shalt thou delight thyself in the LORD; and I will cause thee to ride upon the high places of the earth, and feed thee with the heritage of Jacob thy father: for the mouth of the LORD hath spoken [it].

Fivefold Ministry—apostles, prophets, teachers, evangelists, pastors

H: 08335 shareth {shaw-rayth'}; infinitive of 08334; TWOT - 2472a; n m AV - ministry 1, minister 1; 2
1) ministry, religious ministry, service in the tabernacle Body of Christ
G: 1248 diakonia {dee-ak-on-ee'-ah}; from 1249; TDNT - 2:87,152; n f AV - ministry 16, ministration 6, ministering 3, misc 9; 34
1) service, ministering, esp. of those who execute the commands of others; 2) of those who by the command of God proclaim and promote religion among men; 2a) of the office of Moses; 2b) of the office of the apostles and its administration; 2c) of the office of prophets, evangelists, elders etc.; 3) the ministration of those who render to others the offices of Christian affection esp. those who help meet need by either

collecting or distributing of charities; 4) the office of the deacon in the church; 5) the service of those who prepare and present food

Nave's (3408): minister, Christian (a sacred teacher) —

Called ambassadors for Christ 2Co 5:20; angels of the Church Re 1:20 2:1; apostles Lu 6:13 Re 18:20; apostles of Jesus Tit 1:1; defenders of the faith Php 1:7; elders 1Ti 5:17 1Pe 5:1; evangelists Eph 4:11 2Ti 4:5; fishers of men Mt 4:19 Mr 1:17; laborers Mt 9:38 Phm 1:1 1Th 3:2; lights Joh 5:35; men of God De 33:1 1Ti 6:11; messengers Mal 2:7; Isa 61:6 2Co 6:4; overseers Ac 20:28; pastors Jer 3:15 Joh 21:16-18 Eph 4:11; preachers Ro 10:14 1Ti 2:7 2Pe 2:5; shepherds Jer 23:4; soldiers of Christ Php 2:25 2Ti 2:3,4; stars Re 1:20 2:1; stewards — Tit 1:7; of the grace of God 1Pe 4:10; of the mysteries of God 1Co 4:1; teachers Isa 30:20 Eph 4:11; watchmen Isa 62:6 Eze 33:7; witnesses Ac 1:8 5:32 26:16; Compared to sowers Ps 126:6 Mt 13:3-8 Mr 4:3-20 Lu 8:5-8; Teachers of schools 1Sa 19:20 2Ki 2:3,5,15 4:38 2Ch 15:3 17:7-9 Ac 13:1; Examples to the flock Php 3:17 2Th 3:9 1Ti 4:12 1Pe 5:3; Message of, rejected Eze 33:30-33; God's care of 1Ki 17:1-16 19:1-18 Isa 30:20 Mt 10:29-31 Lu 12:6,7; Defended Jer 26:16-19; Beloved Ac 20:37,38 21:5,6; call of Ex 28:1 Nu 3:5-13 1Sa 3:4-10 1Ki 19:16,19 1Ch 23:13 Isa 6:8-10 Jer 1:5 Am 2:11 Jon 1:1,2 3:1,2 Mt 4:18-22 9:9 Mr 1:17-20 2:14 Lu 10:1,2 Joh 1:43 Ac 13:2,3 20:24 22:12-15 26:14-18 Ro 1:1 10:14,15 1Co 1:1,27,28 9:16-19 2Co 1:1 5:18-20 Ga 1:15,16 Eph 3:7,8 4:11,12 Col 1:1,25-29 4:17 1Ti 1:12-14 2:7 2Ti 1:11 Tit 1:3 Heb 5:4; character and attributes of Le 10:3-11 21:6 Nu 16:9,10 De 32:1-3 1Sa 2:35 12:7 2Ch 6:41 29:11 Ezr 7:10 Ps 68:11 Pr 11:30 Isa 6:5-8 32:20 52:11 Jer 1:7,8 3:15 20:9 Eze 34:1-31 Mal 2:6,7 Mt 10:16-24 11:25,26 13:51,52 20:25-28 23:8-11 24:45 Lu 6:39 10:21 12:42-44 22:27 24:49 Joh 3:27,34 4:36-38 10:2-5,11-15 13:13-17 15:20,21 17:16-18,20 Ac 1:8 4:8,31 6:3,4 20:22-24 Ro 2:21-23 1Co 1:23,27-30 2:2 3:7-10 4:10-13 9:16-23,27 15:10 2Co 2:15-17 3:6-10 4:1-10 5:11,18-20 6:3-7 10:1,2,8 13:10 Ga 2:8 6:17 Php 3:17 1Th 2:3-12 1Ti 3:1-15 5:17,21 6:11,13,14,20,21 2Ti 1:6-8,13,14 2:1-7,14-16,20-26 3:14,16,17 Tit 1:5-9,13,14 2:1,7,8,15 3:1,2,8,9 Heb 5:1-3,12-14 13:6,7,9,17 Jas 3:1,13,16,17 1Pe 4:10,11; duties of Ex 4:12 Le 10:8-11 Jos 1:8 2Ki 17:27,28 2Ch 29:11 Isa 40:1-3,9,11 52:11 57:14 58:1 62:6,7 Jer 1:7,8,17-19 4:15 6:27 15:19-21 23:4,22,28 26:2 Eze 2:6-8 3:8-10,17-21,27 6:11 33:1-9 34:2-31 44:23 Joe 1:13-15 2:17 Jon 1:2 Na 1:15 Hab 2:2 Mal 2:7 Mt 7:6 10:7,11-13,16,25,27,28 16:19 18:5,6,18 20:25-28 28:19,20 Mr 10:43-45 Lu 9:48 22:32 24:48 Joh 3:34 4:35-38 15:27 20:23 21:15-17 Ac 1:21,22 5:20 6:2,4 10:42 16:4 18:9,10 20:28 22:15 26:16-18 Ro 1:14,15 12:3-8 1Co 1:16 4:1,2,21 9:16,17 2Co 1:24 4:1,2,5 5:14,18,20 6:3-10 7:4-9,12,15 8:23 10:8 12:15,19 13:2,10 Ga 1:10 Eph 3:8-10 4:11,12 6:20 Col 4:17 1Th 2:4-8,10-12 3:2 5:12 2Th 3:4 1Ti 1:3,4,11,18,19 2:7 4:6,7,12-16 5:1-3,7-11,19-22 6:3,4,10-14,17-21 2Ti 1:6-8 2:2-7,14-16,23-25 4:1,2,5 1Pe 5:1-4 2Pe 1:12-16; false and corrupt De 13:1-5 18:20-22 1Ki 12:31 2Ch 29:34 30:15 Ne 13:29 Pr 19:27 Isa 3:12 5:20 8:19,20 9:14-16 28:7 29:10,11 30:10 43:27,28 44:20 56:10-12 Jer 2:8 5:13,14,30,31 6:13,14 8:10,11 10:21 12:10 13:20 14:13-16 23:1,2,11,14-16,21,25-39 27:9-18 48:10 50:6 La 2:14 4:13,14 Eze 13:1-23 14:9,10 22:25,26,28 34:1-31 44:8,10 Ho 4:6,8-13 5:1 6:9 9:7,8 Am 2:11,12 Mic 2:11 3:5-7,11 Zep 3:4 Zec 10:3 11:4,5,16,17 13:2-5 Mal 1:6-10 2:1-3,8,9 Mt 5:19 7:15,22,23 15:9,14 20:20-27 23:3,4,13 24:4,5,24,26,48-51 Mr 9:33-35 10:35-37 13:21,22 Lu 6:39 9:46 11:35,46-52 12:45,46 21:8 22:24 Joh 3:10 5:43 10:1,5,8,10-13 Ac 20:29,30 Ro 2:19-25 16:17,18 1Co 3:1-4,10-16,21 11:18,19 2Co 2:17 11:1-31 Ga 1:6-8 5:10 Eph 4:14 Php 1:15,16 3:2 Col 2:4,8,18,19 1Ti 1:3-7,19 4:1-3,7 6:3-5,20,21 2Ti 2:14-18 3:6-9,13 4:3 Tit 1:10-14 3:10,11 Heb 13:9 2Pe 2:1-22 3:16 1Jo 2:18,26 4:1-3,5 2Jo 1:7-10 3Jo 1:10 Jude 1:4-11 Re 2:1,2,12,14,15,18,20-23; promises to, joys of 2Sa 23:6,7 Ps 126:5,6 Jer 1:7-10,17-19 20:11 Da 12:3 Mt 10:28-31 28:20 Lu 12:11,12 24:49 Joh 4:36-38 Ac 1:4,5,8 1Co 9:9,10 2Co 2:14-16 7:6,7 Php 2:16 1Th 2:13,19,20 3:8,9 3Jo 1:4; trials and persecutions of 1Ki 19:1-10 Isa 20:2,3 Eze 24:15-18 Ho 1:2 Am 5:10 7:10-17 Mt 10:16-27 23:34 Joh 13:16 1Co 2:1-4 4:9-13 2Co 6:4-10 7:5 11:23-33 12:7-12 Ga 4:13,14 Eph 3:1,13 (see Absolute 5 for an in-depth definition)

213

Flesh

H: 01320 basar {baw-sawr'}; from 01319; TWOT - 291a; n m AV - flesh 256, body 2, fatfleshed + 01277 2, leanfleshed + 01851 2, kin 2, leanfleshed + 07534 1, mankind + 0376 1, myself 1, nakedness 1, skin 1; 269

1) flesh; 1a) of the body; 1a1) of humans; 1a2) of animals; 1b) the body itself; 1c) male organ of generation (euphemism); 1d) kindred, blood-relations; 1e) flesh as frail or erring (man against God); 1f) all living things
1g) animals; 1h) mankind

G: 4561 sarx {sarx}; probably from the base of 4563; TDNT - 7:98,1000; n f AV - flesh 147, carnal 2, carnally minded + 5427 1, fleshly 1; 151

1) flesh (the soft substance of the living body, which covers the bones and is permeated with blood) of both man and beasts; 2) the body; 2a) the body of a man; 2b) used of natural or physical origin, generation or
relationship; 2b1) born of natural generation; 2c) the sensuous nature of man, "the animal nature"; 2c1) without any suggestion of depravity; 2c2) the animal nature with cravings which incite to sin; 2c3) the physical nature of man as subject to suffering; 3) a living creature (because possessed of a body of flesh)
whether man or beast; 4) the flesh, denotes mere human nature, the earthly nature of man apart from divine influence, and therefore prone to sin and opposed to God
Nave's (1411) depravity of man — General Scriptures concerning Ge 8:21 6:5-7,11-13 8:21 De 32:10 2Ch 6:36 Job 4:17-19 9:2,3,20,29,30 11:12 14:4 15:14-16 25:4-6 Ps 5:9 14:1-3 51:5 53:1-3 58:1-5 94:11 130:3 143:2 Pr 10:20 20:6,9 21:8 Ec 7:20,29 8:11 9:3 Isa 1:5,6 42:6,7 43:8 48:8 51:1 53:6 64:6 Jer 2:22,29 6:7 13:23 16:12 17:9 Eze 16:6 36:25,26 37:1-3 Ho 6:7 14:9 Mic 7:2-4 Mt 7:17 12:34,35 15:19 Mr 7:21-23 Lu 1:79 Joh 1:10,11 3:19 8:23 14:17 Ac 8:23 Ro 2:1 3:9-19,23 5:6,12-14 6:6,17,19,20 7:5,11,13-15,18-21,23, 25 8:5-8,13 11:32 1Co 2:14 3:3 5:9,10 2Co 3:4,5 5:14 Ga 3:10,11,22 5:17,19-21 Eph 2:1-3,11,12 4:17-19,22 5:8,14 Col 1:13,21 2:13 3:5,7 2Ti 2:26 Tit 3:3 Jas 3:2 4:5 1Pe 1:18 2:9,25 1Jo 1:8,10 2:16 3:10 5:19 Re 3:17

Fornication

H: 02181 zanah {zaw-naw'}; a primitive root [highly-fed and therefore wanton]; TWOT - 563; v AV - ...harlot 36, go a whoring 19, ...whoredom 15, whore 11, commit fornication 3, whorish 3, harlot + 0802 2, commit 1, continually 1, great 1, whore's + 0802 1; 93

1) to commit fornication, be a harlot, play the harlot; 1a) (Qal); 1a1) to be a harlot, act as a harlot, commit fornication; 1a2) to commit adultery; 1a3) to be a cult prostitute; 1a4) to be unfaithful (to God) (fig.); 1b) (Pual) to play the harlot; 1c) (Hiphil); 1c1) to cause to commit adultery; 1c2) to force into prostitution; 1c3) to commit fornication
G: 4202 porneia {por-ni'-ah}; from 4203; TDNT - 6:579,918; n f AV - fornication 26; 26
1) illicit sexual intercourse; 1a) adultery, fornication, homosexuality, lesbianism, intercourse with animals etc.; 1b) sexual intercourse with close relatives; Lev. 18; 2) metaphorically, the worship of idols; 2a) of the defilement of idolatry, as incurred by eating the sacrifices offered to idols

Forgive

H: 05375 nasa' {naw-saw'} or nacah (Ps 4 : 6 [7]) {naw-saw'}; a primitive root; TWOT - 1421; v AV - (bare, lift, etc...) up 219, bear 115, take 58, bare 34, carry 30, (take, carry)..away 22, borne 22, armourbearer 18, forgive 16, accept 12, exalt 8, regard 5, obtained 4, respect 3, misc 74; 654

1) to lift, bear up, carry, take; 1a) (Qal); 1a1) to lift, lift up; 1a2) to bear, carry, support, sustain, endure

1a3) to take, take away, carry off, forgive; 1b) (Niphal); 1b1) to be lifted up, be exalted; 1b2) to lift oneself up, rise up; 1b3) to be borne, be carried; 1b4) to be taken away, be carried off, be swept away; 1c) (Piel)
1c1) to lift up, exalt, support, aid, assist; 1c2) to desire, long (fig.); 1c3) to carry, bear continuously; 1c4) to take, take away; 1d) (Hithpael) to lift oneself up, exalt oneself; 1e) (Hiphil); 1e1) to cause one to bear (iniquity); 1e2) to cause to bring, have brought
H: 05545 calach {saw-lakh'}; a primitive root; TWOT - 1505; v AV - forgive 19, forgiven 13, pardon 13, spare 1; 46
1) to forgive, pardon; 1a) (Qal) to forgive, pardon; 1b) (Niphal) to be forgiven
G: 863 aphiemi {af-ee'-ay-mee}; from 575 and hiemi (to send, an intens. form of eimi, to go); TDNT - 1:509,88; v AV - leave 52, forgive 47, suffer 14, let 8, forsake 6, let alone 6, misc 13; 146
1) to send away; 1a) to bid going away or depart; 1a1) of a husband divorcing his wife; 1b) to send forth, yield up, to expire; 1c) to let go, let alone, let be; 1c1) to disregard; 1c2) to leave, not to discuss now, (a topic); 1c21) of teachers, writers and speakers; 1c3) to omit, neglect; 1d) to let go, give up a debt, forgive, to remit; 1e) to give up, keep no longer; 2) to permit, allow, not to hinder, to give up a thing to a person; 3) to leave, go way from one; 3a) in order to go to another place; 3b) to depart from any one; 3c) to depart from one and leave him to himself so that all mutual claims are abandoned; 3d) to desert wrongfully; 3e) to go away leaving something behind; 3f) to leave one by not taking him as a companion; 3g) to leave on dying, leave behind one; 3h) to leave so that what is left may remain, leave remaining; 3i) abandon, leave destitute
G: 5483 charizomai {khar-id'-zom-ahee}; middle voice from 5485; TDNT - 9:372,1298; v AV - forgive 11, give 6, freely give 2, deliver 2, grant 1, frankly forgive 1; 23
1) to do something pleasant or agreeable (to one), to do a favour to, gratify; 1a) to show one's self gracious, kind, benevolent; 1b) to grant forgiveness, to pardon; 1c) to give graciously, give freely, bestow; 1c1) to forgive; 1c2) graciously to restore one to another; 1c3) to preserve for one a person in peril
Nave's (1898): of enemies Ex 23:4,5 Pr 19:11 24:17,29 25:21,22 Ec 7:21 Mt 5:7,39-41,43-48 6:12,14,15 18:21-35 Mr 11:25,26 Lu 6:27-37 11:4 17:3,4 Ro 12:14,17,19-21 1Co 4:12,13 Eph 4:32 Col 3:13 Phm 1:10-18 1Pe 3:9; Sin, forgiveness of Ex 34:6,7 Le 4:20,26,31,35 5:4-13 Nu 14:18,20 15:25 2Sa 12:13 1Ki 8:22-50 Job 10:14 Ps 19:12 25:7,11,18 32:1,2,5 51:9 65:3 79:9 85:2,3 99:8 103:12 130:4 Isa 1:18 6:6,7 43:25,26 44:21,22 55:6,7 Jer 2:22 5:1,7 31:34 33:8 Eze 18:21,22 33:14-16 Mt 1:21 3:6 6:12,14,15 9:2,6 12:31,32 18:23-27,35 26:28 Mr 2:5,7 3:28 11:26 Lu 3:3 5:21,24 12:10 24:47 Joh 8:11 20:23 Ac 2:38 10:36,43 13:38,39 26:16-18 Ro 4:7,8 Eph 4:32 Col 2:13 Heb 8:12 9:22 10:2,17,18 Jas 5:15,20 1Jo 1:7,9 2:1,2,12 5:16 Re 1:5

Fruit of the spirit
Love, joy, peace, longsuffering, gentleness, goodness, faith, meekness, temperance (Gal. 5:22-23)

G

Garden
H: 01588 gan {gan}; from 01598; TWOT - 367a; AV - garden 42; 42; n m/f
1) garden, enclosure; 1a) enclosed garden; 1a1) (fig. of a bride); 1b) garden (of plants); n pr loc
1c) Garden of Eden
H: 01598 ganan {gaw-nan'}; a primitive root; TWOT - 367; v AV - defend 8; 8
1) to defend, cover, surround; 1a) (Qal) to defend; 1b) (Hiphil) to defend

Gifts of the Spirit
Wisdom, knowledge, faith, healing, miracles, prophecy, discerning of spirits, tongues, interpretation of tongues (1 Cor. 12:8-10)

Grace
H: 02580 chen {khane}; from 02603; TWOT- 694a; n m AV - grace 38, favor 26, gracious 2, pleasant 1, precious 1, wellfavoured + 02896 1; 69
1) favor, grace, charm; 1a) favor, grace, elegance; 1b) favor, acceptance
G: 5485 charis {khar'-ece}; from 5463; TDNT - 9:372,1298; n f AV - grace 130, favor 6, thanks 4, thank 4, thank + 2192 3, pleasure 2, misc 7; 156
1) grace; 1a) that which affords joy, pleasure, delight, sweetness, charm, loveliness: grace of speech; 2) good will, loving-kindness, favor; 2a) of the merciful kindness by which God, exerting his holy influence upon souls, turns them to Christ, keeps, strengthens, increases them in Christian faith, knowledge, affection, and kindles them to the exercise of the Christian virtues; 3) what is due to grace; 3a) the spiritual condition of one governed by the power of divine grace; 3b) the token or proof of grace, benefit; 3b1) a gift of grace; 3b2) benefit, bounty; 4) thanks, (for benefits, services, favors), recompense, reward
Nave's (2097): General Scriptures concerning Ge 15:6 20:6 De 7:6-9 9:4-6 Job 10:12 22:2,3 Ps 94:17-19 138:3 143:11 Da 9:18 10:18,19 Joh 6:44,45 17:11,12,15 Ac 4:29,30 26:22 Ro 3:22-24 4:4,5,16 5:2,6-8,15-21 9:10-16 11:5,6 1Co 1:4-8 10:13 15:10 2Co 1:12 Ga 1:15,16 Eph 1:5-9,11,12 2:8,9 3:16 4:7 6:10 Php 1:19 2:13 1Th 1:1 5:28 1Ti 1:14 2Ti 1:1,9 Tit 3:7 1Pe 1:5 4:10 5:10 2Pe 1:2 Jude 1:21,24,25 Re 3:10; growth in Ps 84:7 Pr 4:18 Php 1:6,9-11 3:12-15 Col 1:10,11 2:19 1Th 3:10,12,13 2Th 1:3 Heb 6:1-3 1Pe 2:1-3 2Pe 3:18

H

Harlot (false church)
H: 02181 zanah {zaw-naw'}; a primitive root [highly-fed and therefore wanton]; TWOT - 563; v; AV - ...harlot 36, go a whoring 19, ...whoredom 15, whore 11, commit fornication 3, whorish 3, harlot + 0802 2, commit 1, continually 1, great 1, whore's + 0802 1; 93
1) to commit fornication, be a harlot, play the harlot; 1a) (Qal); 1a1) to be a harlot, act as a harlot, commit fornication; 1a2) to commit adultery; 1a3) to be a cult prostitute; 1a4) to be unfaithful (to God) (fig.); 1b) (Pual) to play the harlot; 1c) (Hiphil); 1c1) to cause to commit adultery; 1c2) to force into prostitution; 1c3) to commit fornication
G: 4204 porne {por'-nay}; from 4205; TDNT - 6:579,918; n f; AV - harlot 8, whore 4; 12
1) a woman who sells her body for sexual uses; 1a) a prostitute, a harlot, one who yields herself to defilement for the sake of gain; 1b) any woman indulging in unlawful sexual intercourse, whether; for gain or for lust; 2) metaph. an idolatress; 2a) of "Babylon," the chief seat of idolatry

Head
H: 07218 ro'sh {roshe}; from an unused root apparently meaning to shake; TWOT - 2097; n m; AV - head 349, chief 91, top 73, beginning 14, company 12, captain 10, sum 9, first 6, principal 5, chapters 4, rulers 2, misc 23; 598
1) head, top, summit, upper part, chief, total, sum, height, front, beginning; 1a) head (of man, animals); 1b) top, tip (of mountain); 1c) height (of stars); 1d) chief, head (of man, city, nation, place, family, priest); 1e) head, front, beginning; 1f) chief, choicest, best; 1g) head, division, company, band; 1h) sum
G: 2776; kephale {kef-al-ay'}; from the primary kapto (in the sense of seizing); TDNT - 3:673,429; n f; AV - head 76; 76
1) the head, both of men and often of animals. Since the loss of the head destroys life, this word is used in the phrases relating to capital and extreme punishment.; 2) metaph.

anything supreme, chief, prominent; 2a) of persons, master lord: of a husband in relation to his wife; 2b) of Christ: the Lord of the husband and of the Church; 2c) of things: the corner stone
Nave's (2806) Christ as head of the Church: Eph 1:22, 23 5:23 Col 1:18, 24; priesthood of Christ — Appointed and called by God Heb 3:1,2 5:4,5; After the order of Melchizedek Ps 110:4 Heb 5:6 6:20 7:15,17; Superior to Aaron and the Levitical priests Heb 7:11,16,22 8:1,2,6; Consecrated with an oath Heb 7:20,21; Has an unchangeable priesthood Heb 7:23,28; Is of unblemished purity Heb 7:26,28; Faithful Heb 3:2; Needed no sacrifice for himself Heb 7:27; Offered himself as a sacrifice Heb 9:14,26; His sacrifice superior to all others Heb 9:13,14,23; Offered sacrifice only once Heb 7:27; Made reconciliation Heb 2:17; Obtained redemption for us Heb 9:12; Entered into heaven Heb 4:14 10:12; Sympathizes with saints Heb 2:18 4:15; Intercedes Heb 7:25 9:24; Blesses Nu 6:23-26 with Ac 3:26; On his throne Zec 6:13; Appointment of, an encouragement to steadfastness Heb 4:14; Typified Melchizedek Ge 14:18-20; Aaron and his sons Ex 40:12-15

Heaven
H: 08064 shamayim {shaw-mah'-yim} dual of an unused singular shameh {shaw-meh'}; from an unused root meaning to be lofty; TWOT - 2407a; n m AV - heaven 398, air 21, astrologers + 01895 1; 420
1) heaven, heavens, sky; 1a) visible heavens, sky; 1a1) as abode of the stars; 1a2) as the visible universe, the sky, atmosphere, etc; 1b) Heaven (as the abode of God)
G: 3772 ouranos {oo-ran-os'}; perhaps from the same as 3735 (through the idea of elevation); the sky; TDNT - 5:497,736; n m AV - heaven 268, air 10, sky 5, heavenly + 1537; 284
1) the vaulted expanse of the sky with all things visible in it; 1a) the universe, the world; 1b) the aerial heavens or sky, the region where the clouds and the tempests gather, and where thunder and lightning are produced; 1c) the sidereal or starry heavens; 2) the region above the sidereal heavens, the seat of order of things eternal and consummately perfect where God dwells and other heavenly beings
Nave's (2288): God's dwelling place De 26:15 1Ki 8:30,39,43,49 1Ch 16:31 21:26 2Ch 2:6 6:18,21,27,30,33,35,39 30:27 Ne 9:27 Job 22:12,14 Ps 2:4 11:4 20:6 33:13 102:19 103:19 113:5 123:1 135:6 Ec 5:2 Isa 57:15 63:15 66:1 Jer 23:24 La 3:41,50 Da 4:35 5:23 Zec 2:13 Mt 5:34,45 6:9 10:32,33 11:25 12:50 16:17 18:10,14 Mr 11:25,26 16:19 Ac 7:49 Ro 1:18 Heb 8:1 Re 8:1 12:7-9 21:22-27 22:1-5; the future dwelling place of the righteous, called a garner Mt 3:12; the kingdom of Christ and of God Eph 5:5; the Father's house Joh 14:2; a heavenly country Heb 11:16; a rest Heb 4:9 Re 14:13; paradise 2Co 12:2,4; the wicked excluded from Ga 5:21 Eph 5:5 Re 22:15; the physical heavens Ge 1:1 Ps 19:1 50:6 68:33 89:29 97:6 103:11 113:4 115:16 Jer 31:37 Eze 1:1 Mt 24:29,30 Ac 2:19,20

Holy
H: 06944 qodesh {ko'-desh}; from 06942; TWOT - 1990a; n m AV - holy 262, sanctuary 68, (holy, hallowed,...) things 52, most 44, holiness 30, dedicated 5, hallowed 3, consecrated 1, misc 3; 468
1) apartness, holiness, sacredness, separateness; 1a) apartness, sacredness, holiness; 1a1) of God; 1a2) of places; 1a3) of things; 1b) set-apartness, separateness
G: 40 hagios {hag-ee-os'}; from hagos (an awful thing) [cf 53, 2282]; TDNT - 1:88,14; adj AV - holy 161, saints 61, Holy One 4, misc 3; 229
1) most holy thing, a saint
Nave's (2389) General Scriptures concerning Ge 17:1 35:2 Ex 19:6 22:31 28:36 39:30 Le 10:8-10 11:44,45,47 19:2 20:7,26 De 13:17 14:2 18:13 26:19 28:9 30:2,10 Jos 7:12,13 Job 5:24 28:28 36:21 Ps 4:4 15:1-5 24:3-5 32:2 37:27 68:13 73:1 85:13 94:15 97:10 119:1-3 Pr 11:23 12:5 16:17 21:8,15,29 22:1 Ec 7:1 Isa 4:3 26:2,8,9 32:17 35:8 51:7 52:1,11 57:2 60:1,21 61:3,9-

11 Mic 6:8 Zep 2:3 Zec 8:3 14:20,21 Mt 5:6,8,29,30,48 12:33 Mr 9:49,50 Lu 1:74,75 6:45 Joh 1:47 4:14 5:14 6:35 15:19 17:23 Ac 24:16 Ro 2:28,29 6:1-23 7:4,6 8:1,4,12 11:16 12:1,2,9 13:12-14 14:17 16:19 1Co 3:16,17 5:7 6:12,13,19,20 7:23 8:12 10:21,31,32 12:31 15:34 2Co 6:14-17 7:1 10:3,5 11:2 13:7,8 Ga 2:17 5:22-25 6:15 Eph 1:4,13,14 2:21,22 4:20-24 5:1,3,8-11 Php 1:10,11 2:15 4:8 Col 1:22 3:5-10,12-15 1Th 2:12 3:13 4:3,4,7 5:5,22,23 2Th 2:13 1Ti 1:5 4:8,12 5:22 6:6,11,12 2Ti 2:16,17,19,21,22 3:17 Tit 1:15 2:9,10,12 Heb 4:3,9 10:22 12:1,10,14,15 13:9 Jas 1:21,27 3:17 4:4 1Pe 1:14-16 2:1,5,9,11,12,24 3:11 4:1,2,6,7 2Pe 1:2-8 3:11,12,14 1Jo 1:6,7 2:1,5,29 3:3,6-10 5:4,5,18,21 2Jo 1:4 3Jo 1:11 Re 14:4,5 18:4 19:8

I

Idolatry

H: 04656 miphletseth {mif-leh'-tseth}; from 06426; TWOT - 1778b; n f; AV - idol 4; 4
1) horrid thing, horrible thing
G: 1495 eidololatreia {i-do-lol-at-ri'-ah}; from 1497 and 2999; TDNT - 2:379,202; n f AV - idolatry 4; 4
1) the worship of false gods, idolatry; 1a) of the formal sacrificial feats held in honor of false gods; 1b) of avarice, as a worship of Mammon; 2) in the plural, the vices springing from idolatry and peculiar to it
Nave's (2486) Licentiousness of Ex 32:6,25 Nu 25:1-3 1Ki 14:24 15:12 2Ki 17:30 23:7 Eze 16:17 23:1-44 Ho 4:12-14 Am 2:8 Mic 1:7 Ro 1:24,26,27 1Co 10:7,8 1Pe 4:3,4 Re 2:14,20-22 9:20,21 14:8 17:1-6; Prayers to idols Jud 10:14 Isa 44:17 45:20 46:7 Jon 1:5; denunciations against Ge 35:2 Ex 20:3-6,23 23:13 34:17 Le 19:4 26:1,30 De 4:15-23,25-28 5:7-9 11:16,17,28 12:31 16:21,22 27:15 28:15-68 30:17,18 31:16-21,29 32:15-26 1Sa 15:23 1Ki 9:6-9 Job 31:26-28 Ps 16:4 44:20,21 59:8 79:6 81:9 97:7 Isa 42:17 45:16 Joe 3:12 Jon 2:8 Mic 5:15 Hab 1:16 Ac 15:20,29 17:16 Ro 1:25 1Co 6:9,10 8:1-13 10:7,14,20-22 1Jo 5:21 Re 21:8 22:15; warnings against, punishments of De 17:2-5 2Ch 28:23 Ne 9:27-37 Ps 78:58-64 106:34-42 Isa 1:29-31 2:6-22 30:22 57:3-13 65:3,4 Jer 1:15,16 3:1-11 5:1-17 7:1 8:1,2,19 13:9-27 16:1 17:1-6 18:13-15 19 22:9 32:35 44:1 48:8 Eze 6:1 7:19 8:5-18 9:1 14:1-14 16 20:1 22:4 23:1 44:10-12 Ho 1:2 2:2-5 4:12-19 5:1-3 8:5-14 9:10 10:1 11:2 12:11-14 13:1-4 14:8 Am 3:14 4:4,5 5:5 Mic 1:1-9 5:12-14 6:16 Zep 1:1 Mal 2:11-13; folly of Ex 32:20 De 4:28 32:37,38 Jud 6:31 10:14 1Sa 5:3,4 12:21 1Ki 18:27 2Ki 3:13 19:18 2Ch 25:15 28:22,23 Ps 96:5 106:20 115:4,5,8 135:15-18 Isa 2:8 16:12 36:18 37:19 40:12-26 41:23,24,26-29 43:9 44:9-20 45:20 46:1,2,6,7 47:12-15 57:13 Jer 2:28 10:3-16 11:12 14:22 16:19,20 48:13 51:17 Da 5:23 Ho 8:5,6 Hab 2:18,19 Zec 10:2 Ac 14:15 17:22,23,29 Ro 1:22,23 1Co 8:4,5 10:19 12:2 Ga 4:8 Re 9:20

Israel

H: 03478 Yisra'el {yis-raw-ale'}; from 08280 and 0410;; n pr m AV - Israel 2489, Israelites 16; 2505
Israel = "God prevails"
1) the second name for Jacob given to him by God after his wrestling with the angel at Peniel; 2) the name of the descendants and the nation of the descendants of Jacob; 2a) the name of the nation until the death of Solomon and the split; 2b) the name used and given to the northern kingdom consisting of the 10 tribes under Jeroboam; the southern kingdom was known as Judah; 2c) the name of the nation after the return from exile

J

Judgment

H: 04941 mishpat {mish-pawt'}; from 08199; TWOT - 2443c; n m AV - judgment 296, manner 38, right 18, cause 12, ordinance 11, lawful 7, order 5, worthy 3, fashion 3, custom 2, discretion 2, law 2, measure 2, sentence 2, misc 18; 421

1) judgment, justice, ordinance; 1a) judgment; 1a1) act of deciding a case; 1a2) place, court, seat of judgment; 1a3) process, procedure, litigation (before judges); 1a4) case, cause (presented for judgment); 1a5) sentence, decision (of judgment); 1a6) execution (of judgment); 1a7) time (of judgment); 1b) justice, right, rectitude (attributes of God or man); 1c) ordinance; 1d) decision (in law); 1e) right, privilege, due (legal); 1f) proper, fitting, measure, fitness, custom, manner, plan

G: 2920 krisis {kree'-sis}; perhaps a primitive word; TDNT - 3:941,469; n f AV - judgment 41, damnation 3, accusation 2, condemnation 2; 48

1) a separating, sundering, separation; 1a) a trial, contest; 2) selection; 3) judgment; 3a) opinion or decision given concerning anything; 3a1) esp. concerning justice and injustice, right or wrong; 3b) sentence of condemnation, damnatory judgment, condemnation and punishment; 4) the college of judges (a tribunal of seven men in the several cities of Palestine; as distinguished from the Sanhedrin, which had its seat at Jerusalem); 5) right, justice

Nave's (2904) the general 1Ch 16:33 Job 14:17 21:30 31:13-15 Ps 9:7 50:3-6 96:13 98:9 Ec 3:17 11:9 12:14 Eze 18:20-28 Da 7:9,10 Am 4:12 Mt 3:12 7:22,23 8:29 10:15 11:22 12:36,37,41,42 13:30,40-43,49,50 16:27 22:11-13 23:14 25:1-46 Mr 4:22 8:38 13:32 Lu 3:17 10:10-14 11:31,32 12:2-5 13:24-29 19:12-26 20:45-47 Joh 5:22 12:48 Ac 2:19-21 10:42 17:31 24:25 Ro 2:5-10,12-16 14:10-12 1Co 3:13 4:5 6:2 2Co 5:10 2Th 1:7,8 2Ti 4:1,8 Heb 6:2 9:27 10:27 1Pe 4:5,7 2Pe 2:4,9 3:7,10-12 1Jo 4:17 Jude 1:6,14,15,24 Re 1:7 6:15-17 11:18 20:11-15 22:12; according to opportunity and works Ge 4:7 Job 34:11 Pr 11:31 12:14 24:11,12 Ps 62:12 Isa 3:10,11 5:1-6,15,16 24:2 28:24-28 59:18 Jer 17:10,11 32:19 Eze 7:3,4,27 9:4-6 16:59 18:4-9,19-32 33:18-20 39:24 Ho 4:9 12:2 Am 3:2 Zec 1:6 Mt 10:14,15 11:24 12:37 21:33-36 23:14 25:14-30 Mr 6:11 14:21 Lu 9:5 10:12-15 11:49-51 12:47,48 13:6-9 19:12-27 20:47 21:1-4 Joh 3:19,20 5:45 9:41 12:48 15:22,24 Ro 2:5-12,27 1Co 3:8,12-15 4:5 2Co 2:15,16 11:15 Ga 6:5-10 Eph 6:7,8 Col 3:25 1Ti 1:13 2Ti 4:14 Heb 2:2,3 10:26-30 12:25 Jas 2:12,13 1Pe 1:17 2Pe 2:20,21 Re 2:23 20:12,13

(see Absolute 2 and Absolute 3 for an in-depth explanation of the difference between God's judgment and man's judgment)

Justification

G: 1347 dikaiosis {dik-ah'-yo-sis}; from 1344; TDNT - 2:223,168; n f AV - justification 2; 2
1) the act of God declaring men free from guilt and acceptable to him; 2) abjuring to be righteous, justification

Nave's (2918) General scriptures concerning Ge 15:6 Ps 32:2 71:16 89:16 Isa 42:21 45:24,25 46:12,13 50:8 51:5,6 53:11 54:17 56:1 61:10 Jer 23:6 Hab 2:4 Zec 3:4 Joh 5:24 Ac 13:39 Ro 1:16,17 2:13 3:21,22,24-26,28,30 4:3-25 5:1,9,11-21 6:22 7:1-25 8:1,30,31,33,34 9:30-32 10:1-21 1Co 1:30 6:11 2Co 5:19,21 Ga 2:14-21 3:6,8,9,11,21,22,24 4:21-31 5:4-6 Eph 6:14 Php 3:8,9 Col 2:13,14 Tit 3:7 Heb 11:4,7 Jas 2:20-23,26

According to "The New Unger's Bible Dictionary," justification is a divine act whereby an infinitely holy God judicially declares a believing sinner to be righteous and acceptable before Him because Christ has borne the sinner's sin on the cross and has become "to us...righteousnss" (1 Cor. 1:30, Rom. 3:24). Justification springs from the fountain of God's grace (Titus 3:4-5). It is operative as the result of the redemption and propitiatory sacrifice of Christ, who has settled all the claims of the law (Rom. 3:24-25; 5:9). Justification is on the basis of faith and not by human merit or works (Rom. 3:28-30; 4:5; 5:1; Gal. 2:16). In this marvelous operation of God, the infinitely holy Judge judicially declares righteous the one who believes in Jesus (Rom. 8:31-34). A justified believer emerges from God's great courtroom with a consciousness that another, his Substitute, has borne his guilt and that he stands without accusation before God (Rom. 8:1, 33-34). Justification makes no one righteous, neither is it the bestowment of righteousness as such, but rather it declares one to be justified whom God sees as clothed with the flesh of His own dear Son, the sinless

Lamb of God. "Therefore, this may be stated as the correct definition of justification: The sinner becomes righteous in God's sight when he is in Christ: he is justified by God freely, all without a cause, because thereby he is righteous in His sight" (L. S. Chafer).

K

Kingdom

H: 04467 mamlakah {mam-law-kaw'}; from 04427; TWOT - 1199f; n f AV - kingdom 110, royal 4, reign 2, king's 1; 117
1) kingdom, dominion, reign, sovereignty; 1a) kingdom, realm; 1b) sovereignty, dominion; 1c) reign
G: 932 basileia {bas-il-i'-ah}; from 935; TDNT - 1:579,97; n f AV - kingdom (of God) 71, kingdom (of heaven) 32, kingdom (general or evil) 20, (Thy or Thine) kingdom 6, His kingdom 6, the kingdom 5, (My) kingdom 4, misc 18; 162
1) royal power, kingship, dominion, rule; 1a) not to be confused with an actual kingdom but rather the right or authority to rule over a kingdom; 1b) of the royal power of Jesus as the triumphant Messiah; 1c) of the royal power and dignity conferred on Christians in the Messiah's kingdom; 2) a kingdom, the territory subject to the rule of a king; 3) used in the N.T. to refer to the reign of the Messiah
Nave's (2962) Compared to a man who sowed good seed Mt 13:24-30,38-43 Mr 4:26-29; to a granule of mustard seed Mt 13:31,32 Mr 4:30,31 Lu 13:18,19; to leaven (yeast) Mt 13:33 Lu 13:21; to a treasure Mt 13:44; to a pearl Mt 13:45; to a net Mt 13:47-50; to a king who called his servants for a reckoning (an audit) Mt 18:23-35; to a householder Mt 20:1-16; to a king who made a marriage feast for his son Mt 22:2-14 Lu 14:16-24; to ten virgins Mt 25:1-13; to a man, traveling into a far country, who called his servants, and delivered to them his goods Mt 25:14-30 Lu 19:12-27; "My kingdom is not of this world," Joh 18:36; And when he was demanded of the Pharisees, when the kingdom of God should come, he answered them and said, The kingdom of God cometh not with observation: Neither shall they say, Lo here! Or, Lo there! For, behold, the kingdom of God is within you. Luke 17:20-21

Knowledge

H: 01847 da`ath {dah'-ath}; from 03045; TWOT - 848c; n m/f AV - knowledge 82, know 6, cunning 1, unwittingly 2 + 01097 2, ignorantly + 01097 1, unawares + 01097 1; 93
1) knowledge; 1a) knowledge, perception, skill; 1b) discernment, understanding, wisdom
G: 1108 gnosis {gno'-sis}; from 1097; TDNT - 1:689,119; n f AV - knowledge 28, science 1; 29
1) knowledge signifies in general intelligence, understanding; 1a) the general knowledge of Christian religion; 1b) the deeper more perfect and enlarged knowledge of this religion, such as belongs to the more advanced; 1c) esp. of things lawful and unlawful for Christians; 1d) moral wisdom, such as is seen in right living
Nave's (2985): Of good and evil Ge 2:9,17 3:22; Is power Pr 3:20 24:5; Desire for 1Ki 3:9 Ps 119:66 Pr 2:1 3:1 12:1 15:14 18:15; Rejected Ho 4:6; Those who reject are destroyed Ho 4:6; Fools hate Pr 1:22,29; A divine gift 1Co 12:8; Is pleasant Pr 2:10; Shall be increased Da 12:4; The earth shall be full of Isa 11:9; The fear (reverence) of the Lord is the beginning of Pr 1:7; Of more value than gold Pr 8:10; The priest's lips should keep Mal 2:7; Of salvation Lu 1:77; Key of Lu 11:52; "Now we know in part" 1Co 13:9-12; Of God more than burnt offering Ho 6:6; Of Christ Php 3:8

L

Language

H: 08193 saphah {saw-faw'} or (in dual and plural) sepheth {sef-eth'}; probably from 05595 or 08192 through the idea of termination (compare 05490); TWOT - 2278a; n f AV - lip 112, bank 10, brim 8, edge 8, language 7, speech 6, shore 6, brink 5, border 3, side 3, prating 2, vain 2, misc 4; 176
1) lip, language, speech, shore, bank, brink, brim, side, edge, border, binding; 1a) lip (as body part); 1b) language; 1c) edge, shore, bank (of cup, sea, river, etc)
G: 1258 dialektos {dee-al'-ek-tos}; from 1256;; n f AV - tongue 5, language 1; 6
1) conversation, speech, discourse, language; 2) the tongue or language peculiar to any people
Nave's (3019) Unity of Ge 11:1,6; Confusion of Ge 11:1-9 10:5,20,31; Dialects of the Jews Jud 12:6 Mt 26:73; Many spoken at Jerusalem Joh 19:20 Ac 2:8-11; Speaking in inspired "tongues" forbidden, in religious assemblies unless there was an inspired interpreter present 1Co 14:2-28; Gift of Mr 16:17 Ac 2:7,8 10:46 19:6 1Co 12:10 14:1; Mentioned in Scripture Ashdod Ne 13:24; Chaldee Da 1:4; Egyptian Ac 2:10 Ps 114:1; Greek Lu 23:38 Ac 21:37; Latin Lu 23:38 Joh 19:20; Lycaonian Ac 14:11; Parthian and other lands Ac 2:9-11; Syrian 2Ki 18:26 Ezr 4:7 Da 2:4

Law

H: 08451 towrah {to-raw'} or torah {to-raw'}; from 03384; TWOT - 910d; n f AV - law 219; 219
1) law, direction, instruction; 1a) instruction, direction (human or divine); 1a1) body of prophetic teaching; 1a2) instruction in Messianic age; 1a3) body of priestly direction or instruction; 1a4) body of legal directives; 1b) law; 1b1) law of the burnt offering; 1b2) of special law, codes of law; 1c) custom, manner; 1d) the Deuteronomic or Mosaic Law
G: 3551 nomos {nom'-os}; from a primary nemo (to parcel out, especially food or grazing to animals); TDNT - 4:1022,646; n m AV - law 197; 197
1) anything established, anything received by usage, a custom, a law, a command; 1a) of any law whatsoever; 1a1) a law or rule producing a state approved of God; 1a1a) by the observance of which is approved of God; 1a2) a precept or injunction; 1a3) the rule of action prescribed by reason; 1b) of the Mosaic law, and referring, acc. to the context. either to the volume of the law or to its contents; 1c) the Christian religion: the law demanding faith, the moral instruction given by Christ, esp. the precept concerning love; 1d) the name of the more important part (the Pentateuch), is put for the entire collection of the sacred books of the OT
Nave's (3033): General Scriptures concerning Ps 19:7-9 119:1-8 Pr 28:4,5 Mt 22:21 Lu 16:17 20:22-25 Ro 2:14,15 7:7,12,14 13:10 1Ti 1:5,8-10 Jas 1:25 1Jo 3:4 5:3; of Moses (Contained in the books of Exodus, Leviticus, Numbers, and Deuteronomy) Given at Sinai #Ex 19:1 De 1:1 4:10-13 33:2 Hab 3:3; Received by the disposition of angels De 33:2 Ps 68:17 Ac 7:53 Ga 3:19 Heb 2:2; Was given because of transgressions until the Messiah arrived Ga 3:19; To be written on door posts De 6:9 11:20; Expounded by the priests and Levites Le 10:11 De 33:10 2Ch 35:3; Formed a constitution on which the civil government of the Israelites was founded, and according to which rulers were required to rule De 17:18-20 2Ki 11:12 2Ch 23; Divine authority for Ex 19:16-24 20:1-17 24:12-18 31:18 32:15,16 34:1-4,27,28 Le 26:46 De 4:10-13,36 5:1-22 9:10 10:1-5 33:2-4 1Ki 8:9 Ezr 7:6 Ne 1:7 8:1 9:14 Ps 78:5 103:7 Isa 33:22 Mal 4:4 Ac 7:38,53 Ga 3:19 Heb 9:18-21; Prophecies in, of the Messiah Lu 24:44 Joh 1:45 5:46 12:34 Ac 26:22,23 28:23 Ro 3:21,22; Epitomized by Jesus Mt 22:40 Mr 12:29-33 Lu 10:27; temporary Jer 3:16 Da 9:27 Mt 5:17-45 Lu 16:16,17 Joh 1:17 4:20-24 8:35 Ac 6:14 10:28 13:39 15:1-29 21:20-25 Ro 3:1,2 7:1-6 8:3 10:4 2Co 3:7-14 Ga 2:3-9 4:30,31 Eph 2:15 Col 2:14-23 Heb 8:4-13 9:8-24 10:1-18 11:40 12:18,19,27

Leaven

H: 07603 s@'or {seh-ore'}; from 07604; TWOT - 2229a; n m AV - leaven 5; 5
1) leaven
G: 2219 zume {dzoo'-may}; probably from 2204; TDNT - 2:902,302; n f AV - leaven 13; 13
1) leaven
Nave's (3047): At the Passover meal Ex 12:19,20 13:3,4,7 23:18; figurative of the hypocrisy of the Pharisees Mt 16:6-12 Mr 8:15 Lu 12:1; Of other evils 1Co 5:6-8 Ga 5:9; Parable of Mt 13:33 Lu 13:21
(see Absolute 7 for an in-depth definition of leaven)

Life

H: 02416 chay {khah'-ee}; from 02421; TWOT - 644a AV - live 197, life 144, beast 76, alive 31, creature 15, running 7, living thing 6, raw 6, misc 19; 501 adj
1) living, alive; 1a) green (of vegetation); 1b) flowing, fresh (of water); 1c) lively, active (of man); 1d) reviving (of the springtime) n m; 2) relatives; 3) life (abstract emphatic); 3a) life; 3b) sustenance, maintenance n f; 4) living thing, animal; 4a) animal; 4b) life; 4c) appetite; 4d) revival, renewal; 5) community
G: 2222 zoe {dzo-ay'}; from 2198; TDNT - 2:832,290; n f AV - life 133, lifetime 1; 134
1) life; 1a) the state of one who is possessed of vitality or is animate; 1b) every living soul; 2) life; 2a) of the absolute fullness of life, both essential and ethical, which belongs to God, and through him both to the hypostatic "logos" and to Christ in whom the "logos" put on human nature; 2b) life real and genuine, a life active and vigorous, devoted to God, blessed, in the portion even in this world of those who put their trust in Christ, but after the resurrection to be consummated by new accessions (among them a glorified body), and to last for ever.
Nave's (3086): Breath of Ge 2:7; Called Spirit of God Job 27:3; Tree of Ge 2:9 3:22,24 Pr 3:18 13:12 Re 2:7; To those who keep the commandments De 4:40 22:7; Vanity of Ec 1:1 2:1 3:1 4:1 5:1 6:1 7:1; To be hated for Christ's sake Lu 14:26; What can a man give in exchange for Mt 16:26 Mr 8:37; The one who loses it will save it Mt 10:39 16:25,26 Lu 9:24 Joh 12:25; brevity and uncertainty of Ge 18:27 47:9 1Sa 20:3 2Sa 14:14 1Ch 29:15 Job 4:19-21 7:6-10,17 8:9 9:25,26 10:9,20,21 13:12,25,28 14:1,2 17:1 Ps 22:29 39:4-6,11 78:39 89:47,48 90:3,5,6,9,10 102:11 103:14-16 144:3,4 146:4 Pr 27:1 Ec 1:4 6:12 Isa 2:22 38:12 40:6,7,24 50:9 51:8,12 64:6 Jas 1:10,11 4:14 1Pe 1:24; everlasting Ps 21:4 121:8 133:3 Isa 25:8 Da 12:2 Mt 19:16-21,29 25:46 Mr 10:30 Lu 18:18,30 20:36 Joh 3:14-16 4:14 5:24,25,29,39 6:27,40,47,50-58,68 10:10,27,28 12:25,50 17:2,3 Ac 13:46,48 Ro 2:7 5:21 6:22,23 1Co 15:53,54 2Co 5:1 Ga 6:8 1Ti 1:16 4:8 6:12,19 2Ti 1:10 Tit 1:2 3:7 1Jo 2:25 3:15 5:11-13,20 Jude 1:21 Re 1:18; from God Ge 2:7 De 8:3 30:20 32:39,40 1Sa 2:6 Job 27:3 34:14,15 Ps 22:29 30:3 68:20 104:30 Ec 12:7 Isa 38:16-20 Ac 17:25-28 Ro 4:17 1Ti 6:13 Jas 4:15; spiritual Joh 3:3-16 5:24-26,40 6:27,33,35,40,47 10:10 11:25,26 14:6 17:2,3 20:31 Ro 6:4,5,8,11,13,22,23 8:10 1Jo 1:1,2

Love

H: 0157 'ahab {aw-hab'} or 'aheb {aw-habe'}; a primitive root; TWOT - 29; v AV - love 169, lover(s) 19, friend(s) 12, beloved 5, liketh 1, lovely 1, loving 1; 208
1) to love; 1a) (Qal); 1a1) human love for another, includes family, and sexual; 1a2) human appetite for objects such as food, drink, sleep, wisdom; 1a3) human love for or to God; 1a4) act of being a friend; 1a4a) lover (participle); 1a4b) friend (participle); 1a5) God's love toward man; 1a5a) to individual men; 1a5b) to people Israel; 1a5c) to righteousness; 1b) (Niphal); 1b1) lovely (participle); 1b2) loveable (participle); 1c) (Piel); 1c1) friends; 1c2) lovers (fig. of adulterers); 2) to like
G: 5368 phileo {fil-eh'-o}; from 5384; TDNT - 9:114,1262; v AV - love 22, kiss 3; 25

1) to love; 1a) to approve of; 1b) to like; 1c) sanction; 1d) to treat affectionately or kindly, to welcome, befriend; 2) to show signs of love; 2a) to kiss; 3) to be fond of doing; 3a) be wont, use to do

G: 26 agape {ag-ah'-pay}; from 25; TDNT - 1:21,5; n f AV - love 86, charity 27, dear 1, charitably+2596 1,

feast of charity 1; 116

1) brotherly love, affection, good will, love, benevolence; 2) love feasts

Nave's (3122): of man for God Ex 20:6 De 5:10 6:5 7:9 10:12 11:1,13,22 13:3 30:6,16,20 Jos 22:5 23:11 Ps 18:1 31:23 37:4 45:10,11 63:5,6 69:35,36 73:25,26 91:14 97:10 116:1 145:20 Pr 8:17 23:26 Isa 56:6,7 Jer 2:2,3 Mt 22:37,38 Mr 12:29,30,32,33 Lu 11:42 Joh 5:42 Ro 5:5 8:28 1Co 8:3 Php 1:9 2Th 3:5 2Ti 1:7 1Jo 2:5,15 3:17,18 4:12,16-21 5:1-3 2Jo 1:6 Jude 1:21; of man for Jesus Mt 10:37,38 25:34-40 27:55-61 Mr 9:41 Lu 2:29,30 7:47 Joh 8:42 14:15,21,23,28 15:9 16:27 17:26 21:17 Ac 21:13 1Co 16:22 2Co 5:6,8,14,15 Ga 5:6,22 6:14 Eph 3:17-19 4:15 6:24 Php 1:9,20,21,23 3:7,8 Col 1:8 2Th 3:5 2Ti 1:13 4:8 Phm 1:5 Heb 6:10 Jas 1:12 2:5 1Pe 1:8 2:7 Re 2:4; of man for man Le 19:18,34 De 10:19 Ps 133:1-3 Pr 10:12 15:17 17:9,17 So 8:6,7 Mt 5:41-47 7:12 10:41,42 19:19 25:34-40 Mr 9:41 12:30-33 Lu 6:31-35 10:30-37 Joh 13:14,15,34,35 15:12,13,17 Ro 12:9,10 13:8-10 1Co 8:1 13:1-13 14:1 16:14 2Co 8:7,8 Ga 5:13,14,22,26 Eph 5:2 Php 1:9 2:2 Col 2:2 3:12 1Th 1:3 3:12 4:9 1Ti 1:5,14 2:15 4:12 6:2 2Ti 2:22 Tit 3:15 Phm 1:12-16 Heb 10:24 Jas 2:8 1Pe 1:22 2:17 3:8,9 4:8 2Pe 1:7 1Jo 2:9-11 3:11,14,16-19,23 4:7,11,12,20,21 5:1,2 2Jo 1:5; of God for man Ge 6:8,9 18:26,28,30,32 32:28 46:4 Ex 3:12 20:21,24 24:2 33:11,12,17,22,23 Le 26:11,12 Nu 5:3 6:27 14:14 22:12 23:20,21 24:1 De 4:7 31:6,8 33:23 Jos 1:5,9 1Sa 2:26 2Sa 22:20 1Ki 6:13 2Ch 15:2 Job 10:12 22:27 29:3-5 Ps 3:8 5:12 11:7 18:19,25,26 24:4,5 25:14 30:7 36:9 37:18,23 41:11,12 44:3 46:7 58:11 68:16,18 75:10 84:11 89:17 92:10 94:19 102:13 112:9 115:12,13,15 132:13,14 147:11 149:4 Pr 3:4,23,32,35 8:35 10:6,22,24 11:20,27 12:2 14:9 16:7 Isa 28:5 30:26 33:17,22 41:10 43:5,21 54:8 60:10 Jer 15:20 La 3:24 Eze 37:27 39:29 48:35 Ho 14:4 Joe 2:26,27 3:16,17,20,21 Am 3:2 Zep 3:15,17 Hag 1:13 Zec 2:5 8:3 9:16 Lu 1:28,30,66 2:52 Joh 14:16-21,23 15:15 Ac 4:33 10:35 Ro 2:29 1Co 1:9 3:21-23 2Co 4:15 10:18 Ga 4:6 Eph 1:6 2:13,14,16,18,19,22 3:12 Ro 5:2 Heb 4:16 10:19,22 11:5 1Pe 2:9 1Jo 1:3 3:19 4:17,18 Re 1:5,6 3:20 19:9 21:3

M

Mercy

H: 02617 checed {kheh'-sed}; from 02616; TWOT - 698a,699a; n m AV - mercy 149, kindness 40, lovingkindness 30, goodness 12, kindly 5, merciful 4, favour 3, good 1, goodliness 1, pity 1, reproach 1, wicked thing 1; 248

1) goodness, kindness, faithfulness; 2) a reproach, shame

H: 07355 racham {raw-kham'}; a primitive root; TWOT - 2146; v AV - ...mercy 32, ...compassion 8, pity 3, love 1, merciful 1, Ruhamah 1, surely 1; 47

1) to love, love deeply, have mercy, be compassionate, have tender affection, have compassion; 1a) (Qal) to love; 1b) (Piel); 1b1) to have compassion, be compassionate; 1b1a) of God, man; 1c) (Pual) to be shown compassion, be compassionate

G: 1653 eleeo {el-eh-eh'-o}; from 1656; TDNT - 2:477,222; v AV - have mercy on 14, obtain mercy 8, show mercy 2, have compassion 1, have compassion on 1, have pity on 1, have mercy 1, have mercy upon 1, receive mercy 1; 31

1) to have mercy on; 2) to help one afflicted or seeking aid; 3) to help the afflicted, to bring help to the wretched; 4) to experience mercy

Nave's (3332): General scriptures concerning 2Sa 22:26 Ps 18:25 37:25,26 85:10 Pr 3:3,4 11:17 12:10 14:21,22,31 20:28 21:21 Ho 4:1 12:6 Mic 6:8 Mt 5:7 23:23 Lu 6:36 Ro 12:8 Col 3:12,13 Jas 2:13; instances of — The prison keeper, to Joseph Ge 39:21-23; Joshua to Rahab Jos 6:25; The Israelites to the man of Beth-el Jud 1:23-26; David to Saul 1Sa 24:10-13,17

Nave's (2069) mercy of God Ge 8:21 18:26-32 19:16 Ex 2:24,25 15:13 20:2,6,22 Ex 22:27 25:17 32:14,34 33:19 34:6,7 Le 26:40-45 Nu 14:18-20 16:48 21:8 De 4:31 5:10,29 7:9 32:29,36,43 Jud 2:18 3:9,15 10:16 2Sa 12:13 14:14 24:14,16 1Ki 8:23 11:39 2Ki 13:23 14:26,27 1Ch 16:34 2Ch 5:13 7:3,6,14 24:19 30:9 36:15 Ezr 9:7-14 Ne 1:10 9:17-20,27-31 Job 11:6 23:2-6 24:12 33:14-30 Ps 18:50 25:6 30:5 31:7 32:1,2,5 36:5 50:21 57:10 Ps 62:12 65:3 69:16 78:4-72 80:1 85:2,3,10 Ps 86:5,13,15 89:2,28 99:8 100:5 103:3,8-14,17 Ps 106:1,43-46 107:1 108:4 111:4 116:5 117:2 118:1-4,29 Ps 119:64,156 130:3,4,7,8 135:14 136:3-26 138:2 145:8,9 Ps 146:7,8 Pr 16:6 28:13 Isa 1:5,18 6:7 12:1 17:6 24:13 Isa 54:9 55:7-9 57:11,15,16,18,19 60:10 65:2,8 Jer 2:9 3:12,22 4:27 5:10 9:24 29:11 30:11 31:20,34,37 Jer 32:18 33:8,11 36:3,6,7 46:28 50:20 51:5 La 3:22,23,31-33 Eze 14:22 16:6,42,63 18:23,31,32 Eze 20:17,42 33:11 36:25 Da 4:22-27 9:4,9 Ho 2:14-23 11:8,9 14:1-8 Joe 2:13,18 3:21 Am 7:3 Jon 4:2,10,11 Mic 7:18,19 Na 1:3 Zep 2:7 Zec 1:16,17 3:9 10:6 Mal 3:6 Mt 6:14 18:11-14,23-27 Lu 1:50,77,78 6:36 15:4-7 Ac 3:19 17:30 26:18 Ro 9:15,18 10:12,13 11:32 15:9 1Co 15:10 2Co 1:3 4:15 12:9 Eph 1:6-8 2:4-7 1Ti 1:13 Tit 3:5 Heb 4:16 8:12 Jas 2:13 4:8 5:11,15 1Pe 1:3 2:10 5:10 2Pe 3:9,15 1Jo 1:9 Re 2:21

Mystery

G: 3466 musterion {moos-tay'-ree-on}; from a derivative of muo (to shut the mouth); TDNT - 4:802,615; n n
AV - mystery 27; 27
hidden thing, secret, mystery; 1a) generally mysteries, religious secrets, confided only to the initiated and not to ordinary mortals; 1b) a hidden or secret thing, not obvious to the understanding; 1c) a hidden purpose or counsel; 1c1) secret will; 1c1a) of men; 1c1b) of God: the secret counsels which govern God in dealing with the righteous, which are hidden from ungodly and wicked men but plain to the godly; 3) in rabbinic writings, it denotes the mystic or hidden sense: of an OT saying, of an image or form seen in a vision, of a dream
Nave's (3502): of redemption De 29:29 Job 15:8 Ps 25:14 Pr 3:32 Am 3:7 Mt 11:25 13:11,35 Mr 4:11 Lu 8:10 Joh 3:8-12 Ro 16:25,26 1Co 2:7-10 2Co 3:12-18 Eph 1:9,10 3:3-5,9,18,19 6:19 Col 1:25-27 2:2 4:3,4 2Th 2:7 1Ti 3:9,16 Heb 5:11 1Pe 1:10-12 Re 10:7
(see Absolute 7 for an in-depth explanation of this term)

N-O

Natural

G: 5591 psuchikos {psoo-khee-kos'}; from 5590; TDNT - 9:661,1342; adj AV - natural 4, sensual 2; 6
1) of or belonging to breath; 1a) having the nature and characteristics of the breath; 1a1) the principal of animal life, which men have in common with the brutes; 1b) governed by breath; 1b1) the sensuous nature with its subjection to appetite and passion

Offering

H: 4503 minchah {min-khaw'}; from an unused root meaning to apportion, i.e. bestow; TWOT - 1214a; n f
AV - offering 164, present 28, gift 7, oblation 6, sacrifice 5, meat 1; 211
1) gift, tribute, offering, present, oblation, sacrifice, meat offering; 1a) gift, present; 1b) tribute; 1c) offering (to God); 1d) grain offering
G: 4374 prosphero {pros-fer'-o};from 4314 and 5342 (including its alternate); TDNT - 9:65,1252; v AV - offer 22, bring unto 10, bring to 4, bring 3, offer up 3, offer unto 1, offer to 1, misc 4; 48
1) to bring to, lead to; 1a) one to a person who can heal him or is ready to show him some kindness, one to a person who is to judge him; 1b) to bring a present or a thing, to reach or

hand a thing to one; 1c) to put to; 2) to be borne towards one, to attack, assail; 2a) to behave one's self towards one, deal with one

Nave's (3659): figurative Ps 51:17 Jer 33:11 Ro 12:1 Php 4:18 Heb 13:15; animal sacrifices a type of Christ

Ps 40:6-8 Heb 10:1-14 Isa 53:11,12 Le 16:21 Joh 1:29 1Co 5:7 2Co 5:21 Eph 5:2 Heb 9:19-28 10:1,11,12 13:11-13 Re 5:6; burnt Le 9:2; Its purpose was to make an atonement for sin Le 1:4 7:1; Ordinances concerning

#Ex 29:15-18 Le 1:1 ... 5:7-10 6:9-13 17:8,9 23:18,26-37 Nu 15:24,25 19:9 28:26-31 29:1; Offered daily, morning and evening Ge 15:17 Ex 29:38-42 Le 6:20 Nu 28:1 ... 29:6 1Ch 16:40 2Ch 2:4 13:11 Ezr 3:3 Eze 46:13-15; -drink Libations of wine offered with the sacrifices Ge 35:14 Ex 29:40,41 30:9 Le 23:13,18 Nu 6:17 15:24 28:5-15,24-31 29:6-11,18-40 2Ki 16:13 1Ch 29:21 2Ch 29:35 Ezr 7:17;free will Must be perfect (whole, complete) Le 22:17-25; Obligatory when signified in a vow De 16:10 23:23; heave Given to the priests' families as part of their benefits Le 10:14 Nu 5:9 18:10-19,24; human sacrifices forbidden Le 18:21 20:2-5 De 12:31; meat Ordinances concerning Ex 29:40,41 30:9 40:29 Le 2:1 ... 5:11,12 6:14-23 7:9-13,37 9:17 23:13,16,17 Nu 4:16 5:15,18,25,26 8:8 15:3-16,24 18:9 28:5,9,12,13,20,21,26-31 29:3,4,14; peace Laws concerning Ex 29:19-22,31 Le 7:11-15,18 9:3,4,15-21 23:19 Nu 6:14 10:10; sin Ordinances concerning Ex 29:10-14 Heb 13:11-13 Le 4:1 ... 5:1 ... 6:1-7,26-30 9:1-21 12:6-8 14:19,22,31 15:30 23:19 Nu 6:10,11,14,16 8:8,12 15:27 28:15,22-24,30 29:5,6,11,16-38; thank Ordinances concerning Le 7:11-15 22:29 De 12:11,12; trespass Ordinances concerning Le 5:1 ... 6:1-7 7:1-7 14:10-22 15:15,29,30 19:21,22 Nu 6:12 Ezr 10:19;

useless when not accompanied by genuine piety 1Sa 15:22 Ps 40:6 50:8-14 51:16,17 Pr 21:3,27 Isa 1:11-14 40:16 66:3 Jer 6:20 7:21-23 14:12 Hos 6:6 8:13 Am 5:21-24 Mic 6:6-8 Mr 12:33; vow Le 7:16,17 22:17-25 De 23:21-23; wave Ordinances concerning Ex 29:22,26-28 Le 7:29-34 8:25-29 9:19-21 10:14,15 23:10,11,17-20 Nu 5:25 6:19,20; wood Fuel for the temple Ne 10:34 13:31

Ordain

H: 03245 yacad {yaw-sad'}; a primitive root; TWOT - 875; v AV - foundation 15, lay 8, founded 8, ordain 2, counsel 2, established 2, foundation + 03117 1, appointed 1, instructed 1, set 1, sure 1; 42

1) to found, fix, establish, lay foundation; 1a) (Qal) to found, establish, begin; 1b) (Niphal); 1b1) to fix or seat themselves close together, sit in conclave; 1b2) to be founded; 1c) (Piel); 1c1) to found; 1c2) to establish, appoint, ordain; 1d) (Pual) to be founded, be laid; 1e) (Hophal) to be founded

G: 2525 kathistemi {kath-is'-tay-mee}; from 2596 and 2476; TDNT - 3:444,387; v AV - make 8, make ruler 6, ordain 3, be 2, appoint 1, conduct 1, set 1; 22

1) to set, place, put; 1a) to set one over a thing (in charge of it); 1b) to appoint one to administer an office; 1c) to set down as, constitute, to declare, show to be; 1d) to constitute, to render, make, cause to be; 1e) to conduct or bring to a certain place; 1f) to show or exhibit one's self; 1f1) come forward as

P

Parable

H: 04912 mashal {maw-shawl'}; apparently from 04910 in some original sense of superiority in mental action; TWOT - 1258a; n m AV - proverb 19, parable 18, byword 1, like 1; 39

1) proverb, parable; 1a) proverb, proverbial saying, aphorism; 1b) byword; 1c) similitude, parable; 1d) poem; 1e) sentences of ethical wisdom, ethical maxims

G: 3850 parabole {par-ab-ol-ay'}; from 3846; TDNT - 5:744,773; n f AV - parable 46, figure 2, comparison 1, proverb 1; 50
1) a placing of one thing by the side of another, juxtaposition, as of ships in battle; 2) metaph.; 2a) a comparing, comparison of one thing with another, likeness, similitude; 2b) an example by which a doctrine or precept is illustrated; 2c) a narrative, fictitious but agreeable to the laws and usages of human life, by which either the duties of men or the things of God, particularly the nature and history of God's kingdom are figuratively portrayed; 2d) a parable: an earthly story with a heavenly meaning; 3) a pithy and instructive saying, involving some likeness or comparison and having preceptive or admonitory force; 3a) an aphorism, a maxim; 4) a proverb; 5) an act by which one exposes himself or his possessions to danger, a venture, a risk
(see Absolute 7 for an in-depth explanation of this term)

Pentecost
G: 4005 pentekoste pen-tay-kos-tay'}; feminine of the ord. of 4004; TDNT - 6:44,826; n f AV - Pentecost 3; 3; Pentecost = "the fiftieth day"
1) the second of the three great Jewish feasts, celebrated at Jerusalem yearly, the seventh week after the Passover, in grateful recognition of the completed harvest
Nave's (3822): Called feast of weeks Ex 34:22 De 16:10; feast of harvest Ex 23:16; day of first fruits Nu 28:26; day of Pentecost Ac 2:1 20:16 1Co 16:8; Institution of Ex 23:16 34:22 Le 23:15-21 Nu 28:26-31 De 16:9-12,16; Holy Spirit given to the apostles on the first day of Ac 2:1

Perfection
H: 08503 takliyth {tak-leeth'}; from 03615; TWOT - 982f; n f AV - end 2, perfection 2, perfect 1; 5
1) end, perfection, consummation, completion, completeness; 1a) end; 1b) completeness
G: 5050 teleiosis {tel-i'-o-sis}; from 5448; TDNT - 8:84,1161; n f AV - performance 1, perfection 1; 2
1) a completing, a perfecting; 1a) fulfilment, accomplishment; 1b) the event which verifies the promise; 1c) consummation, perfection
Nave's (3830): unclassified Scriptures relating to Ge 17:1 De 5:32 18:13 Jos 23:6 1Ki 8:61 1Ch 28:9 29:19 2Ch 6:36 Job 9:20,21 Ps 18:32 37:31,37 101:2 106:3 119:1-3,6,96 Pr 2:21 Ec 7:20 Mt 5:6,48 19:21 Lu 6:40 1Co 2:6 2Co 7:1 13:9,11 Eph 4:11-13 Php 1:10 2:15 3:12-15 Col 1:21,22,28 2:9-11 3:14 4:12 1Th 3:10,13 2Ti 2:1 3:17 Heb 6:1 10:14 13:20,21 Jas 1:4,25 3:2 1Pe 5:10 1Jo 2:5 3:6-10 4:12 5:18
Nave's (4623): sinlessness — General Scriptures concerning Ps 119:3 Ac 24:16 Php 1:9-11 1Th 3:13 5:23 1Pe 4:1,2 1Jo 1:8,10 3:6,9
(see Absolute 1 and Absolute 5 for in-depth explanations of perfection)

Pride
H:1346 ga`avah {gah-av-aw'}; from 01342; TWOT - 299d; n f; AV - pride 9, excellency 3, haughtiness 2, arrogancy 1, highness 1, proud 1, proudly 1, swelling 1; 19
1) pride, majesty, a rising up; 1a) a rising up, swelling (of the sea); 1b) majesty (of Israel); 1c) pride, haughtiness
H:1363 gobahh {go'-bah};from 01361; TWOT - 305b; n m; AV - height 9, high 3, pride 2, excellency 1, haughty 1, loftiness 1; 17
1) height, exaltation; 1a) height; 1b) exaltation, grandeur
1c) haughtiness;
G: 5187 tuphoo {toof-o'-o}; from a derivative of 5188; v
AV - be proud 1, be lifted up with pride 1, highminded 1; 3

1) to raise a smoke, to wrap in a mist; 1a) metaph.; 1a1) to make proud, puff up with pride, render insolent; 1a2) to be puffed up with haughtiness or pride; 2) to blind with pride or conceit, to render foolish or stupid; 2a) beclouded, besotted

G:5243 huperephania {hoop-er-ay-fan-ee'-ah}; from 5244; TDNT - 8:525,1231; n f; AV - pride 1; 1

1) pride, haughtiness, arrogance; 2) the character of one who, with a swollen estimate of his own powers or merits, looks down on others and even treats them with insolence and contempt

G: 212 alazoneia {al-ad-zon-i'-a}; from 213; TDNT - 1:226,36; n f; AV - boasting 1, pride 1; 2

1) empty, braggart talk; 2) an insolent and empty assurance, which trusts in its own power and resources and shamefully despises and violates divine laws and human rights; 3) an impious and empty presumption which trusts in the stability of earthy things

Nave's (3975) General Scriptures concerning Ex 18:10,11 Le 26:19 De 8:11-14,17-20 Jud 9:14,15 1Sa 2:3-5 1Ki 20:11 2Ki 14:9,10 2Ch 25:18,19 Job 11:12 12:2,3 13:2,5 15:1-13 18:3 21:31,32 32:9-13 37:24 Ps 9:20 10:2-6,11 12:4 18:27 31:23 49:11 52:7 73:6,8,9 75:4-6 101:5 119:21,69,70,78 138:6 Pr 3:34 6:16,17 8:13 10:17 11:2,12 12:9,15 13:10 14:21 15:5,10,12,25,32 16:5,18,19 17:19 18:11,12 20:6 21:4,24 25:14,27 26:5,12,16 27:2 28:11,25 29:8,23 30:12,13 Isa 2:11-17 3:16-26 5:8,15 9:9,10 10:5-16 13:11 14:12-16 16:6,7 22:16,19 23:7,9 24:4,21 26:5 28:3 47:4-10 Jer 9:23,24 13:9,15,17 48:7,14,15,29 49:4,16 50:31,32 Eze 16:56 28:2-9,17 30:6 31:10-14 Da 4:37 11:45 Ho 5:5 7:10 10:11 Ob 1:3,4 Na 3:19 Hab 2:4,5,9 Zep 2:10,15 3:11 Mal 4:1 Mt 20:26,27 23:6-8,10-12 Mr 7:21 10:43 12:38,39 Lu 1:51,52 9:46 11:43 14:8,9 18:14 20:45-47 Ro 1:22,29,30 11:17-21,25 12:3,16 1Co 1:29 3:18 4:6-8,10 5:2,6 8:1,2 10:12 13:4 14:38 2Co 10:5,12,18 12:7 Ga 6:3 Eph 4:17 Php 2:3 1Ti 2:9 3:6 6:3,4,17 2Ti 3:2,4 Jas 3:1 4:6 1Pe 5:3,5 1Jo 2:16 Re 3:17,18 18:7,8; Naaman, refusing to wash in the Jordan River 2Ki 5:11-13; Hezekiah, in displaying his resources 2Ki 20:13 2Ch 32:31 Isa 39:2; Uzziah 2Ch 26:16-19; Haman Es 3:5 5:11,13 6:6 7:10; Kings of Tyre Eze 28:2; Nebuchadnezzar Da 4:30-34 5:20

Priesthhood

H: 03548 kohen {ko-hane'}; active participle of 03547; TWOT - 959a; n m AV - priest 744, own 2, chief ruler 2, officer 1, princes 1; 750

1) priest, principal officer or chief ruler; 1a) priest-king (Melchizedek, Messiah); 1b) pagan priests; 1c) priests of Jehovah; 1d) Levitical priests; 1e) Zadokite priests; 1f) Aaronic priests; 1g) the high priest *(see also "ministry")*

Pure

H: 02889 tahowr {taw-hore'} or tahor {taw-hore'}; from 02891; TWOT - 792d; adj AV - clean 50, pure 40, fair 2, purer 1, variant 1; 94

1) pure, clean; 1a) clean (ceremonially - of animals); 1b) pure (physically); 1c) pure, clean (morally, ethically)

G: 2513 katharos kath-ar-os'}; of uncertain affinity; TDNT - 3:413,381; adj AV - pure 17, clean 10, clear 1; 28

1) clean, pure; 1a) physically; 1a1) purified by fire; 1a2) in a similitude, like a vine cleansed by pruning and so fitted to bear fruit; 1b) in a levitical sense; 1b1) clean, the use of which is not forbidden, imparts no uncleanness; 1c) ethically; 1c1) free from corrupt desire, from sin and guilt; 1c2) free from every admixture of what is false, sincere genuine; 1c3) blameless, innocent; 1c4) unstained with the guilt of anything

Nave's (4030): purity of heart Ps 12:6 19:8 24:3-5 51:7 65:3 119:140 Pr 15:26 20:9 21:8 30:12 Isa 1:18,25 6:7 Da 12:10 Mic 6:11 Mal 3:2,3 Mt 5:8 Joh 15:2 Php 4:8 1Ti 1:5 3:9 5:22 2Ti 1:3 2:21,22 Tit 1:15 Heb 9:13,14 10:2 Jas 4:8 1Pe 1:22 1Jo 3:3

R

Reason

H: 03198 yakach {yaw-kahh'}; a primitive root; TWOT - 865; v AV - reprove 23, rebuke 12, correct 3, plead 3, reason 2, chasten 2, reprover + 0376 2, appointed 1, arguing 1, misc 9; 59
1) to prove, decide, judge, rebuke, reprove, correct, be right; 1a) (Hiphil); 1a1) to decide, judge; 1a2) to adjudge, appoint; 1a3) to show to be right, prove; 1a4) to convince, convict; 1a5) to reprove, chide; 1a6) to correct, rebuke; 1b) (Hophal) to be chastened; 1c) (Niphal) to reason, reason together; 1d) (Hithp) to argue
G: 1260 dialogizomai {dee-al-og-id'-zom-ahee}; from 1223 and 3049; TDNT - 2:95,155; v AV - reason 11, dispute 1, cast in the mind 1, muse 1, think 1, consider 1; 16
1) to bring together different reasons, to reckon up the reasons, to reason, revolve in one's mind, deliberate
Nave's (4099): reasoning — with God Job 13:3,17-28; Natural understanding Da 4:36; Not a sufficient guide in human affairs De 12:8 Pr 3:5 14:12; Of the Pharisees Lu 5:21,22 20:5; The gospel cannot be explained by 1Co 1:18-28 2:1-14

Reconciliation

H: 03722 kaphar {kaw-far'}; a primitive root; TWOT - 1023,1024,1025,1026; v AV - atonement 71, purge 7, reconciliation 4, reconcile 3, forgive 3, purge away 2, pacify 2, atonement...made 2, merciful 2, cleansed 1,
disannulled 1, appease 1, put off 1, pardon 1, pitch 1; 102
1) to cover, purge, make an atonement, make reconciliation, cover over with pitch; 1a) (Qal) to coat or cover with pitch; 1b) (Piel); 1b1) to cover over, pacify, propitiate; 1b2) to cover over, atone for sin, make atonement for; 1b3) to cover over, atone for sin and persons by legal rites; 1c) (Pual); 1c1) to be covered over; 1c2) to make atonement for; 1d) (Hithpael) to be covered
G: 2643 katallage {kat-al-lag-ay'}; from 2644; TDNT - 1:258,40; n f AV - reconciliation 2, atonement 1, reconciling 1; 4
1) exchange; 1a) of the business of money changers, exchanging equivalent values; 2) adjustment of a difference, reconciliation, restoration to favor; 2a) in the NT of the restoration of the favor of God to sinners that repent and put their trust in the expiatory death of Christ
Nave's (4108): between God and man Le 8:15 Eze 45:15 Da 9:24 Ro 5:1,10 11:15 2Co 5:18-21 Eph 2:15-18 Col 1:20-22 Heb 2:17

Redemption

H: 01353 g@ullah {gheh-ool-law'}; pass. participle of 01350; TWOT - 300b; n f; AV - redeem 5, redemption 5, again 1, kindred 1, redeem + 04672 1, right 1; 14
1) kindred, redemption, right of redemption, price of redemption; 1a) kin, kindred; 1b) redemption; 1c) right of redemption; 1d) price of redemption, redemption price
G: 629 apolutrosis {ap-ol-oo'-tro-sis}; from a compound of 575 and 3083; TDNT - 4:351,*; n f;
AV - redemption 9, deliverance 1; 10
1) a releasing effected by payment of ransom; 1a) redemption, deliverance; 1b) liberation procured by the payment of a ransom
Nave's (4113): of our souls Ps 111:9 130:7 Mt 20:28 Mr 10:45 Lu 2:38 Ac 20:28 Ro 3:24-26 1Co 1:30 6:20 7:23 Ga 1:4 2:20 4:4,5 Eph 1:7 5:2 Col 1:14,20-22 1Ti 2:6 Tit 2:14 Heb 9:12,15 1Pe 1:18,19 Re 5:9,10

Regeneration

G: 3824 palinggenesia {pal-ing-ghen-es-ee'-ah}; from 3825 and 1078; TDNT - 1:686,117; n f AV - regeneration 2; 2

1) new birth, reproduction, renewal, recreation, regeneration; 1a) hence renovation, regeneration, the production of a new life; consecrated to God, a radical change of mind for the better. The word often used to denote the restoration of a thing to its pristine state, its renovation, as a renewal or restoration of life after death; 1b) the renovation of the earth after the deluge; 1c) the renewal of the world to take place after its destruction by fire, as the Stoics taught; 1d) the signal and glorious change of all things (in heaven and earth) for the better, that restoration of the primal and perfect condition of things which existed before the fall of our first parents, which the Jews looked for in connection with the advent of the Messiah, and which Christians expected in connection with the visible return of Jesus from heaven.

1e) other uses; 1e2) of the restoration of the Jewish nation after exile; 1e3) of the recovery of knowledge by recollection

Nave's (4124): General Scriptures concerning

De 29:4 30:6 1Ki 8:58 Ps 36:9 51:2,7,10 65:3 68:18 87:4,6 110:3 Pr 4:23 12:28 14:27 16:1 Isa 1:16,17,25 4:4 12:3 26:12 29:23 32:3,4,15,17 35:5,6 42:16 43:7 44:3-5 49:9 55:1-3 Jer 13:23 17:13,14 24:7 31:3,33,34 32:38-40 33:6 Eze 11:19,20 16:9 18:31 36:26,27,29 37:1-14 44:7,9 Zec 12:10 Mt 12:33-35,43,44 13:23,33 18:3 Mr 4:20,26-29 5:19,20 10:15 Lu 1:16,17 8:35,38,39 13:21 18:17 Joh 1:4,13,16 3:3-8 4:10,14 5:24 6:44,45,47,50,51,57 8:12,32,36 10:9,10 13:8 15:1,3 17:2 Ac 2:38,47 3:26 11:17,21 15:9 16:14 21:19 26:18 Ro 2:28,29 6:3-23 7:6,24,25 8:2-6,9,13-16 12:2 15:16 1Co 1:9,24,30 2:12,14-16 3:6,7,9 6:11 12:6,13 15:10 2Co 1:21,22 3:3,18 4:6 5:5,17 Ga 2:20 4:29 6:15 Eph 2:1,5,8,10 4:7,8,16,21-24 5:14 Php 1:6 Col 2:11-13 3:9,10 2Th 2:13 Tit 3:5,6 Heb 4:1-12 8:10,11 10:16,17,22,23 Jas 1:18 5:19,20 1Pe 1:2,3,22,23 2:3 2Pe 1:3,4 1Jo 2:27,29 3:9,14 4:7 5:1,4,5,11,12,18

Religion

G: 2356 threskeia {thrace-ki'-ah}; from a derivative of 2357; TDNT - 3:155,337; n f AV - religion 3, worshipping 1; 4

1) religious worship; 1a) esp. external, that which consists of ceremonies; 1a1) religious discipline, religion

Repentance

H: 05164 nocham {no'-kham}; from 05162; TWOT - 1344a; n m AV - repentance 1; 1 repentance, sorrow

G: 3341 metanoia {met-an'-oy-ah}; from 3340; TDNT - 4:975,636; n f AV - repentance 24; 24

1) a change of mind, as it appears to one who repents, of a purpose he has formed or of something he has done

Nave's (4143): (A complete reversal of one's attitude and values, i.e. a turning toward God) — Attributed to God Ge 6:6,7 Ex 32:14 De 32:36 Jud 2:18 1Sa 15:11,29,35 2Sa 24:16 1Ch 21:15 Ps 106:45 110:4 135:14 Jer 15:6 18:8,10 26:3 42:10 Joe 2:13 Am 7:3,6 Jon 3:9,10 Exhortation to Pr 1:23-33 Jer 7:3,5 26:3 Ho 14:1-3 Am 5:4-6 Mt 3:2; exemplified Nu 21:7 2Sa 24:10,17 1Ch 21:17 2Ch 29:6 Ezr 9:4,6,10,13,14 Ne 1:6,7 9:16-37 Job 7:20 9:20 13:23 40:4 42:5 Ps 32:5 38:3,4,18 40:12 41:4 51:1-4,7-17 69:5,10 73:21,22 106:6 119:59,176 130:1-3 Isa 6:5 38:15,17 59:12-15 64:5-7 Jer 3:21,22,25 8:14 14:7,20 31:18,19 La 3:40,41 Da 9:5-7 10:12 Ho 6:1 14:3,8 Jon 3:10 Mic 7:9 Lu 15:17-20 1Co 15:9 2Co 7:9-11 1Pe 2:25

Revelation

G: 602 apokalupsis {ap-ok-al'-oop-sis}; from 601; TDNT - 3:563,405; n f AV - revelation 12, be revealed 2, to lighten + 1519 1, manifestation 1, coming 1, appearing 1; 18

1) a laying bear, making naked; 2) a disclosure of truth, instruction; 2a) concerning things before unknown; 2b) used of events by which things or states or persons hitherto withdrawn from view are made visible to all; 3) manifestation, appearance

S

Sabbath

H: 07673 shabath {shaw-bath'}; a primitive root; TWOT - 2323, 2323c; v AV - cease 47, rest 11, away 3, fail 2, celebrate 1, misc 7; 71
1) to cease, desist, rest; 2) (Qal) to keep or observe the sabbath

H: 07676 shabbath {shab-bawth'}; intensive from 07673; TWOT - 2323b; n f/m AV - sabbath 107, another 1; 108
Sabbath; 1a) sabbath; 1b) day of atonement; 1c) sabbath year; 1d) week; 1e) produce (in sabbath year)

1) The Sabbath as rest was established by God at the time of creation. God blessed the seventh day and **sanctified** it.

> *1 Thus the heavens and the earth were finished, and all the host of them. 2 And on the seventh day, God ended his work which he had made; and he rested on the seventh day from all his work which he had made. 3 And God blessed the seventh day, and sanctified it: because that in it he had rested from all his work which God created and made.* Genesis 2:1-3 (KJS)

2) It was a sign between God and his people that they might understand that it was God who sanctified man and not man.

> *12 And the Lord spake unto Moses, saying, 13 Speak thou also unto the children of Israel, saying, Verily my sabbaths ye shall keep: fir it [is] a sign between me and you throughout your generations; that [ye] may know that I [am] the Lord that doth sanctify you.* Exodus 31:12-13 (KJS)

God's plan of salvation was a salvation as a free gift. Man cannot rest in that free gift, so God gave a commandment that produces a habit of identifying doubt and unbelief while they are simply thoughts, not yet having been acted upon. The Sabbath day was God's way to prepare man to accept so great a rest as that of God doing the work in man to change him.

Lust in the commandment on adultery is the sin as a thought acted upon only in the mind, yet still sin in the eyes of God. Hatred in the commandment on murder is the sin as a thought acted upon though still in the mind. Jesus taught that the sin impacting the mind and not resisted, while not acted out in the flesh, was still sin.

Temptation is not sin, but if temptation is not recognized and those thoughts are allowed to impact and produce results, even in the mind alone, they constitute sin. So it is with doubt. The Sabbath day was ordained by God to teach man to identify the fear produced by thoughts of doubt and unbelief.

Every week, one day was set aside with a commandment to rest, carry no burden, or do no work. The habit this should have formed in the people was one of identifying the thoughts that are contrary to God's Word. Man would have found that the flesh could not rest but that the spirit man could.

If God was seeking a day of vacation for the flesh only, He would not have called for a year of Sabbath. To let the ground of an entire nation sit unused for one entire year would not produce rest in any man! It would produce fear and it would show man how little he knew about trusting God. It would show man that he has not learned to deal with doubt and unbelief God's way.

It is no wonder that the Christian community, which still preaches the other nine commandments from the pulpits, cannot rest in its salvation as a finished work. Christianity has ignored the sign commandment because man's intellect does not understand it.

In the New Testament, the writer to the Hebrews stated that Israel could not enter into her rest because of unbelief, and warned the New Testament Church that she would come to the same testing. It is further stated that there remains a keeping of Sabbath to the people of God.

3) Yearly Sabbath. Every six years, God commanded Israel to keep a year of Sabbath by allowing the ground to remain unplanted. They were to plant no crop that could feed and protect them from famine. Once committed to keeping the yearly Sabbath, they would have had to trust only in God for the next two years.

> *20 And them that had escaped from the sword carried he away to Babylon; where they were servants to him and his sons until the reign of the kingdom of Persia: 21 To fulfil the word of the LORD by the mouth of Jeremiah, until the land had enjoyed her sabbaths: [for] as long as she lay desolate she kept sabbath, to fulfil threescore and ten years.* 2 Chronicles 36:20-21 (KJS)

The people of Israel never voluntarily kept their yearly Sabbath. God made them keep it when they were carried away into Babylon. They were a nation for four hundred ninety years and they owed God one year of every seven. They were carried away for seventy years. The prophet Jeremiah prophesied that the seventy years in Babylon were the Sabbath fulfillment. That is how important the Sabbath is to God.

4) The Sabbath as Feast.

> *27 Also on the tenth [day] of this seventh month [there shall be] a day of atonement: it shall be an holy convocation unto you; and ye shall afflict your souls, and offer an offering made by fire unto the LORD. 28 And ye shall do no work in that same day: for it [is] a day of atonement, to make an atonement for you before the LORD your God. 29 For whatsoever soul [it be] that shall not be afflicted in that same day, he shall be cut off from among his people. 30 And whatsoever soul [it be] that doeth any work in that same day, the same soul will I destroy from among his people. 31 Ye shall do no manner of work: [it shall be] a statute for ever throughout your generations in all your dwellings. 32 It [shall be] unto you a sabbath of rest, and ye shall afflict your souls: in the ninth [day] of the month at even, from even unto even, shall ye celebrate your sabbath.* Leviticus 23:27-32 (KJS)

There is a day coming that will bring the Christian Church to a time of keeping Sabbath. While the world is resting in the flesh, the people of God will be resting in God. There will be no torment, no judgment, just rest. This will not be a time that the flesh will see a reason to rest, but faith in God will create rest in the soul.

Nave's (4230): Signifying a period of rest Ge 2:2,3 Le 23:1 25:1 26:34,35; unclassified Scriptures relating to Ge 2:2,3 Ex 16:5,23-30 20:8-11 23:12 31:13-17 34:21 35:2,3 Le 16:29-31 19:3,30 23:1-3,27-32 24:8 26:2,34,35 Nu 15:32-36 28:9,10 De 5:12-15 2Ki 4:23 1Ch 9:32 2Ch 36:21 Ne 9:13,14 10:31 13:15-22 Ps 92:1-15 118:24 Isa 1:13 56:2,4-7 58:13,14 66:23 Jer 17:21,22,24-27 La 1:7 2:6 Eze 20:12,13,16,20,21,24 22:8 23:38 44:24 46:1,3 Ho 2:11 Am 8:5

Mt 12:1-8,10-12 24:20 Mr 2:27,28 6:2 16:1 Lu 4:16,31 6:1-10 13:10-17 14:1-6 23:54,56 Joh
5:5-14 7:21-24 9:1-34 19:31 Ac 13:14,27,42,44 15:21 16:13 17:2 18:4 Col 2:16 Heb 4:4,9

Sacrifice
H: 02077 zebach {zeh'-bakh}; from 02076; TWOT - 525a; n m AV - sacrifice 155, offerings
6, offer 1; 162
1) sacrifice; 1a) sacrifices of righteousness; 1b) sacrifices of strife; 1c) sacrifices to dead
things; 1d) the covenant sacrifice; 1e) the Passover; 1f) annual sacrifice; 1g) thank offering
G: 2378 thusia {thoo-see'-ah}; from 2380; TDNT - 3:180,342; n f AV - sacrifice 29; 29
1) a sacrifice, victim
Nave's (4239): figurative Isa 34:6 Eze 39:17 Zep 1:7,8 Ro 12:1 Php 2:17 4:18; Of self-denial
Php 3:7,8; Of praise Ps 116:17 Jer 33:11 Ho 14:2 Heb 13:15

Saint
H: 06918 qadowsh {kaw-doshe'} or qadosh {kaw-doshe'}; from 06942; TWOT - 1990b; adj
AV - holy 65, Holy One 39, saint 12; 116
1) sacred, holy, Holy One, saint, set apart

Salvation
H: 03444 y@shuw`ah {yesh-oo'-aw}; passive participle of 03467; TWOT - 929b; n f AV -
salvation 65, help 4, deliverance 3, health 3, save 1, saving 1, welfare 1; 78
1) salvation, deliverance; 1a) welfare, prosperity; 1b) deliverance; 1c) salvation (by God);
1d) victory
G: 4991 soteria {so-tay-ree'-ah}; feminine of a derivative of 4990 as (properly, abstract)
noun; TDNT - 7:965,1132; n f
AV - salvation 40, the (one) be saved 1, deliver + 1325 1, health 1, saving 1, that (one) be
saved + 1519 1; 45
1) deliverance, preservation, safety, salvation; 1a) deliverance from the molestation of
enemies; 1b) in an ethical sense, that which concludes to the souls safety or salvation; 1b1)
of Messianic salvation; 2) salvation as the present possession of all true Christians; 3) future
salvation, the sum of benefits and blessings which the Christians, redeemed from all earthly
ills, will enjoy after the visible return of Christ from heaven in the consummated and
eternal kingdom of God.
Nave's (4259): unclassified Scriptures relating to Ge 12:1,3 Ex 15:2 De 30:19,20 32:15 2Sa
14:14 1Ki 8:41-43 1Ch 16:35 2Ch 6:41 Ps 3:8 36:8,9 37:39 46:4 63:5,6 65:4 68:18-20 86:13
90:14 91:16 95:1 98:2,3 106:8 107:9 121:1-8 132:16 Pr 1:20,21 8:1-5 9:1-6 Isa 1:18 2:5 25:6,7
29:18,19,24 32:1-4 35:8 44:3 45:17 46:12,13 49:10,11 50:10 51:4,5 52:10,15 55:1-3,6,7 56:1,6-
8 57:18,19 61:1-3 63:9 Jer 3:23 21:8 Eze 18:32 Joe 2:32 Am 5:4 Zec 14:8 Mal 4:2 Mt 1:21 3:9
11:28-30 18:14 21:31 22:9,10,14 23:37 24:14 28:19 Mr 2:17 16:15,16 Lu 2:10,31,32 3:6
5:31,32 7:47 13:29,30 14:16-24 15:2,4-32 19:10 24:47 Joh 1:7 3:14-17 4:14,22 5:40 6:35,37
7:37,38 10:16 11:51,52 12:32 15:4,5 Ac 2:39 4:12 5:20 11:17,18 13:26,38,39,47 15:7-9,11
16:17,30,31 20:21 28:28 Ro 1:5,14,16,17 2:26 3:21-26,28-30 4:1-25 5:1,2,15-21 7:24,25 9:30-
33 10:4,8-13 11:1-36 15:9,16 1Co 1:18 6:11 2Co 5:17,20 6:1,17 7:10 Ga 1:4 2:16 3:1-28 Eph
1:9,10,13 2:1,3-5,8,9,14,15,17 3:6,9 5:14 Php 2:12 3:7-11 Col 1:5,6,20-23,26,27 3:11 1Th 5:8-
10 2Th 2:13,14 1Ti 1:13,15,16 2:3-6 4:10 2Ti 1:9,10 2:10 3:15 Tit 2:11 3:3-7 Heb 1:14 2:3,10
4:1-10 5:9 7:25 Jas 1:21 1Pe 1:5,9,10 2Pe 3:9,15 1Jo 2:25 4:9,10 5:11 Jude 1:3 Re 3:17,18,20
5:9 7:9,10 14:6 21:6 22:17; conditions of Mt 3:2 18:3 19:16-21 24:13 Mr 1:4 Lu 3:8 14:25-33
18:18-26 Joh 3:3-12,14-18 5:24 6:28,29,47 9:35 11:25,26 12:36 20:31 Ac 2:38 3:19,23;
Plan of Mr 4:11 Joh 6:37,44,45,65 17:4 18:11 19:28-30 Ac 3:18 17:3 Ro 1:16,17 10:3-9
16:25,26 1Co 1:21-25 2:7-9 2Co 5:18,19 Ga 4:4,5 Eph 1:3-23 2:4-10 3:1-11 6:19 Col 1:19-
23,26,27 2Th 2:13,14 1Ti 3:16 2Ti 1:9,10 Heb 2:9,10,14-18 6:17-20 Re 5:2-5 10:7
(see Absolute 6 for an in-depth explanation of salvation)

Sanctification

H: 06942 qadash kaw-dash'}; a primitive root; TWOT - 1990; v AV - sanctify 108, hallow 25, dedicate 10, holy 7, prepare 7, consecrate 5, appointed 1, bid 1, purified 1, misc 7; 172
1) to consecrate, sanctify, prepare, dedicate, be hallowed, be holy, be sanctified, be separate; 1a) (Qal); 1a1) to be set apart, be consecrated; 1a2) to be hallowed; 1a3) consecrated, tabooed; 1b) (Niphal); 1b1) to show oneself sacred or majestic; 1b2) to be honoured, be treated as sacred; 1b3) to be holy; 1c) (Piel); 1c1) to set apart as sacred, consecrate, dedicate; 1c2) to observe as holy, keep sacred; 1c3) to honour as sacred, hallow; 1c4) to consecrate; 1d) (Pual); 1d1) to be consecrated; 1d2) consecrated, dedicated; 1e) (Hiphil); 1e1) to set apart, devote, consecrate; 1e2) to regard or treat as sacred or hallow; 1e3) to consecrate; 1f) (Hithpael); 1f1) to keep oneself apart or separate; 1f2) to cause Himself to be hallowed (of God); 1f3) to be observed as holy; 1f4) to consecrate oneself
G: 38 hagiasmos hag-ee-as-mos'}; from 37; TDNT - 1:113,14; n m; AV-holiness 5, sanctification 5; 10; 1) consecration, purification; 2) the effect of consecration
2a) sanctification of heart and life
Nave's (4268): All Israel sanctified Ex 19:10,14; The Lord is the Sanctifier Ex 31:13 Le 20:8 21:8 22:9; Tabernacle sanctified by God's presence Ex 29:43 40:34,35; unclassified Scriptures relating to Ex 31:13 33:16 Le 21:1-23 Jer 1:5 Eze 37:28 Joh 17:17,19 Ac 26:17,18 Ro 15:16 1Co 1:2,30 6:11 13:1-13 2Co 1:21,22 Ga 2:20 6:14 Eph 1:3,4 3:19 4:7,12,13,15,16 5:25-27 Col 2:11 1Th 4:3,4 5:23 2Th 2:13,14 2Ti 2:11,21 Heb 2:11 9:14 10:10,14 12:10 13:12,21 1Pe 1:2 2Pe 1:2-4 1Jo 1:9 Jude 1:24 Re 7:14
According to "The New Unger's Bible Dictionary" sanctification is defined as separation from the secular and sinful and setting apart for a sacred purpose. As the holiness of God means His separation from all evil, so sanctification, in the various Scripture applications of the term, has a kindred lofty significance.
In the OT economy, things, places, and times, as well as persons, were sanctified, i.e., consecrated to holy purposes (Gen. 2:3; Ex. 13:2; 40:10-13, etc.). These rites, however, when applied to persons were efficacious only in a ceremonial and legal sense and did not extend to the purifying of the moral and spiritual nature. They were types and shadows of the dispensation of grace, being reminders to the Jews of the necessity of spiritual cleansing but also of the gracious purpose of God to actually accomplish the work. So David prayed not only, "Purify me with hyssop, and I shall be clean," but also "Create in me a clean heart, O God, and renew a right spirit within me" (Psalm 51:7-10).
Although in the OT, as well as in the NT, men are sometimes called upon to sanctify themselves, i.e., to consecrate themselves truly to God by their own free will (Ex. 19:22; Lev. 11:44; 20:7-8; 1 Pet. 3:15), the thought everywhere prevails that inward cleansing is the work of God.
The NT presents the concept of sanctification in both positional and experiential aspects. Positional sanctification is the possession of everyone "in Christ." The great epistles of the NT first present the marvels of saving grace manifested in the believer's position and then close with an appeal for life consonant with this divinely wrought position (Rom. 12:1; Eph. 4:1; Col. 3:1-2). Positional sanctification is just as complete for the weakest and youngest believer as it is for the strongest and oldest. It depends only upon one's union with and position "in Christ." All born-again believers are "saints" and are "sanctified" (Acts 20:32; 1 Cor. 1:2; 6:11; Heb. 10:10; 14; Jude 3).
The basis of experiential sanctification, or actual holiness of life, is positional sanctification, or what one is in Christ. Only those "in Christ," that is, regenerate and thus concomitantly sanctified, are candidates for experiential sanctifications. This aspect of sanctification is effected by faith that reckons upon one's position in Christ (Rom. 6:1-10). One's position is true whether or not he reckons or counts it as true. But it becomes experientially real only in proportion as one reckons it to be true (Rom. 6:11).

Satan

H: 07854 satan {saw-tawn'}; from 07853; TWOT - 2252a; n m AV - Satan 19, adversary 7, withstand 1; 27

1) adversary, one who withstands; 1a) adversary (in general - personal or national); 2) superhuman adversary; 2a) Satan (as noun pr)

G: 4567 Satanas {sat-an-as'}; of Aramaic origin corresponding to 04566 (with the definite affix); TDNT - 7:151,1007; n pr m AV - Satan 36; 36

1) adversary (one who opposes another in purpose or act), the name given to; 1a) the prince of evil spirits, the inveterate adversary of God and Christ; 1a1) he incites apostasy from God and to sin; 1a2) circumventing men by his wiles; 1a3) the worshippers of idols are said to be under his control; 1a4) by his demons he is able to take possession of men and inflict them with diseases; 1a5) by God's assistance he is overcome 1b) a Satan-like man

Nave's (4291): Called Abaddon (Hebrew: Destroyer) Re 9:11; The accuser of our brethren Re 12:10; The adversary 1Pe 5:8; Beelzebul Mt 12:24 Mr 3:22 Lu 11:15; Belial 2Co 6:15; The Devil Mt 4:1 Lu 4:2,6 Re 20:2; Our common enemy Mt 13:39; Evil spirit 1Sa 16:14; The father of all lies Joh 8:44; Great red dragon Re 12:3; The liar Joh 8:44; The murderer Joh 8:44; That old serpent Re 12:9 20:2; The power of darkness Col 1:13; The prince of this world Joh 12:31 14:30 16:11;

Of demons Mt 12:24; Of the power of the air Eph 2:2;

Satan 1Ch 21:1 Job 1:6 Joh 13:27 Ac 5:3 26:18 Ro 16:20; The spirit that works in all disobedient people Eph 2:2; The tempter Mt 4:3 1Th 3:5; The god of this world 2Co 4:4; Unclean spirit Mt 12:43; Kingdom of, to be destroyed 2Sa 23:6,7

Sin

H: 02403 chatta'ah {khat-taw-aw'} or chatta'th {khat-tawth'}; from 02398; TWOT - 638e; n f AV - sin 182, sin offering 116, punishment 3, purification for sin 2, purifying 1, sinful 1, sinner 1; 296

1) sin, sinful; 2) sin, sin offering; 2a) sin; 2b) condition of sin, guilt of sin; 2c) punishment for sin; 2d) sin-offering; 2e) purification from sins of ceremonial uncleanness

G: 266 hamartia {ham-ar-tee'-ah}; from 264; TDNT - 1:267,44; n f AV - sin 172, sinful 1, offense 1; 174

1) equivalent to 264; 1a) to be without a share in; 1b) to miss the mark; 1c) to err, be mistaken; 1d) to miss or wander from the path of uprightness and honour, to do or go wrong; 1e) to wander from the law of God, violate God's law, sin; 2) that which is done wrong, sin, an offence, a violation of the divine law in thought or in act; 3) collectively, the complex or aggregate of sins committed either by a single person or by many

Nave's (4613): Progressive De 29:19 1Ki 16:31 Ps 1:1 Isa 5:18 30:1 Jer 9:3 16:11,12 Ho 13:2 2Ti 3:13; No escape from the consequences of Ge 3:8-12 Isa 28:18-22 Am 9:1-4 Mt 23:33 Heb 2:3; Attempt to cover, vain Isa 29:15 59:6; Secret sins Ps 19:12 44:21 64:2 90:8 Ec 12:14 Eze 8:12 11:5 Mt 10:26 Lu 8:17 12:2,3 Joh 3:20 Ro 2:16 Eph 5:12; Fools mock at Pr 14:9; unclassified Scriptures relating to, defining, illustrating

#De 29:18 2Ch 12:14 Job 14:4 22:5 Ps 25:11 95:10 Pr 4:23 24:8,9 Ec 5:6 Isa 1:6,18 44:20 Jer 7:24 17:9 Eze 20:16 Mt 5:28 7:17,18 12:31,33-35 13:24,25,38,39 15:2-20 Mr 3:29 Lu 6:45 12:10 Joh 8:34,44 Ro 5:12-21 7:7,13 14:23 1Co 5:6 Eph 2:1,2 Heb 3:13 12:15 Jas 1:14,15 2:10,11 4:1-3,17 2Pe 1:4 1Jo 3:4,6,8-10,15 5:16,17; confession of Le 16:21 Nu 14:40 2Sa 24:10,17 1Ch 21:17 2Ch 29:6 Ezr 9:4-7,10-15 Ne 1:6-9 9:2,3,5-38 Job 7:20 9:20 13:23 40:4 42:5 Ps 32:5 38:3,4,18 40:11,12 41:4 51:2-5 69:5 73:21,22 106:6 119:59,60,176 130:3 Isa 6:5 26:13 59:12-15 64:5-7 Jer 3:21,22,25 8:14,15 14:7,20 31:18,19 La 1:18,20 3:40-42 Da 9:5,6,8-11,15 Lu 15:17-21 1Co 15:9 Jas 5:16 1Jo 1:8-10; forgiveness of Ex 34:6,7 Le 4:20,26,31,35 5:4-13 Nu 14:18,20 15:25 2Sa 12:13 1Ki 8:22-50 Job 10:14 Ps 19:12 25:7,11,18 32:1,2,5 51:9 65:3 79:9 85:2,3 99:8 103:12 130:4 Isa 1:18 6:6,7 43:25,26 44:21,22 55:6,7 Jer 2:22 5:1,7 31:34

33:8 Eze 18:21,22 33:14-16 Mt 1:21 3:6 6:12,14,15 9:2,6 12:31,32 18:23-27,35 26:28 Mr 2:5,7 3:28 11:26 Lu 3:3 5:21,24 12:10 24:47 Joh 8:11 20:23 Ac 2:38 10:36,43 13:38,39 26:16-18 Ro 4:7,8 Eph 4:32 Col 2:13 Heb 8:12 9:22 10:2,17,18 Jas 5:15,20 1Jo 1:7,9 2:1,2,12 5:16 Re 1:5; fruits of Ge 3:7-24 4:9-14 6:5-7 De 29:18 1Ki 13:33,34 Job 4:8 5:2 13:26 20:11 Ps 5:10 9:15,16 10:2 94:23 141:10 Pr 1:31 3:35 5:22,23 8:36 10:24,29-31 11:5-7,18,19,27,29 12:13,14,21,26 13:5,6,15 22:8 27:8 28:1 29:6 30:20 Isa 3:9,11 9:18 14:21 50:11 57:20,21 Jer 2:17,19 4:18 5:25 7:19 14:16 21:14 Eze 11:21 22:31 23:31-35 Ho 8:7 10:13 12:14 13:9 Mic 7:13 Mr 7:21-23 Ac 9:5 Ro 5:12-21 7:5 1Co 3:3 6:9-11 Ga 5:19-21 6:7,8 1Pe 4:3; known to God Ge 3:11 4:10 18:13 Ex 16:8,9,12 Nu 12:2 14:26,27 De 1:34 31:21 32:34 Jos 7:10-15 Job 10:14 11:11 13:27 14:16,17 20:27 34:21,22,25 24:23 Ps 44:20,21 69:5 90:8 94:11 Ec 5:8 Isa 29:15 Jer 2:22 16:17 29:23 Eze 21:24 Ho 5:3 7:2 Am 5:12 9:1-4,8 Hab 2:11 Mal 2:14 Mt 10:26 22:18 26:46 Lu 6:8 Joh 4:17-19 5:42 6:64 13:11 Re 2:23; national, punishment of Ge 6:5-7 7:21,22 Le 26:14-38 De 9:5 Job 34:29,30 Isa 19:4 Jer 12:17 25:31-38 46:28 Eze 16:49,50 Jon 1:2; separates from God De 31:17,18 Jos 7:12 2Ch 24:20 Job 13:24 23:3,8,9 Ps 78:59-61 Isa 59:1,2 64:7 Eze 23:18 Ho 9:12 Am 3:2,3 Mic 3:4 Mt 7:23 25:41 Lu 13:27 Ro 8:7 Heb 12:14

Soul

H: 05315 nephesh {neh'-fesh}; from 05314; TWOT - 1395a; n f AV - soul 475, life 117, person 29, mind 15, heart 15, creature 9, body 8, himself 8, yourselves 6, dead 5, will 4, desire 4, man 3, themselves 3, any 3, appetite 2, misc 45; 751
1) soul, self, life, creature, person, appetite, mind, living being, desire, emotion, passion; 1a) that which breathes, the breathing substance or being, soul, the inner being of man; 1b) living being; 1c) living being (with life in the blood); 1d) the man himself, self, person or individual; 1e) seat of the appetites; 1f) seat of emotions and passions; 1g) activity of mind; 1g1) dubious; 1h) activity of the will; 1h1) dubious; 1i) activity of the character; 1i1) dubious
G: 5590 psuche {psoo-khay'}; from 5594; TDNT - 9:608,1342; n f AV - soul 58, life 40, mind 3, heart 1, heartily + 1537 1, not tr 2; 105
1) breath; 1a) the breath of life; 1a1) the vital force which animates the body and shows itself in breathing; 1a1a) of animals; 1a12) of men; 1b) life; 1c) that in which there is life; 1c1) a living being, a living soul; 2) the soul; 2a) the seat of the feelings, desires, affections, aversions (our heart, soul etc.); 2b) the (human) soul in so far as it is constituted that by the right use of the aids offered it by God it can attain its highest end and secure eternal blessedness, the soul regarded as a moral being designed for everlasting life; 2c) the soul as an essence which differs from the body and is not dissolved by death (distinguished from other parts of the body)

Spirit

H: 07307 ruwach {roo'-akh}; from 07306; TWOT - 2131a; n f AV - Spirit or spirit 232, wind 92, breath 27, side 6, mind 5, blast 4, vain 2, air 1, anger 1, cool 1, courage 1, misc 6; 378
1) wind, breath, mind, spirit; 1a) breath; 1b) wind; 1b1) of heaven; 1b2) quarter (of wind), side; 1b3) breath of air; 1b4) air, gas; 1b5) vain, empty thing; 1c) spirit (as that which breathes quickly in animation or agitation); 1c1) spirit, animation, vivacity, vigor; 1c2) courage; 1c3) temper, anger; 1c4) impatience, patience; 1c5) spirit, disposition (as troubled, bitter, discontented); 1c6) disposition (of various kinds), unaccountable or uncontrollable impulse; 1c7) prophetic spirit; 1d) spirit (of the living, breathing being in man and animals); 1d1) as gift, preserved by God, God's spirit, departing at death, disembodied being; 1e) spirit (as seat of emotion); 1e1) desire; 1e2) sorrow, trouble; 1f) spirit; 1f1) as seat or organ of mental acts; 1f2) rarely of the will; 1f3) as seat especially of moral character; 1g) spirit of God; 1g1) as inspiring ecstatic state of prophecy; 1g2) as impelling prophet to utter instruction or warning; 1g3) imparting warlike energy and executive and

administrative power; 1g4) as endowing men with various gifts; 1g5) as energy of life; 1g6) ancient angel and later Shekinah

G: 4151 pneuma {pnyoo'-mah}; from 4154; TDNT - 6:332,876; n n AV - Spirit 111, Holy Ghost 89, Spirit (of God) 13, Spirit (of the Lord) 5, (My) Spirit 3, Spirit (of truth) 3, Spirit (of Christ) 2, human (spirit) 49, (evil) spirit 47, spirit (general) 26, spirit 8, (Jesus' own) spirit 6, (Jesus' own) ghost 2, misc 21; 385

1) a movement of air (a gentle blast); 1a) of the wind, hence the wind itself; 1b) breath of nostrils or mouth; 2) the spirit, i.e. the vital principal by which the body is animated; 2a) the rational spirit, the power by which the human being feels, thinks, decides; 2b) the soul; 3) a spirit, i.e. a simple essence, devoid of all or at least all grosser matter, and possessed of the power of knowing, desiring, deciding, and acting; 3a) a life giving spirit; 3b) a human soul that has left the body; 3c) a spirit higher than man but lower than God, i.e. an angel; 3c1) used of demons, or evil spirits, who were conceived as inhabiting the bodies of men; 3c2) the spiritual nature of Christ, higher than the highest angels and equal to God, the divine nature of Christ; 4) of God; 4a) God's power and agency distinguishable in thought from his essence in itself considered; 4a1) manifest in the course of affairs; 4a2) by its influence upon the souls productive in the theocratic body (the church) of all the higher spiritual gifts and blessings; 4a3) God the Holy Spirit; 5) the disposition or influence which fills and governs the soul of any one; 5a) the efficient source of any power, affection, emotion, desire, etc.

Nave's (2393) Holy Spirit — General Scriptures concerning Ge 1:2 6:3 41:38 Ex 31:3 35:31 Nu 27:18 Ne 9:20 Job 16:19 32:8 33:4 Ps 51:11,12 103:9 139:7 Isa 4:4 6:8 11:2 28:6 30:1 32:15 40:13 42:1 44:3,4 48:16 51:12 54:13 59:19,21 61:1 63:10,11,14 Eze 36:27 37:9,14 39:29 Joe 2:28,29 Mic 2:7 3:8 Hag 2:5 Zec 4:1-7 12:10 Mt 1:18,20 3:11,16,17 4:1 10:20 12:28 28:19 Mr 1:10 12:36 13:11 Lu 1:15,35,67 2:25-27 3:22 4:18 11:13 12:12 24:49 Joh 1:9,32,33 3:5,6,34 4:14 6:45,63 7:38,39 14:16,17,26 15:26 16:7-14 20:22 Ac 1:2,5,8,16 2:2-4,33,38 4:8,31 5:3,4,9,32 6:5 7:51 8:15-19 9:31 10:19,20,44-47 11:15,16,24 13:2,4,9,52 15:8,28 16:6,7 19:2-6 20:28 Ro 1:4 5:3-5 8:1-27 9:1 11:33,34 14:17 15:13,16,18,19,30 1Co 2:4,10-14 3:16 6:11,19 12:3-11 2Co 1:22 3:3,6,8,17,18 5:5 6:4,6 13:14 Ga 3:2,3,14 4:6 5:5,17,18,22,23,25 6:8 Eph 1:12-14,17 2:18,22 3:5,16 4:3,4,30 5:9,18 6:17,18 Php 1:19 2:1 Col 1:8 1Th 1:5,6 4:8,9 5:19 2Th 2:13 1Ti 4:1 2Ti 1:7,14 Tit 3:5,6 Heb 2:4 3:7 6:4 9:14 10:15,29 1Pe 1:2,11,12,22 3:18 4:14 2Pe 1:21 1Jo 2:20 3:24 4:2,13 5:6-8 Jude 1:19,20 Re 1:4 2:7,11,29 4:5 5:6 11:11 14:13 19:10 22:17; withdrawn from incorrigible sinners Ge 6:3 De 32:30 Ps 51:11 Pr 1:24-28 Jer 7:29 Ho 4:17,18 5:6 9:12 Mt 15:14 Lu 13:7 Ro 1:24,26,28

T

Tabernacle/Temple

H: 04908 mishkan {mish-kawn'}; from 07931; TWOT - 2387c; n m AV - tabernacle 119, dwelling 9, habitation 5, dwellingplaces 3, place 1, dwelleth 1, tents 1; 139

1) dwelling place, tabernacle; 1a) dwelling-place; 1b) dwellings

G: 4633 skene {skay-nay'}; apparently akin to 4632 and 4639; TDNT - 7:368,1040; n f AV - tabernacle 19, habitation 1; 20

1) tent, tabernacle, (made of green boughs, or skins or other materials); 2) of that well-known movable temple of God after the pattern of which the temple at Jerusalem was built

Nave's (4808) Pattern of, revealed to Moses Ex 25:9 26:30 39:32,42,43 Ac 7:44 Heb 8:5; Materials for, voluntarily offered Ex 25:1-8 35:4-29 36:3-7; Workmen who constructed it were inspired Ex 31:1-11 35:30-35; Description of the frame Ex 26:15-37 36:20-38; The outer covering Ex 25:5 26:7-14 36:14-19; The second covering Ex 25:5 26:14 35:7,23 36:19 39:34; The curtains of Ex 26:1-14,31-37 27:9-16 35:15,17 36:8-19,35,37; The courtyard of Ex 27:9-17 38:9-16,18 40:8,33; The Holy Place of Ex 26:31-37 40:22-26 Heb 9:2-6,8; The Most Holy Place Ex 26:33-35 40:20,21 Heb 9:3-5,7,8; The furniture of Ex 25:10-40 27:1-

8,19 37:1 38:1-8; Completed Ex 39:32; Dedicated Nu 7:1; Sanctified Ex 29:43 40:9-16 Nu
7:1; Anointed with holy oil Ex 30:25,26 Le 8:10 Nu 7:1; Sprinkled with blood
#Le 16:15-20 Heb 9:21,23; Filled with the cloud of glory Ex 40:34-38; Strangers (foreigners)
forbidden to enter Nu 1:51; Tribes encamped around, while in the wilderness Nu 2:1; The
Lord reveals himself at Le 1:1 Nu 1:1 7:89 12:4-10 De 31:14,15; Symbol of spiritual things
Ps 15:1 Heb 8:2,5 9:1-12,24;

Tongue
H: 03956 lashown {law-shone'} or lashon {law-shone'}; also (in plural) feminine l@shonah
{lesh-o-naw'} from 03960; TWOT - 1131a; n m AV - tongue 98, language 10, bay 3, wedge
2, babbler 1, flame 1, speaker + 0376 1, talkers 1; 117
1) tongue; 1a) tongue (of men); 1a1) tongue (literal); 1a2) tongue (organ of speech); 1b)
language; 1c) tongue (of animals); 1d) tongue (of fire); 1e) wedge, bay of sea (tongue-
shaped)
G: 1100 glossa {gloce-sah'}; of uncertain affinity; TDNT - 1:719,123; n f AV - tongue 50; 50
1) the tongue, a member of the body, an organ of speech; 2) a tongue; 1a) the language or
dialect used by a particular people distinct from that of other nations
Nave's (4985) Language Ge 10:5,20 Isa 66:18 Re 7:9; Confusion of Ge 11:1-9; Gift of Ac 2:1-
18,33 10:46 19:6 1Co 12:10,28,30 14:1
Nave's (4986) tongues (the gift) — The miraculous gift granted according as God pleases
1Co 12:10,28,30 13:8 14:2-19,21-28,39

Truth
H: 0530 'emuwnah {em-oo-naw') or (shortened) 'emunah {em-oo-naw'}; from 0529;
TWOT - 116e; n f AV - faithfulness 18, truth 13, faithfully 5, office 5, faithful 3, faith 1,
stability 1, steady 1, truly 1, verily 1; 49
1) firmness, fidelity, steadfastness, steadiness
G: 225 aletheia {al-ay'-thi-a}; from 227; TDNT - 1:232,37; n f AV - truth 107, truly + 1909
1, true 1, verity 1; 110
1) objectively; 1a) what is true in any matter under consideration; 1a1) truly, in truth,
according to truth; 1a2) of a truth, in reality, in fact, certainly; 1b) what is true in things
appertaining to God and the duties of man, moral and religious truth; 1b1) in the greatest
latitude; 1b2) the true notions of God which are open to human reason without his super-
natural intervention; 1c) the truth as taught in the Christian religion, respecting God and
the execution of his purposes through Christ, and respecting the duties of man, opposing
alike to the superstitions of the Gentiles and the inventions of the Jews, and the corrupt
opinions and precepts of false teachers even among Christians; 2) subjectively; 2a) truth as
a personal excellence; 2a1) that candor of mind which is free from affection, pretence,
simulation, falsehood, deceit
Nave's (5033) Saints should worship God in Joh 4:24 Ps 145:18; Serve God in Jos 24:14 1Sa
12:24; Walk in the presence of God in 1Ki 2:4 2Ki 20:3; Esteem, as inestimable Pr 23:23;
Love Zec 8:19; Speak, to one another Zec 8:16 Eph 4:25; Write, upon the tables of the heart
Pr 3:3; The fruit of the Spirit is in Eph 5:9; God's servants should speak 2Co 12:6 Ga 4:16;
Teach in 1Ti 2:7; Is in Christ 1Ti 2:7; The ekklesia (body of Christ) is the pillar and ground
of 1Ti 3:15; Satan is devoid of Joh 8:44; Is one of God's attributes De 32:4 Isa 65:16; He
keeps, forever Ps 146:6

V-W

Veil
H: 07289 radiyd {raw-deed'}; from 07286 in the sense of spreading; TWOT - 2120a; n m AV
- veil 1, vails 1; 2

1) something spread, wide wrapper or large veil
G: 2665 katapetasma {kat-ap-et'-as-mah}; from a compound of 2596 and a congener of 4072; TDNT - 3:628,420; n n AV - veil 6; 6
1) a veil spread out, a curtain; 1a) the name given to the two curtains in the temple at Jerusalem, one of them at the entrance to the temple separated the Holy Place from the outer court, the other veiled the Holy of Holies from the Holy Place

Wilderness

H: 01696 dabar {daw-bar'}; a primitive root; TWOT - 399; v AV - speak 840, say 118, talk 46, promise 31, tell 25, commune 20, pronounce 14, utter 7, command 4 misc 38; 1143
1) to speak, declare, converse, command, promise, warn, threaten, sing; 1a) (Qal) to speak; 1b) (Niphal) to speak with one another, talk; 1c) (Piel); 1c1) to speak; 1c2) to promise; 1d) (Pual) to be spoken; 1e) (Hithpael) to speak; 1f) (Hiphil) to lead away, put to flight
H: 04057 midbar {mid-bawr'}; from 01696 in the sense of driving; TWOT - 399k,399L; n m AV - wilderness 255, desert 13, south 1, speech 1, wilderness + 0776 1; 271
1) wilderness; 1a) pasture; 1b) uninhabited land, wilderness; 1c) large tracts of wilderness (around cities); 1d) wilderness (fig.); 2) mouth; 2a) mouth (as organ of speech)
G: 2048 eremos {er'-ay-mos}; of uncertain affinity; TDNT - 2:657,255; adjective AV - wilderness 32, desert 13, desolate 4, solitary 1; 50
1) solitary, lonely, desolate, uninhabited; 1a) used of places; 1a1) a desert, wilderness; 1a2) deserted places, lonely regions; 1a3) an uncultivated region fit for pasturage; 1b) used of persons; 1b1) deserted by others; 1b2) deprived of the aid and protection of others, especially of friends, acquaintances, kindred; 1b3) bereft; 1b3a) of a flock deserted by the shepherd; 1b3b) of a women neglected by her husband, from whom the husband withholds himself

Will Worship

G: 1479 ethelothreskeia {eth-el-oth-race-ki'-ah}; from 2309 and 2356; TDNT - 3:155,337; n f AV - will worship 1; 1
1) voluntary, arbitrary worship; 1a) worship which one prescribes and devises for himself, contrary to the contents and nature of faith which ought to be directed to Christ; 1b) said of the misdirected zeal and the practice of ascetics

Wisdom

H: 02451 chokmah {khok-maw'}; from 02449; TWOT - 647a; n f; AV - wisdom 145, wisely 2, skilful man 1, wits 1; 149
1) wisdom; 1a) skill (in war); 1b) wisdom (in administration); 1c) shrewdness, wisdom; 1d) wisdom, prudence (in religious affairs); 1e) wisdom (ethical and religious)
G: 4678 sophia {sof-ee'-ah}; from 4680; TDNT - 7:465,1056; n f; AV - wisdom 51; 51
1) wisdom, broad and full of intelligence; used of the knowledge of very diverse matters; 1a) the wisdom which belongs to men; 1a1) spec. the varied knowledge of things human and divine, acquired by acuteness and experience, and summed up in maxims and proverbs; 1a2) the science and learning; 1a3) the act of interpreting dreams and always giving the sagest advice; 1a4) the intelligence evinced in discovering the meaning of some mysterious number or vision; 1a5) skill in the management of affairs; 1a6) devout and proper prudence in intercourse with men not disciples of Christ, skill and discretion in imparting Christian truth; 1a7) the knowledge and practice of the requisites for godly and upright living; 1b) supreme intelligence, such as belongs to God; 1b1) to Christ; 1b2) the wisdom of God as evinced in forming and executing counsels in the formation and government of the world and the scriptures
Nave's (5183) spiritual unclassified Scriptures relating to De 32:29 Job 5:27 8:8,10 12:2,3,7-13,16,17,22 28:12-28 32:9 42:5 Ps 2:10 9:10 76:1 107:43 111:10 Pr 1:5,7,21-33 2:1-20

3:13-26,34,35 4:4-13,18-22 5:12 7:2-4 8:1-36 9:1-6,9-12 10:8,13,14,21,23 11:9,12 12:1,8,15
13:14-16 14:6-8,16,18,33 15:2,7,33 16:16,20-24 17:10,24 18:15 19:8,20 21:11 22:17-21
23:12,19,23 24:13,14 28:5,7 29:3 Ec 8:1,5 9:13-18 10:12 12:11 Isa 2:3 11:9 29:24 33:6 Jer
9:23,24 31:34 Da 11:32,33 12:3,4,10 Ho 6:3,6 14:9 Mt 6:22,23 7:24,25 11:19 25:1-13 Mr
12:32-34 Lu 1:17 7:35 11:34-36 Joh 7:17 8:32 10:4,14 17:3,8,25 Ac 6:10 Ro 15:14 16:19 1Co
2:6-16 3:18 8:3 13:11 14:20 2Co 2:11 8:7 Ga 4:9 Eph 4:11-13 5:15-17 Php 3:7-10 Col 3:10,16
1Th 5:4,5 1Ti 2:4 2Ti 3:15 Jas 3:13 1Jo 4:6; Spiritual, from God Ex 4:11,12 8:9,10 De
4:5,6,35,36 29:4 1Ch 22:12 Ne 9:20 Job 4:3 11:5,6 22:21,22 32:7,8 33:16 35:10,11 36:22
38:36,37 Ps 16:7 19:1,2 25:8,9,12,14 32:8 36:9 51:6 71:17 94:12 112:4 119:130 Pr 1:23 2:6,7
3:5,6 Ec 2:26 Isa 11:1-3 30:21 42:6,7,16 48:17 54:13 Jer 24:7 Da 1:17 2:20-23 Mt 11:25-27
13:11 16:16,17 Lu 1:76-79 12:11,12 21:15 24:32,45 Joh 1:1,4,5,7-9,17 6:45 8:12,31,32 9:5,39
12:46 14:7 16:13,14 17:6,26 18:37 Ro 1:19,20 1Co 1:30 2:9-14 12:8 2Co 4:6 Php 3:15 Col
1:26-28 2Ti 1:7 Jas 3:17 2Pe 1:2-5,8,12 3:18 1Jo 2:20,27 5:20; worldly Ge 3:6,7 Job 4:18-21
5:13 11:2,12 37:24 Pr 3:7 15:21,22 16:25 17:2,10 18:1 20:18 21:20,22,30 24:3-7 28:11 Ec 1:18
2:1-26 7:11-13,16-25 8:1,16,17 10:2,3,10 Isa 5:21 28:24-29 29:14-16 47:10,11 Jer 8:7-9
9:23,24 49:7 Mt 6:23 7:24-27 11:25 Lu 10:21 16:8 Ro 1:21-23 1Co 1:17-26 2:1-14 3:18-20
8:1,2 2Co 1:12 Col 2:8 1Ti 6:20,21

Word

H: 01697 dabar {daw-baw'}; from 01696; TWOT - 399a; n m AV - word 807, thing 231,
matter 63, acts 51, chronicles 38, saying 25, commandment 20, misc 204; 1439
1) speech, word, speaking, thing; 1a) speech; 1b) saying, utterance; 1c) word, words; 1d)
business, occupation, acts, matter, case, something, manner (by extension)
G: 3056 logos {log'-os}; from 3004; TDNT - 4:69,505; n m AV - word 218, saying 50,
account 8, speech 8, Word (Christ) 7, thing 5, not tr 2, misc 32; 330
1) of speech; 1a) a word, uttered by a living voice, embodies a conception or idea; 1b) what
someone has said; 1b1) a word; 1b2) the sayings of God; 1b3) decree, mandate or order;
1b4) of the moral precepts given by God; 1b5) Old Testament prophecy given by the
prophets; 1b6) what is declared, a thought, declaration, aphorism, a weighty saying, a
dictum, a maxim; 1c) discourse; 1c1) the act of speaking, speech; 1c2) the faculty of speech,
skill and practice in speaking; 1c3) a kind or style of speaking; 1c4) a continuous speaking
discourse—instruction; 1d) doctrine, teaching; 1e) anything reported in speech; a
narration, narrative; 1f) matter under discussion, thing spoken of, affair, a matter in
dispute, case, suit at law; 1g) the thing spoken of or talked about; event, deed; 2) its use as
respect to the mind alone; 2a) reason, the mental faculty of thinking, meditating, reasoning,
calculating; 2b) account, i.e. regard, consideration; 2c) account, i.e. reckoning, score; 2d)
account, i.e. answer or explanation in reference to judgment; 2e) relation, i.e. with whom as
judge we stand in relation; 2e1) reason would; 2f) reason, cause, ground; 3) In John,
denotes the essential Word of God, Jesus Christ, the personal wisdom and power in union
with God, his minister in creation and government of the universe, the cause of all the
world's life both physical and ethical, which for the procurement of man's salvation put on
human nature in the person of Jesus the Messiah and shone forth conspicuously from His
words and deeds. A Greek philosopher named Heraclitus first used the term *Logos* around
600 B.C. to designate the divine reason or plan which coordinates a changing universe. This
word was well suited to John's purpose in John 1.
Nave's (5193) Called book Ps 40:7 Re 22:19; Compared To seed Mt 13:3-8,18-23,37,38 Mr
4:3-20,26-32 Lu 8:5-15; To a two-edged sword Heb 4:12; Searching of, commanded Joh 5:39
7:52; Texts of, to be written on door-posts De 6:9 11:20; Not to be added to, or taken from
De 4:2 12:32 Re 22:18,19; Conviction of sin from reading 2Ki 22:9-13 2Ch 17:7-10 34:1;
Fulfilled by Jesus Mt 5:17 Lu 24:27 Joh 19:24; Testify of Jesus
#Joh 5:39 Ac 10:43 18:28 1Co 15:3; The standard of the judgment Joh 12:48 Ro 2:16; Not to
be handled deceitfully 2Co 4:2; inspiration of Ex 19:7 20:1 24:4,12 25:21 31:18 32:16

34:27,32 Le 26:46 De 4:5,14 11:18 31:19,22 2Ki 17:13 2Ch 33:18 Job 23:12 Ps 78:5 99:7
147:19 Ec 12:11 Isa 30:12,13 34:16 59:21 Jer 30:2 36:1,2,27,28,32 51:59-64 Eze 11:25 Da
10:21 Ho 8:12 Zec 7:12 Mt 22:31,32 Lu 1:1-4,68-73 Ac 1:16 28:25 Ro 3:1,2 1Co 2:12,13 7:10
14:37 Eph 6:17 Col 3:16 1Th 2:13 4:1-3 1Ti 6:3-5 2Ti 3:16,17 Heb 1:1,2 3:7,8 4:12 5:12 1Pe
1:11,12 2Pe 1:21 3:2,15 1Jo 1:1-5 Re 1:1,2,11,17-19 2:7 19:10 22:6-8

Workmanship

G: 4161 poiema {poy'-ay-mah}; from 4160; TDNT - 6:458,895; n n; AV - thing that is made
1, workmanship 1; 2
1) that which has been made; 2) a work; 2a) of the works of God as creator

Works

H: 04639 ma`aseh {mah-as-eh'}; from 06213; TWOT - 1708a; n m AV - work 189,
needlework + 07551 5, acts 4, labor 4, doing 4, art 3, deed 3, misc 23; 235 1) deed, work; 1a)
deed, thing done, act; 1b) work, labor;
1c) business, pursuit; 1d) undertaking, enterprise; 1e) achievement; 1f) deeds, works (of
deliverance and judgment); 1g) work, thing made; 1h) work (of God); 1i) product
G: 2041 ergon {er'-gon}; from a primary (but obsolete) ergo (to work); TDNT - 2:635,251;
n n AV - work 152, deed 22, doing 1, labor 1; 176
1) business, employment, that which any one is occupied; 1a) that which one undertakes to
do, enterprise, undertaking; 2) any product whatever, any thing accomplished by hand, art,
industry, or mind; 3) an act, deed, thing done: the idea of working is emphasized in opp. to
that which is less than work
Nave's (5196) insufficiency of, for salvation Ps 49:7,8 127:1,2 Ec 1:14 Isa 43:26 57:12 64:6
Eze 7:19 33:12-19 Da 9:18 Mt 5:20 Lu 17:7-10 18:9-14 Ac 13:39 Ro 3:20-31 4:1-22 8:3
9:16,31,32 11:6 1Co 13:1-3 Ga 2:16,19,21 3:1-29 4:9-11 5:2,4,6,18 6:15 Eph 2:8,9 Php 3:3-9
Col 2:20-23 2Ti 1:9 Tit 3:4,5 Heb 4:3-10 6:1,2 9:1-14 Jas 2:10,11

World

H: 08398 tebel {tay-bale'}; from 02986; TWOT - 835h; n f AV - world 35, habitable part 1;
36
1) world
G: 2889 kosmos {kos'-mos}; probably from the base of 2865; TDNT - 3:868,459; n m AV -
world 186, adorning 1; 187
1) an apt and harmonious arrangement or constitution, order, government; 2) ornament,
decoration, adornment, i.e. the arrangement of the stars, 'the heavenly hosts', as the
ornament of the heavens. 1 Pet. 3:3; 3) the world, the universe; 4) the circle of the earth, the
earth; 5) the inhabitants of the earth, men, the human race; 6) the ungodly multitude; the
whole mass of men alienated from God, and therefore hostile to the cause of Christ; 7)
world affairs, the aggregate of things earthly; 7a) the whole circle of earthly goods, endow-
ments riches, advantages, pleasures, etc, which although hollow and frail and fleeting, stir
desire, seduce from God and are obstacles to the cause of Christ; 8) any aggregate or
general collection of particulars of any sort; 8a) the Gentiles as contrasted to the Jews
(Rom. 11:12 etc); 8a) of believers only, John 1:29; 3:16; 3:17; 6:33; 12:47; 1 Cor. 4:9; 2 Cor.
5:19
Nave's (5198) worldliness — General Scriptures concerning 1Sa 8:19,20 Job 20:4-29 21:11-
15 Ps 49:16-18 73:2-22 Pr 14:12,13 15:21 21:17 23:20,21 27:1,7 Ec 1:8 2:1-12 6:11,12 8:15-17
10:19 11:9,10 Isa 22:12,13 24:7-11 28:4 32:9-11 47:7-9 Ho 9:1,11,13 Am 6:3-7 8:10 Mic 2:10
6:14 Hag 1:6 Mt 6:25-34 10:39 13:22 16:25,26 18:1-4 22:2-6 24:38,39 Mr 4:19 8:35-37 9:33-
36 Lu 8:14 9:46-48 12:19 14:17-24 16:1-13,19-25 17:26-29,33 21:34 Joh 5:44 12:25,43 15:19
Ro 12:2 1Co 7:29-31 10:6 15:32 Php 3:18,19 Col 3:2,5 1Ti 5:6 2Ti 2:4,22 3:2-7 Tit 2:12 3:3

Heb 11:24-26 Jas 2:1-4 4:4,9 5:5 1Pe 1:14,24 2:11 4:3,4 2Pe 2:12-15,18 1Jo 2:15-17 Jude 1:11-13,16,19

Worship

H: 7812 shachah {shaw-khaw'}; a primitive root; TWOT - 2360; v AV - worship 99, bow 31, bow down 18, obeisance 9, reverence 5, fall down 3, themselves 2, stoop 1, crouch 1, misc 3; 172
1) to bow down; 1a) (Qal) to bow down; 1b) (Hiphil) to depress (fig); 1c) (Hithpael); 1c1) to bow down, prostrate oneself; 1c1a) before superior in homage; 1c1b) before God in worship; 1c1c) before false gods; 1c1d) before angel
G: 4352 proskuneo {pros-koo-neh'-o}; from 4314 and a probable derivative of 2965 (meaning to kiss, like a dog licking his master's hand); TDNT - 6:758,948; v AV - worship 60; 60
1) to kiss the hand to (towards) one, in token of reverence; 2) among the Orientals, esp. the Persians, to fall upon the knees and touch the ground with the forehead as an expression of profound reverence; 3) in the NT by kneeling or prostration to do homage (to one) or make obeisance, whether in order to express respect or to make supplication; 3a) used of homage shown to men and beings of superior rank; 3a1) to the Jewish high priests; 3a2) to God; 3a3) to Christ; 3a4) to heavenly beings; 3a5) to demons
Nave's (5201): To be rendered only to God Ex 20:3 De 5:7 6:13 Mt 4:10 Lu 4:8 Ac 10:26 14:15 Col 2:18 Re 19:10 22:8; unclassified Scriptures Ge 35:2,3 Ex 3:5,6 5:1 15:2 19:10-13,21-24 20:24-26 24:1,2 25:8,22 28:34,35 29:43 30:19-21 34:8 40:34,35 Le 10:3 16:2 Nu 17:4 Jos 5:15 1Ki 8:3-11 2Ki 17:36 1Ch 16:29 2Ch 5:13,14 7:1 30:27 Ezr 3:10-13 Ne 10:39 Ps 5:7 22:22 24:3-6 26:6-8 27:4 29:2 35:18 36:8 42:4 48:9 51:19 55:14 63:1,2 65:4 66:4,13,14 77:13 84:1-4,10 89:7 92:13,14 93:5 95:6 98:2,3 100:1-4 103:1-4 107:6-8,32 116:12-14,17 118:18,19 119:108 122:1 126:1-3 132:7,13,14 138:2 149:1 Ec 5:1,2 Isa 1:11-15 2:3 4:5 12:5,6 25:9 29:13-16 30:29 38:20 40:31 43:22-24 49:13 52:9 56:6,7 66:1,2 Jer 31:11,12 Eze 22:8 Ho 6:6 Am 5:21-24 Mic 4:2 Hab 2:20 Zep 3:18 Zec 8:21,22 Mal 3:3,4 Mt 18:19,20 Lu 4:8 Joh 4:23,24 Ac 2:1-4 17:24,25 1Co 11:13,20-22 14:15-17 Php 3:3 1Ti 2:8 Heb 10:25 12:28 1Pe 2:5 Re 11:1 14:6,7 15:4; commanded Ge 35:1 Ex 23:17,18 34:23 De 12:5-7,11,12 16:6-8 31:11-13 33:19 2Ki 17:36 Ps 45:11 76:11 96:8,9 97:7 99:5 Joe 1:14,15 2:15-17 Na 1:15 Hag 1:8 Zec 14:16-18 Mt 8:4 Mr 1:44 Lu 5:14 Heb 10:25 Re 14:7 19:10
"God [is] a Spirit : and they that worship him must worship [him] in spirit and in truth ." John 4:24

Sources:

Brown, Francis, S.R. Driver, and Charles A. Briggs, eds. *The Brown-Driver-Briggs-Gesenius Hebrew and English Lexicon.*

Conner, Kevin J. *The Tabernacle of Moses.* Portland, Oregon: BT Publishing, 1976.

Thayer, Joseph H. *Thayer's Greek-English Lexicon of the New Testament.*

Webster's Dictionary. Springfield, Massachusetts: Merriam-Webster, Inc., Publishers.

Unger, Merrill F. *The New Unger's Bible Dictionary.* Chicago, Illinois: Moody Press, 1988.

W. E. Vine. *An Expository Dictionary of New Testament Words.* Nashville, Tennessee: Royal Publishers, Inc., 1940.

Absolutes of God
Order Form

Postal orders: P.O Box 204
Lecompton, KS 66050

Telephone orders: 785-887-6845

E-mail orders: rr.ricley@juno.com

Please send *Absolutes of God* to:

Name: _____

Address: _____

City: _____ State: _____

Zip: _____

Telephone: (_____) _____

Book Price: $14.99

Shipping: $3.00 for the first book and $1.00 for each additional book to
cover shipping and handling within US, Canada, and Mexico.
International orders add $6.00 for the first book and $2.00 for
each additional book.

Or order from:
ACW Press
5501 N. 7th. Ave. #502
Phoenix, AZ 85013

(800) 931-BOOK

or contact your local bookstore

This book was produced as a study aid for use in seminars for Pastors, evangelists and church workers in West Africa. A portion of the purchase price is used to subsidize these books which are provided either free of charge or at a greatly reduced price for the Ministers of West Africa, by the West African Center for Ministerial Studies.

If you cannot afford to pay full retail price, a number of these books have been set aside to assure availability to anyone. You can get one by contacting our United States office listed in this book.

This book is also available in French or Ewe translations.

If you would like to donate the book you have purchased after reading it, it may be mailed to our United States office listed in this book or to West African Center for Ministerial Studies P.O. Box 11708 Community 11 Tema, Ghana West Africa.

Thank you.
Ron Ricley